BACKCOUNTRY
SKI & SNOWBOARD
ROUTES

OREGON

BACKCOUNTRY SKI & SNOWBOARD ROUTES

OREGON

CHRISTOPHER VAN TILBURG

THE MOUNTAINEERS BOOKS

THE MOUNTAINEERS BOOKS
is the nonprofit publishing arm of The Mountaineers,
an organization founded in 1906 and dedicated to the exploration,
preservation, and enjoyment of outdoor and wilderness areas.

1001 SW Klickitat Way, Suite 201, Seattle, WA 98134

© 2011 by Christopher Van Tilburg

First edition, 2011

Manufactured in the United States of America

Copy Editor: Jane Crosen
Cover and Book Design: Peggy Egerdahl
Cartographer: Pease Press Cartography

All photographs by the author unless otherwise noted
Cover photograph: *Backcountry powder skier skis steep terrain.*
    © Scott Cramer/Getty Images
Frontispiece: *Climbing to high country powder, Tam McArthur Rim*
    (Jonas Tarlan)
Maps shown in this book were produced using National Geographic's *TOPO!* software.
    For more information go to www.national geographic.com/topo

Library of Congress Cataloging-in-Publication Data
Van Tilburg, Christopher.
  Backcountry ski & snowboard routes : Oregon / Christopher Van Tilburg.
    p. cm.
  Includes bibliographical references and index.
  ISBN 978-1-59485-516-0 (ppb)
  1. Backcountry skiing—Oregon—Guidebooks. 2.
Snowboarding—Oregon—Guidebooks. 3. Oregon—Guidebooks. I. Title.
  GV854.V25 2011
  796.9309795—dc23

                          2011024424

ISBN (paperback): 978-1-59485-516-0
ISBN (e-book): 978-1-59485-517-7

CONTENTS

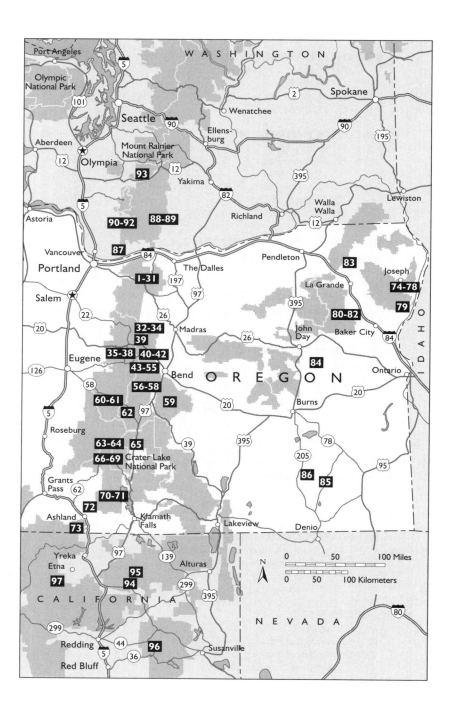

Symbol	Description	Symbol	Description
▪▪▪▪▪▪▪	Featured ascent and descent (via same route)	Ⓟ	Trailhead parking
••••••••••	Descent (when separate)	▪	Landmark
▬ ▬ ▬ ▬	Alternate route	▲	Peak
----------	Other trail	•——————•	Chairlift
←——→	Direction of descent and/or return	Ⓖ	Camp spot
———————	Highway	Λ	Campground
———————	Local road		Body of water
=======	Dirt road	———	Stream
(5) (84)	Interstate	┼	Gate
(50) (495)	U.S. highway		Elevation contours (usually 40-foot intervals)
(58) (242)	State highway	←	Gentle terrain
123	Forest road	←	Steep terrain
/123/	Trail number		
N ↑	North		

PREFACE

I WAS FIVE YEARS OLD WHEN I first skied down the field in our backyard in rural southwest Washington. Wearing red rubber rain boots, I put my feet atop Dad's 205-centimeter red skis and we careened down the cow pasture to the barn. We hiked back up and did it again and again. I became soaked from the heavy wet snow affectionately known as Pacific Northwest Crud and Cascade Cement. I vaguely remember an ear-to-ear smile. Once inside, Mom had a cup of hot chocolate waiting for me by a crackling warm fire.

A few years later my parents bought me my own short red skis and matching boots. We walked up the slope at Summit Ski Area on Mount Hood and glided back down. First I went straight down, suspended by my arms between my parents' legs. Later I began going down by myself, straight down. Then I graduated to the T-bar. On my first ride up, the wood bar nearly knocked me over. The bar came across my shoulder blades and hit Dad across his knees so that he had to hunch over to keep me from falling off.

From grade school through high school, I skied resorts all over the Pacific Northwest, the Rockies, British Columbia, and Europe with my family and friends. We'd trek by train, car, and airplane to make tracks on the world's mountains. For us it wasn't about racing or the once-yearly trip. It was a deeply ingrained routine family activity.

Off to college and later medical school, I kept skiing and jumped to snowboarding, which back then was new, exciting, and constantly developing. I spent a year in Europe and eventually returned to the Pacific Northwest and the famed Cascade Range. I began seeking out new challenges: hiking the resorts before and after the season and dipping into the sidecountry. I climbed the famous trifecta of snowclad volcanoes: Mounts Hood, Adams, and St. Helens. Eventually, I was spending more time in the backcountry than in-area, I was snowboarding, and I was making turns year-round. I tried snowshoes, experimented with snowboarding in mountaineering boots, made short approach skis, and eventually built a split snowboard from one of the first kits made by Voile. My enchantment with backcountry snowboarding and my passion for writing culminated in *Backcountry Snowboarding*, an instructional guide published by The Mountaineers Books back in 1998. It is still in print today.

Eventually, like some ski and snowboard mountaineers, I didn't limit myself to one tool, but schooled myself on many techniques of ascent and descent. I dabbled in telemark skiing; learned to climb glaciers, rock, and ice; and geared up with alpine touring boots and binders.

In my enthusiasm for the mountains, I began researching new routes, particularly descents in my home mountains. And, as part of my nature as both journalist and physician, I kept a descent log of the explorations, gathered magazine accounts of routes, and collected mountaineering books, new and old. I began compiling a list of routes—not just summit bags or gnarly lines, but everything I could ski or snowboard. Those of us who deal with Pacific Northwest weather regularly know that if you want to make turns, you don't always get a summit bid due to weather. Sometimes a 500-foot slope in the trees yields a primo descent. So as I continued to climb, glide, and document, my collection grew to routes for skiers and snowboarders, for all levels, in all weather conditions, and for all seasons.

The first book, *Backcountry Ski Oregon, Including Southwest Washington: Classic Descents for Skiers and Snowboarders*, was published in 2001. I included basic routes, summit bids, and a few obscure adventures. Over the last decade, I've skied and snowboarded many more routes and, in fact, return to my favorites annually. And I continue to keep a log, which has culminated in this new book, nearly double the number of routes.

Now I spend dozens of days skiing and snowboarding every year. I'm in the mountains often with my daughters, parents, siblings, and friends in the Pacific Northwest and beyond. I climb and descend on a snowboard, on alpine touring skis, and on Nordic gear—although I still log the most days on snow in Oregon on alpine touring gear. I now make part of my living on skis as a doctor at Oregon's busiest resort, Mount Hood Meadows. And I volunteer with the oldest mountain rescue unit in the country, Hood River Crag Rats, which finds me sometimes traipsing in the backcountry in the middle of the night, in the middle of a storm.

So this new volume compiles many, many years of skiing and snowboarding the high peaks of Oregon, with a smattering of southwest Washington and northern California routes tossed in because of their proximity. It's an all-seasons, all-skills, and all-weather guide to the best powder, corn, crud, and cement.

It was impossible for me to ski and snowboard all these routes in all conditions in the year prior to publication of this volume. I owe many thanks for the assistance of friends, family, and colleagues who helped with this book as well as the previous incarnation. My parents, Wayne and Eleanor, taught me how to ski. My daughters, Skylar and Avrie, enthusiastically participated in many mountain adventures. My colleagues at the Pacific Northwest's many ski patrols, winter resorts, mountain rescue units, mountaineering and ski clubs, and U.S. Forest Service ranger districts continue to help make Oregon's mountains accessible and safe. For contributing images, thanks to Jennifer Donnelly, Mark Flaming, Stefan Gumperlein, Pete Keane of timberlinemtguides.com, Won Kim, Nick Pope, Jonas Tarlan of ThreeSistersBackcountry.com, Peter Van Tilburg, and Dave Waag of offpiste.com.

In particular, I want to thank the skilled crew at The Mountaineers Books. I had the pleasure of working with editor in chief Kate Rogers, project editor Janet Kimball, copyeditor Jane Crosen, graphic designer Peggy Egerdahl, and mapmaker Ben Pease.

Have fun. Be safe.

Christopher Van Tilburg
Cloud Cap Inn, Mount Hood, Oregon

ABOUT THESE
MOUNTAINS

THERE'S ONE THING unique about skiing and snowboarding in Oregon: we make turns year-round. We have powder in winter, smooth silky corn in spring, and reliable firn—the granular, compact glacial snow—in summer. An early-season snowfall followed by Indian summer yields a white harvest in fall. The year I spent crafting this book, I skied three feet of powder on Mount Hood on October 27.

The Oregon mountains are a majestic yet sorted lot. Many of these routes are on the perennially snowcapped stratovolcanoes, the famed Cascade Range. The string is part of the Ring of Fire, which lines the Pacific Coast with dormant, extinct, and active volcanoes. Mount Hood vents sulfur gas from fumaroles near the summit, and Mount St. Helens steams and burps gas from the crater.

In winter, trails are snow covered and the lower routes yield easy access to steep but short runs in thick conifer forests. We have bluebird days of clear, cold weather, but in midwinter we also have rain up high. Spring brings our share of deep dry powder, but not endless days of white smoke. In spring and summer the approaches are marked by the ubiquitous basalt and andesite lava, dirt single track, and blown-down trees. Depending on the time of year, the approach may be an easy skin over snow or a trek on dirt, mud, and sand. The approach trails to the high summer snowfields can be a long slog from the car or an easy walk through our famous old-growth Douglas fir, western red cedar, and mountain hemlock forests. Out east, the Ponderosa pine and lodgepole pine forests mark the approaches in the Wallowa and Elkhorn mountains.

Please use common sense. This book is not intended as a substitute for careful planning, professional training, or your own good judgment. It is incumbent upon any user of this guide to assess his or her own skills, experience, fitness, and equipment. Readers will recognize the inherent dangers in skiing, snowboarding, and backcountry terrain and assume responsibility for their own actions and safety.

Changing or unfavorable conditions in weather, roads, trails, waterways, etc., cannot be anticipated by the author or publisher but should be considered by any outdoor participants, as trails may become dangerous or slopes unstable due to such altered conditions. Likewise, be aware of any changes in public jurisdiction, and do not access private property without permission.

The publisher and author are not responsible for any adverse consequences resulting directly or indirectly from information contained in this book.

Glaciers and permanent snowfields are located on many peaks and provide media for many of our descents on skis or snowboards.

Although most skiers and snowboarders venturing into the backcountry are experts at mountain resorts, this introduction provides an overview of equipment, skills, and hazards for backcountry adventures.

EQUIPMENT

Unlike a day of riding chairlifts, a backcountry tour requires a cadre of gear. Specialty skis and snowboards for uphill travel, essential safety gear, and clothing are key to an enjoyable, safe outing.

Cold temps and dry snow—a perfect start to a powder day

Skis and Snowboards, Boots and Bindings

This book is designed for all snow gliders. Skiers may use one of several types of ski and binding systems. Alpine touring (aka ski mountaineering or randonée) gear, or AT for short, is great for a wide variety of conditions and terrain. For ascent, AT bindings allow the toe of the boot to be attached but the heel to move freely. This allows for uphill skiing. When at the top of the run, the heel can be locked down for descent. The boots look like alpine downhill ski boots with a few modifications. The boots have a "walk" mode, which allows flexible upper cuff for uphill travel comfort. The cuff can be locked into a "ski" mode, so it is stiff for descent. The boots also have a lugged sole for climbing up rocks and across dirt trails.

Many prefer the dynamic and unique turn of telemark gear. Telemark boots have a soft flex at the ball of the foot. They are connected at the toe of the boot, for uphill and downhill skiing. Many telemark bindings have a cable that runs around the heel of the boot for added control and support. But the heel of the boot does not lock down to the ski. Hence, the moniker "free-heel skiing."

A few lower-angle routes are suitable for light Nordic gear, steel-edged cross-country skis with or without scales on the bases. Like telemark gear, these skis are connected at the toe of the boot and the heel does not lock down. But the skis are usually skinnier and lighter; the boots are lightweight as well and don't offer the support of AT or telemark boots.

A few who may be just starting out, or occasionally venturing into the backcountry, may even use their downhill ski gear with ski mountaineering adapters in the bindings to allow a free heel for ascent. When ready to ski down, the adapters are removed and stashed in your pack.

And for the mountaineer who wants to take along skis for the occasional summer descent, firn gliders (named for the compact, granular snow on glaciers) are small 120-centimeter skis that you can throw on your pack for the hike up; put them on at the top, and glide down on the summer corn. These are exclusively used by skiers ascending peaks in their boots during summer when glacial snow is firm.

Except for the occasional summer bootpack (a compacted trail of boot prints you hike up while carrying your skis or snowboard) or sidecountry route, snowboarders need a means of ascent. Many riders use snowshoes because they are readily available and relatively inexpensive; they work okay in deep snow but are much slower than skis and take a lot of energy. Short approach skis are an alternative but one that is not wildly popular. They sometimes work well for snowboarders who tour with skiers and who want to use a skin track; however, approach skis don't float very well in deep snow. In either case, the snowboard must be carried on a rider's backpack during ascent. A splitboard solves the problem: with these, backcountry snowboarders no longer need a separate mode of ascent. Splitboards are snowboards with a seam lengthwise. The bindings are removed, the board is separated into two skis, and the bindings are reattached in ski mode. This allows a splitboarder, with skins attached, to ski uphill much like telemark or alpine touring skiers. When atop the slope, the splitboard is reassembled into snowboard mode for the ride down.

For snowboard boots and bindings, most riders will use soft boots with strap bindings, because these are the most widely available. Some will use soft boots with step-in bindings, but they are falling in popularity. My recommendation for backcounty snowboarding in Oregon, especially in the spring and summer, is to use plastic mountaineering boots with plate bail bindings on a splitboard.

Whether you use AT skis, telemark skis, or a splitboard, all require climbing skins for ascent. These are swaths of nylon fabric with adhesive on one side allowing the skins to be stretched and adhered to the underside of the ski or snowboard. Tiny hairs on the skin's surface allow the ski or snowboard to slide up the slope, then grip and not slide back down.

In addition, you will need adjustable ski poles. These allow you to hike in variable terrain—steep slopes, rocky crags, and ice. They are also handy to collapse and stash in your pack. Some backcountry ski poles have an option for self-arrest grips, which help slow a fall on steep ice if you are not carrying an ice ax; these are not, however, a good substitute for an ice ax when climbing glaciers or steep snow. Other adjustable ski poles can be used, in a pinch, as avalanche probes, but a real probe is a more functional option if you are searching for a buried partner.

This is a very brief overview of backcountry ski and snowboard gear. You'll need some formal instruction and experience before you become proficient. For more tips on uphill travel and on organizing and using tools for ascent, see the Backcountry Wisdom section.

Essentials

In addition to ski and snowboard gear, you should carry, and know how to use, backcountry safety gear for every one of these routes, year round. This includes essentials like food, water, map, compass, global positioning system (GPS), altimeter, cell phone, firestarter, first-aid and repair kits, extra clothes, sunscreen, sunglasses, headlamp, and emergency shelter. Mandatory avalanche gear includes a transceiver, shovel, and probe. Optional avalanche equipment includes an under-snow breathing apparatus backpack (Avalung) or an avalanche airbag backpack. I always carry a basic emergency, first-aid, and survival kit as well. A complete equipment list is outlined in Appendix B.

You need to learn to use this equipment and practice regularly before you attempt these routes. Formal instruction is especially important for avalanche rescue, navigation, and survival. Consult avalanche and mountain safety texts and take a course in avalanche safety and general mountaineering. To learn more about mountain travel, refer to one of the books listed in Appendix A.

Clothing

Fortunately, clothing nowadays is warm, durable, and relatively inexpensive. You probably have a closet full of backcountry-worthy clothing. However, there are a few key points worth discussing, especially for those just venturing beyond winter resorts. Backcountry weather can be wildly variable. Even on the clearest, sunniest day, you can get caught by a brisk chilly wind or step knee-deep into a stream. Layering is the essential clothing management system for the backcountry. For the most part, clothing will be synthetic: it's cheap, durable, warm when wet, quick-drying, and functional. Cotton generally doesn't work in the wilderness because it's not warm and doesn't retain heat when wet. Down is the standard high-altitude insulator, but in the Pacific Northwest rain and wet snow, if down gets wet, it doesn't work well. Generally synthetics are favored over down unless you are high, dry, and cold.

Some natural fibers, like silk and wool, work well as underlayers. However, wool is not as durable, takes a bit longer to dry than synthetics, and is not quite as warm when wet.

Start with an underlayer of polyester or polypropylene (or silk or wool). For mid-layers, a fleece sweater or fleece vest provides some added warmth. I prefer full-zip sweaters for ease of taking on and off. For outerwear you have a couple of choices. I'm never without a windproof and waterproof "hard-shell" jacket and pants in the backcountry. After all, in the Pacific Northwest, you never know when it will rain or the wind will show up. "Soft-shell" jackets and pants are becoming popular. These provide minimal wind and rain protection, but give some warmth and allow you to ventilate excess heat and moisture more efficiently than a hard shell. Some back-country travelers carry a soft-shell jacket instead of a sweater and hard-shell parka, thus utilizing one piece of clothing instead of two. But, be advised, for foul weather you should have hard-shell outergear. I typically tour in soft-shell mountaineering pants and carry hard-shell wind-and-rain pants in my pack.

Along with basic clothing, you'll need accessories. I recommend good ski socks, lightweight gloves for uphill, heavy gauntlet gloves for downhill and foul weather, an under-helmet hat, a neck gaiter, a helmet, goggles, and sunglasses.

Glacier Travel Gear

In the case of steep routes such as glaciers, you should carry extra traction and extra safety gear. For the occasional steep pitch on an otherwise moderate route, you can get extra traction from ski or splitboard crampons. These clip to the ski binding and, when used with skins, stick into hard snow to keep the ski or splitboard from sliding back. Occasionally instep crampons can be used for boots. In addition, self-arrest grip poles provide a slight margin of safety. If you fall, a pick on the end of a ski pole helps stop a slide.

For most glacier travel, steep snow, and ice, you will need the basic glacier gear of a helmet, an ice ax, and full-frame boot crampons. Crampons are used for climbing ice too steep and hard to skin up or hike up in boots. They usually have ten or twelve spikes and can be fitted for ski and mountaineering boots, if you are using the latter for snowboarding. An ice ax is used to self-arrest if you fall on steep slopes and start sliding. Once sliding, it's nearly impossible to stop yourself without an ice ax, which is dug into the snow to stop your fall. In this book, only a half-dozen routes may require this gear, like the summit climbs and mountaineering routes of the more technical Cascade volcanoes.

A few routes—especially summit routes in the Cascade volcanoes—require more advanced equipment. Routes requiring mountaineering gear—rope, climbing harness, snow anchors, and crevasse rescue gear (prusik cords, carabiners, a pulley, and other hardware)—are generally beyond the scope of this book. You should be well versed in glacier travel and crevasse rescue techniques before undertaking any advanced climbing route.

For more on glacier travel, read *Mountaineering: The Freedom of the Hills*, eighth edition, the definitive book, listed in Appendix A.

Electronic Locating and Communication Devices

Locating devices can be confusing and overwhelming. You may not choose to take all these devices; some are essential though, while others are optional. Here's a brief description of the different choices. Keep in mind that electronics don't always work due to many factors. Weak or cold batteries limit transmission power. Heavy clouds, thick forests, and deep canyons can block the signal. Also, there's a lot of electromagnetic radiation in the world, and you can't escape it on a backcountry tour. And the devices can be so complicated that you may forget how to use them. Lithium batteries

Check and recheck your gear. And remember: it's useless if you don't know how to use it.

work the best in cold weather and for prolonged use. But they are expensive, and not all devices are designed to work on lithium batteries. Some avalanche beacons, for example, require alkaline batteries.

Avalanche Beacon. An avalanche beacon is a small transceiver that broadcasts a signal 50 meters. If you get caught in an avalanche, your partner needs to switch his or her beacon to receive, to allow them to home in on your signal and your location. This is only practical for partner rescues. If you do not know how to use an avalanche beacon, you are not ready for the backcountry.

Personal Locator Beacon. A personal locator beacon, or PLB, is much like the emergency position-indicating remote beacons (EPIRBs) used on ships and emergency locator transmitters used on airplanes.When you buy a PLB, you register the unique serial number with the national emergency management service. Then, if you are in trouble and activate the unit, the PLB sends an emergency signal via satellites with the unit's unique serial number and GPS location. This notifies the emergency management agency that you are in trouble, and gives your location. Unfortunately, these units are costly—and you need to manually activate them. If you are caught in an avalanche or injured, you might not be able to reach the PLB to activate it. When they come down in price, PLBs may become the ultimate in location devices, but they require instruction, practice, and experience to operate them.

Locating Messenger Service. Somewhat similar to PLBs, a product made by one company, SPOT, uses satellites to transmit GPS coordinates. The SPOT locator works by sending your GPS location, via satellite signal, to a web page. A friend or family member can track your progress. The unit has an emergency button that, if activated, sends an emergency message to the company, which can then call your local sheriff.

Mountain Locator Unit. Unique to Oregon's Mount Hood, the Mountain Locator Unit, or MLU, is available for rental. It was developed after a 1986 accident that claimed the lives of several climbers. If activated, it broadcasts a distress signal for several miles. Essentially an animal tracker or a large version of an avalanche beacon, the MLU transmits a stronger signal and on a separate frequency than an avalanche beacon. To find you, a rescue agency must know you are in trouble and know you have an MLU. This is because the search-and-rescue group coming after you would need to get the MLU receiver to search for you. It can be fairly complicated to mount an MLU search: Two teams at different locations need to use the receiver antenna to find the vector with the strongest signal from the transmitting MLU. Then, the two teams each take a compass bearing, and those bearings are plotted on a map. Where the two bearings intersect is the approximate location of the distressed party. I've used this on one rescue in Oregon with success, and it is worth considering if you are climbing above timberline on Mount Hood and don't have access to other safety electronics.

RECCO. The RECCO is a small microwave reflector sewn into ski and snowboard clothing, and sometimes affixed to snowboard boots. So if you are lost, a team with a RECCO search unit can send out a signal, which bounces off your reflector and points the team to your location. The range is quite long and can be searched for from a helicopter. The reflectors are inexpensive and already part of some snow clothing. However, as with the MLU, a search team needs to (a) know you are missing, (b) know you have a RECCO reflector, and (c) have a RECCO search unit. A few of the larger winter resorts in Oregon have them.

Cell Phone/Satellite Phone. Cell phones and satellite phones often work throughout the mountains of Oregon, and even above timberline—but not always. Deep canyons, heavy trees, clouds, severe cold, and low batteries can limit reception and transmission.

Global Positioning System. A Global Position System, or GPS, receiver helps you pinpoint your location using navigational satellites. They are inexpensive and easy to use. But they do require some practice. As with cell phones, reception can be limited by weather, geography, and batteries.

Wrist-top Computer. Many backcountry aficionados use a wrist-top altimeter/ barometer/compass. Some brands are very accurate; however, you should carry a standard liquid-filled compass as backup.

VHF/UHF Radio. When phones and GPS units don't work because they rely on cell towers and satellites respectively, radios can be an excellent emergency device. Radios can be used to communicate via public channels like FRS, GMRS, or CB frequencies. VHF/UHF "ham" radios can be extremely useful, especially if you are in an area where a local ham operator or snowmobile club has set up a repeater. This can extend the range so that you have a chance of reaching someone sitting at their base station at home who can call 911 for you. Usually, radios work via line of sight, so on a clear day a five-watt radio can transmit 20 miles or more. In bad weather or thick trees, they have less range, sometimes under a mile. Also, small family radios, which are usually a half or one watt, may only transmit a mile or two. Either way, if you are broadcasting a distress call, someone on the other end needs to be listening.

All said, an avalanche beacon is mandatory. The best combination for emergencies, considering price and ease of use, is a cell phone and GPS. Tell rescuers that you are lost or hurt and describe your location.

PREPARATION AND PLANNING

Backcountry travel is significantly more hazardous than inbounds skiing and snowboarding. Although most skiers and snowboarders who spend time in resorts have a basic idea of how bad and how beautiful the weather can be in Oregon, the backcountry is a whole new ball game. This guidebook assumes the reader is skilled in backcountry travel. The following section covers the fundamentals you should know before heading into the backcountry. This should be a refresher. If not, seek formal instruction, practice regularly, and go with experienced partners to hone your skills.

Education

If you are new to the backcountry, take a general backcountry ski or snowboard course and an entry-level mountaineering course that covers glacier travel. These are usually weekend courses offered by climbing clubs or guide services. They will give you an excellent overview of safety, clothing, equipment, and techniques.

An avalanche course is a must. Many guide services offer this training in a weekend course. It is usually part classroom and part fieldwork on snow.

Also consider hiring one of the many guide services. In fact, several routes in this book, including Mount Hood, Mount Bailey, Tam McArthur Rim near Bend, and the Wallowa Mountains, have guided backcountry tours. Think about taking a guided trip as an introduction to these volcanoes and mountain ranges. You will learn new skills, make friends, and get to know an area with a seasoned guide.

To complement the route descriptions provided here you can consult rangers, topographic maps, other guidebooks, seasonal updates, and Internet chat forums, blogs, and trip reports. Although this book may be a fixture in your vehicle or kitchen, don't plan to carry it in your pack. You should be able to find your way with a map, a compass, a global positioning system, and an altimeter. A list of resources is outlined in Appendix A.

Road Conditions

The roads can be quite hazardous in Oregon, and not just in the mountains. Ice, snow, and our famous Pacific Northwest freezing rain are especially treacherous. Always check the road reports before driving, carry emergency supplies in your vehicle, and be advised on traction requirements. In Oregon, use www.tripcheck.com for the road report; you can also view cameras mounted at mountain passes and winter resorts to get a better idea of the conditions. There are comparable websites and phone numbers where you can check road conditions in California and Washington, listed in the area overviews for those states.

In Oregon, the Snow Zone signs are important to follow for safety. The Oregon Department of Transportation (ODOT) defines traction tires as tires (studded or otherwise) that qualify for use in severe snow conditions, designated by the snowflake-in-a-mountain emblem on the sidewall.

"CARRY CHAINS OR TRACTION TIRES" means you must have tire chains in your car available to put on if you need them, or use traction tires. "CHAINS REQUIRED: TRACTION TIRES ALLOWED ON VEHICLES UNDER 10,000 GVW" means you must use chains or traction tires. Four-wheel-drive or all-wheel-drive vehicles are exempt if they weigh less than 6500 pounds; use traction, mud-and-snow, or all-weather tires on all four wheels; carry chains; are not towing; and are driven safely.

Finding Good Snow

Oregon's weather can be somewhat predictable, fortunately. Forecasting and reading weather in the field is a complex science that takes several years to master. The most complete source for Oregon skiers and snowboarders is the Northwest Weather and Avalanche Center, www.nwac.us. Another great source is the National Weather Service at www.nws.gov. Alternatively, check out Jeff Renner's short book *Mountain Weather*, published by The Mountaineers Books.

Early morning recon on ice-hard suncups, South Sister

Many types of snow exist on Oregon's mountains. We all know that powder is fresh snow. But even that can be described as "heavy" or "wet" when it has a large water content, or light and dry when it has a low water content. Here is an overview of snow terms used in this book:

Corn is the consolidated firm snow that occurs in spring. At this time of year, the snow freezes hard overnight, then warms during the day; corn occurs when the snowpack has softened in the first few inches, usually by midmorning. Slush describes the condition when the sun melts the top 6 to 12 inches into soft, thick snow. Firn is the granular, coarse, old snow found on glaciers and permanent snowfields in summer. Ice, although used widely to denote any firm snow, really refers to hard frozen water, not snow. Unconsolidated snow is soft powder that does not metamorphose into ice or slush. It is light and dry, usually days after a snow, and sometimes called hoar frost or "loud powder" because it is noisy when skied through. "Mashed potatoes" or "Cascade crud" generally denotes heavy, soft, dense snow that is cut up by other skiers or by rain, or is otherwise bumpy. When the crud becomes thicker and denser, it's called "Cascade cement." Windblown is usually smooth, often firm snow that is transported by wind and packed tightly on a slope. Breakable crust is a firm 1- or 2-centimeter crust caused by either sun exposure or rain, which breaks into softer snow below when skied.

Learn the Oregon snow and weather patterns, and keep a close eye on seasonal and weekly variations. Watch the snowfall, temperature, and wind. Especially learn the effects of prolonged sun or rain on the snowpack. In the Pacific Northwest, we typically get storms from the Pacific, and we know in advance when they are coming. Occasionally, local weather systems or rapidly advancing storms can surprise us. But for the most part, pay a little attention to the weather, and you should be able to find the best snow.

I tend to watch the one- and three-day forecasts. Much beyond three days, in my opinion, things change so rapidly that I don't find it particularly useful. I do pay attention to the weather all winter, even when I'm out of town, to keep track of Oregon's snowpack. Since I'm in Oregon's mountains all year, every month and sometimes every week, it's important for me to know, for example, if we have a few days of rain up high or a big windstorm that loads some of the cornices.

In Oregon, storms usually come from the Pacific Ocean. Southwest storms that come from the tropics are warm and wet, the so-called Pineapple Express. These bring heavy, wet, gooey snow or sometimes rain to the Cascades. Usually, these are not storms for dumping loads of snow on the mountains. If we do get snow, it is usually up in the high mountains. Storms from west-southwest or west-northwest are cooler and drier but still have a lot of moisture. These usually dump the most snow in the Oregon mountains. The storms that dip down from the Canadian north are usually very cold and bring less moisture, although what snow falls usually is light and dry.

Watch both the freezing level and the snow level. In winter, the snow level is usually 1000 feet below the freezing level. Dry and plentiful snow is usually found 1000–2000 feet above the freezing level, which corresponds to 2000–3000 feet above the snow level. The air temperature here is about 20–25 degrees F.

In spring and summer, watch the temperature, since timing is everything. Many routes must be climbed in the early-morning hours when the snow is firm, which makes for easy ascent. Once the snow heats up and turns to slush, hiking is very difficult. Moreover, the best descent is midmorning when the snow softens to corn but before it turns to slush. If it doesn't freeze the night before, the snow may not freeze and turn to corn; thus you could have a slushy hike up and a slushy ride down. The colder it is, the longer it takes to warm up the snow to corn. If it is cloudy and windy, it may stay frozen all day in spring, and never soften to corn.

Aspect is another important function of snow conditions. East- and south-facing slopes heat up and get slushy quickly in the spring and summer afternoons. North slopes in spring hold their firm corn longer, sometimes all day. In winter, shaded north-facing slopes often have good snow, even days after a winter storm.

In addition to snow and weather, the yearly and seasonal variations in these mountains can be dramatic. Some approach trails may be covered by snow in winter; this makes a longer approach but often allows you to ski or snowboard all the way back to your vehicle. In summer, lava or dirt can significantly speed your approach time, but you will be hiking, not riding or skiing, back out to your vehicle. Always call ahead to check road and trail conditions.

Permits

Nowadays, you need a permit for almost every route in this book, at all times of the year. The permit situation for any particular trailhead or sno-park may be complicated and may change from year to year. You may hear some squabbling in the parking lot about permits and the associated fees. Keep in mind that permits limit overuse of the land and pay for upkeep of trails, parking areas, and toilets. They also defray the cost of rangers and search-and-rescue.

For good or ill, there are three general types of permits required on these routes plus some additional ones in national parks and on Washington and California volcanoes. Make sure you check well in advance to confirm the requirements listed in this book.

A **Wilderness Permit** is required for all of the wilderness areas. These are usually available at self-serve boxes at trailheads and are often free, with a few exceptions (including Mounts Adams, St. Helens, and Shasta). In addition to the Wilderness Permit, some areas have a climber's registration form for ascent above timberline. This is to assist with rescues and with resource management, so fill it out accurately. Remember to sign out on your way home if required.

A **Sno-Park Pass** is required for winter and spring at most trailheads designated as Winter Recreation Areas to help defray costs of plowing. These are available at outdoor stores, ranger stations, and ski areas. In Oregon, a $30 permit is required from November 1 to April 30. Washington, California, and Idaho Sno-Park Passes are honored in Oregon, provided they are on vehicles with corresponding license plates.

A **Northwest Forest Pass** is now required on many routes year-round as part of the recreation fee program. The pass is good in all Oregon and Washington national forests for parking at trailheads. The cost is $30 annually. These are available at outdoor stores, ranger stations, and self-serve dispensaries at selected trailheads. In parking areas where a Northwest Forest Pass and Sno-Park Pass are both required, usually the Sno-Park will suffice from November 1 to April 30.

A **national park entrance fee** is required for Mount Rainier National Park, Crater Lake National Park, and Lassen Volcanic National Park. If climbing above 10,000 feet on Mount Rainier, a separate **climbing fee and permit** are required. If you plan to camp on the Muir Snowfield, just a **backcountry camping permit** is required.

A special, rather complex, **climbing permit and fee** are required for Mount St. Helens, as noted in that section. In addition, as mentioned above, Mounts Adams, Shasta, and Rainier all have climbing fees. The first two are combined with a wilderness permit.

Ski Area Uphill Traffic and Sidecountry Access

While researching a prior edition of this book, I came across *Northwest Ski Trails*, written by Ted Mueller and published in 1968 by The Mountaineers Books, containing descriptions of ski resorts and backcountry routes in the Pacific Northwest. As backcountry skiing and snowboarding surged in the 1990s and 2000s, guidebooks proliferated, but they included mostly out-of-area routes. However, many backcountry skiers and snowboarders get their start by hiking and descending ski area slopes before, during, or after the season. I have included some in-area routes (routes that lie within ski area permit boundaries) because they are an important part of backcountry winter culture and history.

More and more, skiers and snowboarders are climbing ski runs during lift operation, called "in-area uphill traffic." This allows skiers and snowboarders to get exercise, to try out new gear, and to practice skills within the relative safety of ski resorts. Some resorts allow in-area uphill traffic during the ski season; many have strict regulations prohibiting or limiting it. For example, Mount Bachelor Ski Resort in Bend designates two uphill routes inbounds. Others prohibit all uphill traffic altogether, as at Mount Hood Meadows Winter Resort, where uphill traffic has been disallowed due to safety. That resort designated two uphill routes also, but they are outside the resort boundary. Because winter resorts usually lie on public land leased from the Forest Service and occasionally on private land, the resort management is allowed by law to set these rules, and enforce them, with the help of law enforcement if needed.

In addition to regulating uphill traffic, resorts regulate access to the backcountry. Some resorts allow a skier or snowboarder to ride a lift, then access the backcountry—the area beyond the boundary but adjacent to the resort—through a control gate. This is the so-called "sidecountry," sometimes called "slackcountry," or "lift-access backcountry." Access to the sidecountry, however, is also strictly regulated by the resorts.

Some ski areas have "soft boundaries"—intermittently open boundaries, via control gates that allow a skier and snowboarder to ride the lift, then hike or ski out of bounds, if the ski patrol opens the gates. Mount Bachelor's access gate to the Kwohl Butte is an example. A few resorts have "open boundaries," allowing one to exit the resort any time; one of these is Timberline Lodge, which allows skiers and snowboarders to hike to the top of the Palmer chairlift, or catch a chairlift ride, and then climb to the summit of Mount Hood. Others winter resorts have "hard boundaries," which disallow any out-of-bounds touring.

Just to make things more confusing, a few ski areas have areas within the boundary of their permit area, which they call the "outback" or "back side." So if in question, check the ski resort website, trail map, and ski patrol.

Be advised, skiers and snowboarders should obey the ski resort rules—the rules are in place for good reason, and ignoring them just makes access difficult for others in the future. Resort skiers and snowboarders heading out of bounds in Oregon illegally have been arrested and fined, and have lost their season pass privileges. (The Oregon laws pertaining to skiers and snowboarders are outlined in Appendix C.) We all should treat uphill traffic and the sidecountry with the same respect we do the deep mountains. Sidecountry equals backcountry. Before heading uphill in a ski resort, or heading into the sidecountry, check with the ski patrol at the resort. Unfortunately, because of ease of access, sometimes less-skilled skiers and snowboarders are tempted to jaunt out of bounds, which is replete with the full cadre of mountain hazards: avalanches, cliffs, unmarked obstacles, and variable snow conditions.

Planning a Trip

Before I go, I mentally run through the following brief checklist. If you are a list person, make a list. Otherwise, just try to remember everything.

- Eat a big breakfast. That's the only way to start a backcountry day.
- Check your local ski resort's snow phone, the avalanche and weather report, the telemetry data, and the road conditions. Although this seems like a lot, if you bookmark them on your computer, you can pull them up quickly. Once you get in the habit of checking them throughout the season or all year, you can quickly get the info you need.
- Organize and pack your ski gear, food, and water. Make sure phone and radio are charged; GPS and avalanche beacon should have fresh batteries.
- Gas up your car. I always head into the mountains with a full tank.
- Let someone know where you are going.
- Get your partner. Although I tour occasionally by myself, it's always safer and more fun to go with a friend.
- Be ready to turn around. When planning a trip, if the roads, weather, or snowpack look dangerous at any time for any reason, you shouldn't be afraid to bail.

MOUNTAIN SAFETY

Mountain hazards are myriad, including avalanche dangers. There is not space here to do much more than list the hazards and synopsize what you already know. There are four primary skills that are essential to master: navigation, surviving a night out, self-reliance in an emergency, and traveling safely in avalanche conditions. You should master these skills, or at least be proficient enough to use them in an emergency.

This guide to Oregon's mountain wilderness assumes the reader is well-versed in backcountry mountain travel at all times of year including winter, and proficient in skiing or snowboarding in expert terrain in many snow and weather conditions. Beginner routes included here correspond with advanced or expert routes in a comparable cross-country or snowshoe guide. For an approximate measure of ability, readers should be able to safely make turns on the most difficult ski run in their local ski area, in the most difficult weather and snow conditions. In other words, if you can ski or snowboard a black diamond run, in ice, in a whiteout, and you have experience in the mountain wilderness, you are probably ready for the backcountry. Although the routes include many summit climbs and descents, they are limited to basic mountaineering and glacier travel. They do not include technical rock, ice, or crevasse travel.

Weather and Terrain Hazards

Mountain weather and routefinding are what cause most people to get into trouble. More so than injuries, most mountain rescue callouts in winter are for people lost in storms—climbers, skiers, snowboarders, snowshoers, and snowmobilers. The weather turns bad, and they lose their way. And, without navigation skills and the appropriate tools, routefinding is difficult if not impossible.

Keep in mind that if you get lost, you may not be readily rescued, and you may be billed for search-and-rescue costs (see Appendix C).

Always carry and know how to use a map, a compass, a GPS, and an altimeter. Above all, try to stay on route and if bad weather rolls in, consider aborting the tour. Turning around is tough, but if conditions are lousy for finding your way, they likely won't be that great for skiing or snowboarding. Thus, mountain safety skill number 1: **Be able to navigate in a storm.**

If you do get lost or hurt, or simply caught in foul weather, you should be able to spend the night in the winter mountain wilderness. Spending the night out in an emergency is possible. Some have survived many nights in mountain storms on Mount Hood. The key survival shelter is a ranger trench or snow cave. Know how to build one. And you should carry the essential survival equipment listed in Appendix B. Especially important are warm clothes, hard-shell windproof and waterproof parka and pants, a bivouac (bivy) sack and/or tarp, and extra food and water. With these basics, you should be able to survive a night on the mountains in a snow cave or ranger trench. Mountain safety skill number 2: **Be able to spend a night out in the mountains, in a snow trench or snow cave and with adequate food, water, clothing, and a bivouac sack.**

If you don't quite have the skills, go with a guide, take a course, go with experienced people, study books, and always use caution and good judgment.

Weather can pose additional environmental problems. Cold weather can lead to hypothermia, when the core body temperature cools dangerously low, and frostbite, when skin actually freezes. Cold-weather injuries can be debilitating. Moderate to severe hypothermia can lead to having trouble concentrating, walking, speaking, and following directions. Severe frostbite can render a hand or foot unusable, which may make it impossible to ski or hike down out of the mountains.

The sun and heat can lead to dehydration, sunburn, heat exhaustion, heat stroke, and snow blindness. Sun and heat illness can surprise even skilled alpinists.

Hazards such as lightning, rockfall, icefall, tree wells, deep snow, high altitude, and crevasses are daily issues with these routes. This leads to mountain safety skill number 3: **Be well versed in emergency survival, field repair of equipment, and emergency first aid.** And, always give yourself a margin for safety. If the snow, weather, or terrain conditions are questionable, stay in-area or find another activity off the mountain.

Finally, two big problems in the mountain wilderness are avalanches and crevasses. Mountain safety skill number 4: **Be knowledgeable about how to avoid avalanches and crevasses**, the subject of the two following sections.

Avalanche Safety

Avalanche safety is paramount with skiers and snowboarders. You should learn the general guidelines for safety and use the Northwest Weather and Avalanche Center at www.nwac.us to get the general recommendations for that day. Keep in mind, the avalanche report is general and does not offer specifics. Also remember an avalanche beacon, shovel, and probe will only help you save your buried buddy; they won't keep you from getting caught. Avoiding avalanches in the first place is the primary method of safety. If you are pulling out your avalanche beacon, your primary and secondary avoidance tactics have failed. My favorite avalanche safety books are listed in Appendix A. Take a course, read the course book every fall, and go with skilled and safe partners. Here is a summary of avalanche avoidance broken down into several sections that cover safe uphill and downhill travel, what to do if you are caught by an avalanche, and what to do if your partner is caught by an avalanche.

Travel in Safe Terrain. Terrain is a key factor in safe travel, and understanding slope angle is one of the primary elements of avalanche safety. Most avalanches occur between 30 and 40 degrees of slope. Carry an inclinometer; some compasses have them included. You can always descend slopes under 30 degrees even if avalanche danger is high.

Slope aspect is another key factor. North-facing slopes take longer to consolidate in the winter, and thus danger can persist for several weeks after a storm. South-facing slopes heat up quickly in the spring and summer, and thus wet slides can occur in the hot afternoons. The shape of the slope contributes to instability also: convex slopes are more likely to slide.

Anchors, like trees and rocks, offer some protection, but usually only if they are too thick to ski through. Higher elevations are usually colder and have more snow. After windstorms or several days of persistent winds, leeward slopes and cornices can be loaded with unstable wind-deposited snow. Terrain traps are especially dangerous, because they can be unexpected; in a small gully, even a small slide can bury a person.

Travel in Safe Weather. Weather can cause significant destabilization of the snow. We all know that storms bring new snow, and thus avalanches. Most large slab avalanches occur during or after big storms. But wind is a key factor in avalanches too, because wind can deposit loose snow on slopes.

In addition, the sun, especially in spring and summer, can bear down on slopes, especially those facing south, and destabilize the snow, bringing wet slides that are slushy in the bright spring and summer sun. Rain brings weight but not much stability to the snowpack. Temperature is a key factor too, just like the sun. Dramatic warming or cooling can cause snowpack instability.

Travel in Safe Snow Conditions. The snowpack can vary with layers throughout the season. Unless you are a snow scientist, it is advisable to check conditions before you go, and follow the conditions all season long. The weather and avalanche reports are vital information before heading out on a tour. Assimilate it with your knowledge of conditions. Once on a tour, check for signs of recent avalanche activity, ask others in the parking lot for info, and plan your route for the safest line.

While touring, dig a quick pit or do a pole test regularly to check the snowpack layers. Sometimes the safest, smartest decision is to stay home, or pick low-angle slopes in the trees.

For safe travel uphill, here are a few tips:

- Avoid skinning up open slopes or gullies.
- Stick to ridges.
- Stick to areas of thick trees.
- Cross slopes very low or high.
- Avoid crossing above your partners.
- Spread out, cross hazards singly.
- Avoid cornices.
- Check for escape routes.
- Avoid slopes between 30 and 40 degrees if conditions are dangerous.

For safe travel downhill, follow these guidelines:

- Stay on low-angle slopes.
- Use islands of safety wisely.
- Check for escape routes.
- Stay in voice and visual contact.
- Descend slopes singly, using a spotter.
- Stay within your skill level.
- Use the correct tool: for example, a wide, long snowboard or wide, long skis for deep powder.

If You Are Caught. If you do get caught by an avalanche, it is vital that you yell to your partners. Stay on your feet and ski out to the side. Don't try to outrun the avalanche. If knocked down, try to self-arrest by jamming your ice ax or ski pole into the snowpack that is under the avalanche. You might be able to arrest your slide and let the avalanche continue without dragging you into the sliding snow. If self-arrest doesn't work and you get caught in the avalanche, fight with all your might to stay on top of the sliding snow; usually this is accomplished by using a swimming motion with your arms and by kicking your feet. If you can, jettison your skis or snowboard—but keep your pack on, as it has essential survival gear and will help protect your back.

If you have a specialty backpack, insert an Avalung mouthpiece when you start to go down, or pull the ripcord for a backpack airbag system. As you slow down, one hand should punch to the surface to alert your rescuer of your location, and the other should make an air pocket. We know that creating an air pocket is the key to survival in prolonged burials. We also know that if you can get a hand to the surface, this is the fastest way for your partner to find you. Above all, if buried, stay calm.

If Your Partner Is Caught. If your partner is buried, prevent another accident and two burials: Always approach the avalanche slope cautiously. Watch your partner and mark the point where last seen. Once the slope is safe, begin a hasty search; sometimes you may find your partner quickly if his or her hand or ski pole is sticking out of the snow. Then, quickly begin a beacon search. When you locate the strongest signal, probe to confirm the burial location and dig, carefully. Hopefully, you'll never need these skills. But make sure to reread your favorite avalanche book and/or the instruction manual for your beacon every year. And do some beacon drills before heading out for a tour.

Glacier Travel

Glacier skiing and snowboarding can be magical: wide-open, endless permanent snowfields offer great turns, nearly every month of the year. However, glaciers are big, flowing masses of ice and snow and have some inherent dangers.

Crevasses are cracks in the snow that may be gigantic open chasms or may be hidden underneath surface snow. Seracs are towers of ice that pile up on the glacier. Glide cracks are fissures in the snowpack that appear in summer on permanent snow-fields as they melt and creep downhill. Unlike crevasses, which appear on glaciers, glide cracks are usually small. Glaciers also can be marked by steep, hard ice and suncups—large depressions in the snow from repeated sun exposure.

There is not space here to explain skills of glacier travel. The best way to learn them is to take a basic mountaineering course. This will teach you how to climb with the safety of crampons and ice ax. It will also show you the fundamentals of crevasse rescue, if you or your partner falls into a crevasse. Extrication requires specialized equipment: a rope, pickets or other anchors, carabiners, prusik cords or mechanical ascenders, and a harness.

Risk and Responsibility

A final note: Oregon is a relative hotbed for risk and responsibility discussions. We were the first state to enact a law that allows sheriff departments to bill for search-and-rescue against an irresponsible and/or unprepared person requiring rescue, including backcountry skiers and snowboarders. (In 2007, lawmakers also tried to mandate locating devices for climbing above 10,000 feet on Mount Hood but this law failed.)

In addition, a second law, the Skier Responsibility Act, governs winter resort rules, which all skiers and snowboarders must follow if skiing inbounds or accessing the sidecountry. The ski resorts can make their own rules for uphill traffic, backcountry access, and pre- and postseason use.

Both laws—the Skier Responsibility Act and the search-and-rescue law—are listed in Appendix C. Be safe. Be smart.

Whenever you enter the backcountry, you take risks. Subjective risks are those largely in your control: the ability to plan, prepare, travel safely, avoid hazards, and turn back when conditions are dangerous. Objective risks are the ones always present: rock and ice fall, crevasses, and altitude. Make sure you know and understand the risks, and mitigate risk through education, routine practice, a lot of experience, and good judgment.

Rescue is never guaranteed. Foul weather, lack of communication, severe terrain, dangerous snow conditions, and lack of resources, especially a dearth of skilled mountain rescuers, all can delay rescue.

Skinning up for ascent on a first-generation splitboard, Mount Hood

BACKCOUNTRY WISDOM

In medicine, my other career, we often offer "pearls," or short tips or words of wisdom learned from years of working in the profession. From three decades of exploring the world's mountains on one plank and two, here are pearls I've learned from colleagues, professionals, and partners.

Packing and Planning

- Stay organized so you can jettison work and hit the mountain on a powder day when your buddy calls at 6:00 AM . Keep your gear clean, dry, waxed, and ready to roll.
- Avalanche gear is useless if you don't know how to use it. Practice by hiding one beacon in your backyard or in the grocery store; then go find it.
- Pack light and keep your backpack tidy and organized so you can find things on the mountain, especially in a snow, wind, or rain storm. Use freezer bags or stuff sacks to organize gear. I pack my first-aid, survival, and repair gear in a one-quart freezer bag. I can see everything, and it's small enough to stuff into a small pack or coat pocket.
- Bring plenty of food and water, but also make sure you leave the trailhead fully hydrated and nourished. Eat a big breakfast before you head out on a backcountry tour.
- Always pack a hard-shell jacket, windproof and waterproof.
- Wear a helmet for safety and warmth. And never leave your goggles in the car, no matter how sunny it seems.
- Down doesn't handle sweat, rain, or wet snow very well. Bring synthetic layers. My favorites are medium-loft fleece, Primaloft insulation, polyester silk-weight long underwear, and socks that are a wool and synthetic blend.
- Probe ski poles are not a good substitute for a regular avalanche probe.
- Use an aluminum avalanche shovel, not plastic.
- You can save weight by carrying a compact aluminum shovel and compact 2-meter probe.
- Hot tea is a great treat on the mountain; bring a small thermos.
- Bring food you like. The quick prepackaged energy bars are okay on short notice, but usually a sandwich, nuts, dried fruit, and jerky hit the spot.
- On returning home, always put your clothes and boots out to dry, replace batteries, and fix broken equipment. It might be a powder day in the morning.

Skinning

- Glide with your skins. Don't pick up your feet and walk.
- Before you peel your skins, engage your ski brakes (move your bindings from skin mode to ski mode). That way if you drop your ski without the skin on, there's less chance it will careen down the mountain.

- To save time and energy, learn to peel your skins without unfastening your boot toe from the binder.
- Don't drop your skins in the snow. If they get wet or frozen they won't stick to your skis, rendering them nearly useless. It might not matter for one run. But if you plan to yo-yo (make several laps on one slope) or if you have an emergency and you need to put your skins back on, you need to make sure they are functional.
- After you peel your skins, stick them in your coat or in your pack to help keep them as dry as possible.
- If your skins don't stick, tape them to your skis in an emergency. Duct tape, first-aid tape, or hockey tape work best.
- Use skin wax to keep warm, wet snow from sticking to your skins.
- On long tours or multiday trips, you may want to employ a "no sweating" rule, so you don't get wet with sweat. Dress for climbing so that you don't overheat. Often this means a light layer with a vest, sweater, or soft-shell jacket.
- Keep breaks short; otherwise you are likely to cool down. If I'm out on a short two-hour tour for a couple of runs, I might stop two or three times for only a few minutes, just long enough for a quick bite and drink.

Snowboarding
- If you are serious about snowboarding in the backcountry, get a splitboard. It takes only a little practice to become efficient at converting from split to solid and vice versa.
- For Oregon's mountains, due to the long approach trails and numerous glaciers, my favorite setup for backcountry snowboarding is crampon-compatible plastic mountaineering boots with wire-bail plate bindings. Soft boots and strap bindings are not versatile for scrambling over rocks or climbing glaciers. I've used plastic mountaineering boots in soft bindings, which work okay too. I've also used clicker boots, which work well for splitboarding but are not that great for cramponing or long dirt approach trails.

TRAIL ETIQUETTE

One of the most elusive skills in mountain backcountry travel is etiquette. Other skills, for avalanche safety or mountain bivouacs, you can learn by taking a course and practicing. But etiquette for ski and snowboard mountaineers can be difficult to figure out. Local practices and customs vary around the West. And even for well-traveled backcountry skiers and snowboarders, we may not know the local vibe or the local system, like which direction to ski a trail, for example. Here are some of the basics.

We should all travel lightly on the land, "leave no trace." The old mantra "Take nothing but pictures, leave nothing but footprints" holds true.

Try to carry out all your litter, and if you have to relieve yourself, pick a place off trail and away from streams and water sources. Another mantra: "Pack it in, pack it out."

Think hard about bringing your dog: Pets are not necessarily as aware as humans when it comes to cliffs, avalanches, and toileting.

When parking, be careful you don't block others—with snow-covered parking lots, everyone needs a bit more space. Be cognizant that snowplows will need as much room as possible to get around you. Sometimes big banks of snow prohibit adequate parking, and during midwinter storms you may need to improvise or park down the road and walk to the trailhead.

If you are ascending by bootpacking or via snowshoes, please don't walk or snowshoe in the skin track. It makes it very bumpy for skiers and can ruin the skin track.

Hopefully you find yourself on a clean slope with no other tracks, or maybe a shot with only a few tracks. Either way, don't tear up the whole slope. Try to keep turns tight and leave some pow for the next skier or snowboarder. Who knows, you may be the one hiking up for another lap. Ski and snowboard close to the track already laid down on a slope. This technique, aka "powder farming," allows the most fresh tracks per slopes. If you are the last to hike the slope that morning, you'll appreciate the people who left you fresh shots.

HOW TO USE THIS BOOK
Route Selection

These routes are for both skiers and snowboarders. Sure, some wide-open spring corn or slush snowfields are perfect for a snowboard descent. Some rolly-polly routes with sections of flats are better for telemark and alpine touring skis. And for the low-angle beginner routes, metal-edged Nordic touring skis suffice. But most routes are suitable for all forms of backcountry skiing and snowboarding. Let's face it, many of us ski *and* snowboard, ski with telemark *and* alpine tour setups, tour with company of mixed persuasions, or, at a minimum, share our uphill skin track with a splitboarder or skier.

Most snowboarders will want to tour with a splitboard, although a few will climb with snowshoes or, fewer yet, with approach skis. For skiers, most of these routes are appropriate for either alpine touring or telemark gear. Nordic touring skis, metal edges with fish scales, are adequate for several low-angle routes. In summer, when bootpacking or cramponing, you can sometimes rip tracks carrying your alpine skis and solid snowboard on your pack—especially the summer routes up Mount Adams or St. Helens. Finally, although not wildly popular in the United States, firn gliders work just as well for descending a smooth, solid snowfield after a midsummer climb.

These routes have been selected with a few basic concepts in mind, beside the fact that they are great thrills for all glissé alpinists, suitable for any form of gliding down on snow. First, they provide something for everyone, from beginners looking to make their first backcountry turns in Oregon, to ski and snowboard mountaineers wanting to climb to the summits. Some guidebooks specifically focus on advanced routes. I too was once a beginner, and, being a physician and father, I wanted to be

Dawn patrol, South Sister (Nick Pope)

able to steer those just starting out to safer, low-angle routes. (Keep in mind a beginner backcountry skier or snowboarder should be an expert in resort conditions. And a ski and snowboard mountaineer should be experienced in the backcountry and have a full set of mountaineering and glacier travel skills.)

Second, these routes provide a good selection for year-round riding. Some are primarily routes for spring and summer, Oregon's busiest backcountry ski and snowboard season, while others are snow-covered only in winter, particularly the low-angle, low-elevation routes. A few gems can be ridden throughout the year, depending on conditions.

Third, most of these routes are aesthetic tours: thrilling, beautiful, peaceful, fun, and/or easy to reach via car and on foot. Highly technical routes beyond basic glacier travel or descents that require hours of schlogging to and from the snow have been omitted, with the exception of a few routes like North Sister and Three Fingered Jack, included for completeness. Summits requiring technical rock-climbing skills, like Mounts Washington, Jefferson, or Thielsen, have been omitted, but are options for rock climbers and mountaineers. Local hills that get enough snow for only a one-week window of turns—like those in the Columbia Gorge—have also been omitted.

I have been on these mountains at all times of year, in multiple conditions, and in all forms of ascent and descent: alpine skis, cross-country skis, snowboard, splitboard, snowshoes, crampons, bike, boots, and, where roads and laws allow, a truck. Some of them I have climbed recently, others a while ago. I have researched routes at different times of the year and in different conditions. I corroborated and supplemented findings with other books, magazine reports, maps, trip reports on Internet forums and websites, and, importantly, conversations with colleagues. I have attempted to keep the route descriptions useful without dating them by including seasonal landmarks. I also have not made these descriptions so detailed as to take out some of the adventure. And it is impossible to cover every bit of ground described here, in every season, since the last edition of this book.

Area Overviews

To more easily reference the routes, the book is divided into twelve geographic sections. Each section begins with an overview that includes important resources for the area.

Overview maps listed for each region are generally of two types. Some cover an entire area to provide a good lay of the land, including roads and large drainages. The U.S. Forest Service offers forest, ranger district, and wilderness area maps. Geo-Graphics wilderness maps and Green Trails provide excellent detail of many Oregon wilderness areas and show topography as well. The Geo-Graphics maps are among my favorites and may sometimes be the only map you need, aside from the USGS topo(s) listed for the route. DeLorme's Oregon (and California and Washington) state atlases are helpful in driving to the trailheads.

USGS topographic maps are the standard for routefinding, either the 7.5-minute series or CD-ROM versions of the same, such as those produced by National

Geographic. These maps cover a very small area, and sometimes more than one is needed to cover the whole route, but they are the most detailed topographic maps available. You'll see more info below on how maps are used in the routes.

Phone numbers and websites are listed for information centers, ranger districts, avalanche information, weather conditions, and road conditions, and ski area snow reports. The local U.S. Forest Service ranger district should have the most up-to-date local conditions. Always call ahead to check route conditions and road access. The rangers usually know snow and weather conditions as well. If you can talk to a backcountry ranger, that's a bonus. Ski patrollers also have a good idea of conditions and sometimes are well-versed in backcountry routes.

The best source for weather and avalanche info online is the Northwest Weather and Avalanche Center, accessed by phone or via the website with links to mountain telemetry data for temperature, precipitation, and wind speed in some areas. For backcountry routes near ski areas, resort snow phone and website reports are other ways to get snow and weather conditions.

For some areas, I've listed guides, backcountry huts, and courses.

For a comprehensive list of resources, see Appendix A.

Route Information

Each route description begins with essential information to help you plan your trip and compare routes.

On many routes, I've included alternate start points. Some roads are closed or unplowed in winter. The winter start point may be at the end of the plowed road, whereas in summer you may be able to drive right to the trailhead. The route information will list both start points, trail distances, and trail times.

Start Point: The elevation at the parking lot and trailhead.

High Point: The summit or the goal for the ascent.

Trail Distance: The approximate round-trip mileage from the parking area to the top and back.

Trail Time: The approximate time for a round-trip tour. This is a very rough estimate of hours and doesn't include time for prolonged rest stops, time to hike back up to make another run, or endless yo-yos if you find a good stash of snow. Your time will depend on what kind of shape you are in, weather, snow, trail conditions, seasonal variances, your group, and many other factors. It is a very approximate generalization.

In general, time estimates are based on experience and three basic rates of travel. For steep terrain, time is based roughly on 1 hour per 1000-foot elevation gain, which is a good clip for mountaineering. Some may climb at a slower pace. For approach trails, the time is based on about 2–4 miles/hour on dirt trail and 1–2 miles/hour on snow. Again, this is a moderately fast pace. Those hiking rates mean you're hiking fast to get to higher ground, not lollygagging.

Skill Level: This is a general recommendation for the ability required to meet the challenges of the route. Skill level is variable and quite subjective. For simplicity and to account for differences among riders, I've consolidated ascent and descent difficulty, avalanche hazard and general mountain hazards, routefinding, and such into four very general categories.

Beginner routes are most often safe, close to roads and civilization, and have low-angle slopes. They are mostly in or around ski areas or on cross-country trails. For those riders with basic skill in backcountry winter travel and new equipment, these routes are a good place to start. Remember, beginners in the backcountry should be advanced intermediates or experts in resorts: you should be able to safely descend a black diamond run in any condition, including ice, in any weather, including a whiteout. So, on your first day with new gear, pick one of the beginner routes.

Intermediate routes are for those with some additional skill and experience who want to try more challenging routes. They usually have moderate slope angle and may require some routefinding and avalanche risk assessment. They may involve a whole day, mitigating avalanche risk, routefinding, and traversing exposed terrain.

Advanced routes are for backcountry riders with significant experience under their belts, especially in avalanche safety, survival, and navigation. These routes are generally longer, steeper, and higher in elevation. Snow and terrain conditions may be variable. Advanced routes often include ascent and descent of a peak, glacier travel, and an overnight. Many are above timberline. Many require routefinding. Almost all require significant survival skills if you get caught in a storm or injured.

Expert routes are the most difficult in this book and may require glacier travel, scrambling, routefinding, avalanche risk, and long approaches. There are only a few expert routes, and if you don't get to these, don't worry. There are plenty of turns to be made in the intermediate and advanced routes. If you do want to tackle an expert route but don't quite have the skills, hire a guide.

Best Season: The generally recommended time of year to try this route. Although many of these can be done year-round, certain seasons for some tours make them great fun and have better chance of good snow. Remember to call ahead to check conditions as snow, terrain, weather, approach trail conditions, stream crossing, and water runoff can be wildly variable from seasonal or yearly changes.

Maps: These are the topographic maps that are essential for backcountry travel and routefinding. United States Geologic Survey (USGS) 1:24,000 (7.5-minute) maps are available at most outdoor stores or forest headquarters. You can order directly through USGS at www.usgs.gov/pubprod, where you can buy printed maps or download digital scans of topo maps. Many people will choose mapping software to print their own maps as well as download them into their GPS. An excellent mapping program is published by National Geographic along with the USGS. The Oregon map package covers all routes except those in Washington and California, which require additional software.

Getting There: Each route includes brief, general directions from the nearest town easily recognizable from an auto map. Always call ahead to check on road conditions and access.

The Route: The route description is general without trying to describe every detail. Some needs to be left for your exploration. Keep in mind, seasonal and yearly variations cause change in terrain, snowpack, water, and weather; trails, snowfields, landmarks, and vegetation may be quite different from year to year. Confirm the route with a ranger or others knowledgeable about the conditions. Correlate this book's descriptions with maps, hopefully those as up-to-date as available.

A NOTE ABOUT SAFETY

Safety is an important concern in all outdoor activities. No guidebook can alert you to every hazard or anticipate the limitations of every reader. Therefore, the descriptions of roads, trails, routes, and natural features in this book are not representations that a particular place or excursion will be safe for your party. When you follow any of the routes described in this book, you assume responsibility for your own safety. Under normal conditions, such excursions require the usual attention to traffic, road and trail conditions, weather, terrain, the capabilities of your party, and other factors. Keeping informed on current conditions and exercising common sense are the keys to a safe, enjoyable outing.

The Mountaineers Books

Opposite: High alpine exposure on Oregon's highest peak (Pete Keane)

MOUNT HOOD SOUTH

THE AMERICAN INDIANS CALLED IT WY'EAST, son of the Great Spirit. In 1792, British Lieutenant William Broughton spied the bold peak from the Columbia River and named it after Rear Admiral Samuel Hood of the British Navy. We know it as Mount Hood, a name synonymous with Oregon mountaineering. At 11,239 feet it is one of the most-climbed mountains in the Pacific Northwest and the world. With numbers often compared to Mount Fuji in Japan, Mount Hood has some 10,000 climbers attempting it every year. It is a big majestic snow-clad volcano jutting from endless miles of green forested hills. With proximity to Portland and permanent snowfield and glaciers, it offers turns year round within easy reach of the Rose City.

The first ascent was by Portland climbers William Buckley, W. Chittenden, James Deardorf, Henry Pittock, and L. Powell in 1857. Although the *Oregonian* newspaper editor Thomas Dryer was reported to have reached the summit in 1854. In 1894, the Portland climbing club, The Mazamas, was formed on the summit; still active today, they offer climbing and ski and snowboard mountaineering trips for members. The first ski descent from the summit was probably Sylvain Saudan in 1971.

The south side offers year-round skiing and snowboarding; Timberline Lodge is the launching pad for many ascents, especially during the spring and summer. Mount Hood's south side gives access to a huge variety of routes: beginner backcountry tours, lift-access backcountry trips, ski and snowboard mountaineering routes, and technical climbs. All are within a day's adventure. Since road access goes to Timberline Lodge Ski Area at 6000 feet and chairlift drops one off at 8500 feet, access to snow at higher elevations is relatively easy.

MOUNT HOOD SOUTH MAPS

The single best map for an overview of the area is the Geo-Graphics Mount Hood Wilderness Map, a 1:30,000-scale map with 40-foot contours and 2000-meter UTM Grid for GPS use. The U.S. Forest Service Mount Hood National Forest map covers the most area, but doesn't give much detail or any relief lines. The Green Trails series has a close-up climbing map that covers the summit route. If you're a map junkie, here's a complete list for Mount Hood:

   USFS Mount Hood National Forest
   USFS Zigzag Ranger District
   USFS Mount Hood Wilderness
   USFS Mount Hood National Forest North
   Geo-Graphics Mount Hood Wilderness
   National Geographic Trails Illustrated Mount Hood
   Cross-Country Ski and Snowshoe Trails, Mount Hood, Oregon
   Green Trails Mount Hood No. 462
   Green Trails Mount Hood Climbing No. 462S

PRIMARY INFORMATION CENTERS/RANGER DISTRICTS

* Mount Hood National Forest Headquarters, Portland, OR: (503) 668-1700, www.fs.fed.us/r6/mthood
* Zigzag Ranger District: (503) 622-3191

AVALANCHE/WEATHER/ROAD CONDITIONS

- Northwest Weather and Avalanche Center: (503) 808-2400, www.nwac.us
- Oregon DOT Trip Check: (800) 977-6368, www.tripcheck.com. (Check the Government Camp pass camera, which points to US 26 for real-time road conditions and temperatures during daylight hours.)

SKI AREA SNOW REPORTS

- Timberline Lodge: (503) 222-2211, www.timberlinelodge.com
- Mount Hood Meadows: (503) 227-7669, www.skihood.com
- Ski Bowl: (503) 222-2695, www.skibowl.com
- Summit: (503) 272-0256, www.summitskiarea.com

OVERNIGHT SHELTERS

- Silcox Hut: (503) 222-2211, www.timberlinelodge.com

PERMITS

- Wilderness permits and climber's registrations are required for all routes in the Mount Hood Wilderness Area. This begins above Timberline Lodge Ski Area on the south side. Free, self-issued permits and climber's registrations are available at Timberline Ski Area's Wy'east Day Lodge.
- A Sno-Park Pass is required for all routes between November 1 and April 30.

GUIDES AND COURSES

- Timberline Mountain Guides: (541) 312-9242, www.timberlinemtguides.com
- The Mazamas: (503) 227-2345, www.mazamas.org

SPECIAL NOTES

For south-side routes that climb above 9000 feet, you should be aware of the Mount Hood Triangle. If you follow the fall line down from high on the south side—Palmer Glacier, the summit, or Illumination Rock—you will descend the Zigzag Glacier and risk going over the Mississippi Head Cliffs. The correct route down is a slight traverse to the left that generally follows magnetic south on your compass. In a storm or whiteout, it may seem odd not to descend the fall line, but trust your compass! Head south.

Mountain Locator Units are available for a nominal charge for south-side mountaineers. The Mountain Locator Unit is an animal tracker that was made available for use on the south side after an accident in 1986. It is carried by a climber and is activated by pulling a pin if one is lost. If search-and-rescue is actively looking for a lost climber, a receiver is activated that homes in on the transmitter to aid in locating the lost person. It is not designed for immediate rescue, and it is not an avalanche beacon. It only helps rescuers find someone who has been reported missing. You may choose to carry one per party, especially if you are attempting the summit. You can rent locators in Government Camp at Mount Hood Inn, (503) 272-3205, or at mountaineering shops in Portland. Alternatively, carry a GPS and cell phone.

1 Tom, Dick, and Harry Mountain

Start Point : Mirror Lake trailhead, 3400 feet
High Point : Tom, Dick, and Harry Mountain, 5000 feet
Trail Distance : 5 miles
Trail Time : 3 hours
Skill Level : Intermediate
Best Season : Winter
Map : USGS Government Camp

Tom, Dick, and Harry Mountain is about the closest terrain to Portland for decent turns and, when compared to other below-timberline south-side routes, fairly steep. Only a short hike from the road, it is ideal for a half-day tour. However, because the route is relatively low in elevation, the snow quality is often suspect in warm temperatures or after rain. When the sky finally does dump snow, the steep shots here are avalanche prone. Nonetheless, if you are a weather-savvy, avalanche-aware off-piste enthusiast with only a half-day to spare, you can get great turns here. On sunny weekends, this basin may be crowded with snowshoers and cross-country skiers, so share the trail.

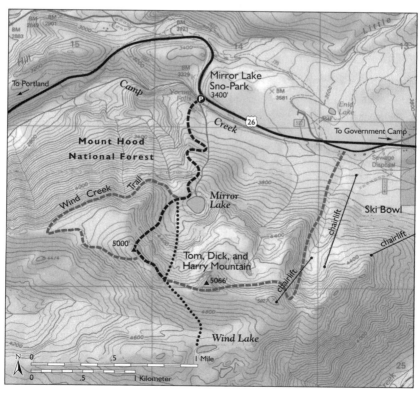

Don't pass up good snow: the closest turns to Rose City

GETTING THERE. From Portland, drive east on US 26 about 60 miles toward Government Camp. About a mile before Government Camp, park at the Mirror Lake Sno-Park on the south side of the road.

THE ROUTE. From the sno-park, follow Mirror Lake Trail 664 for 1.5 miles to the wide clearing of Mirror Lake. This trail is fairly narrow and may have skin or snowshoe tracks. At Mirror Lake, you will have a good view of the bowl and ridge. Skirt the lake to the right, pass through a thick grove of trees, and climb 800 feet to the ridge. Stay to the right near trees as much as possible, and evaluate avalanche hazard on the way up.

Alternatively, continue on Trail 664 as it becomes the Wind Creek Trail for 1.5 miles, heading west, then back east to gently climb the ridge. This is longer and doesn't allow you to check out slope conditions on the way up.

Yet another option is to hike up Ski Bowl lifts to the top of the ski area and traverse west to Tom, Dick, and Harry Mountain and the bowl that opens up below. Because you will be skiing or snowboarding within the ski area boundary, check with the ski patrol about access if you want to make this approach during the ski season.

From the ridge you have several options to glide down. The west end of Tom, Dick, and Harry offers 25-degree slopes. Toward the east end of the ridge the slopes steepen, and you will find some chutes among the rock bands. You can also ski the back side toward Wind Lake.

Ride the slope down to Mirror Lake; then you may need to skin or snowshoe back across the flat trail to the trailhead.

2 Glade Trail

Start Point :	Blossom Lane Sno-Park, 4000 feet
High Point :	Timberline Lodge, 6000 feet
Trail Distance :	6 miles
Trail Time :	3 hours
Skill Level :	Beginner
Best Season :	Winter
Map :	USGS Mount Hood South

The Glade Trail is an old ski trail that connects Timberline Lodge Ski Area with Government Camp; it's the path of an old tramway that long ago used a refurbished city bus suspended from a cable to ferry people from the small town to the antique lodge. The tramway is long gone, but the Glade Trail remains. It is most often ridden one-way from Timberline, but it is an easy up-and-back for beginners, especially for your first tour or when you're testing new gear. The Glade Trail is one of the gentlest routes in this book, so choose a day with fresh dry snow or firm cold corn to make this trip worthwhile. With its low elevation, slush is common on this trail; it can be a slow-motion trip down. And early or late in the season, the trail can have scant snow cover. But because of the low-angle slope, it is a pretty safe bet when avalanche danger exists on steeper slopes higher up.

GETTING THERE. From Portland, drive east on US 26 about 60 miles to Government Camp. Take the first Government Camp exit and continue east through town on Government Camp Loop Road. Turn left on Meldrum Street, which becomes Blossom Lane. The Glade Trail begins at the end of the road, which dead-ends into a parking area marked with a trailhead sign.

THE ROUTE. From the trailhead, follow the well-marked trail through the woods. It meanders through the trees, then opens up to an old powerline swath. After 2 miles it comes near the bottom of the Blossom lift in the Timberline Lodge Ski Area. Continue skinning on the edge of the ski run to Timberline Lodge, where you can get a cup of java or cocoa.

The famed Glade Trail, ideal for a shake-down tour with new gear

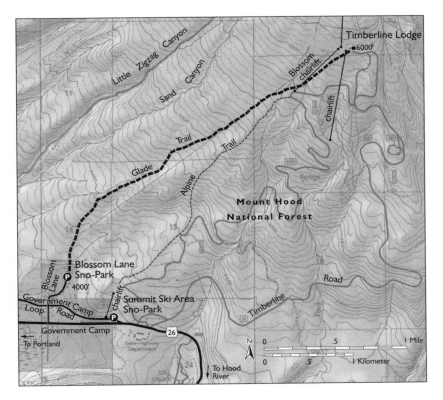

Then turn around for the glide down. From Timberline, make turns down the resort ski run called Glade toward the Blossom chairlift. About 100 yards before the bottom of Blossom, look for the sign and the wide-open powerline clearing of the Glade Trail.

3 Alpine Trail

Start Point	Government Camp, 4000 feet
High Point	Timberline Lodge, 6000 feet
Trail Distance	6 miles
Trail Time	3 hours
Skill Level	Beginner
Best Season	Winter
Map	USGS Mount Hood South

The Alpine Trail is another old ski trail that connects Timberline Lodge Ski Area with Government Camp. It is slightly shorter and steeper than the Glade Trail

(Route 2), so it sees more downhill traffic. Like the Glade Trail, Alpine often sees one-way riders from Timberline and also is a relatively safe tour when there is avalanche danger or foul weather pummels the upper mountain. If the snow is good, several runs may be warranted. Since it is shorter and steeper, choose Alpine first; then, if you have time, do Glade too. Another option is to combine this trip with a half day of resort skiing or snowboarding.

Soaking up sun during a quick break at tree line

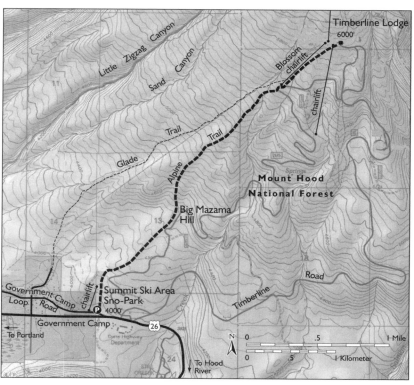

GETTING THERE. From Portland, drive east on US 26 about 60 miles to Government Camp. Take the second Government Camp exit and park in the Summit Sno-Park at Summit Ski Area.

THE ROUTE. From Summit Ski Area, hike up the east flank of the ski run via the West Leg Trail to the top of the chairlift. Stay well clear of ski runs and watch for downhillers. The Alpine Trail starts at the top of and behind the chairlift. Follow the well-marked trail through the woods. In about a mile, you will come to a steep section called Big Mazama Hill. The trail continues through the woods, ending up 2 miles later at the bottom of the Blossom chairlift. Continue hiking up to Timberline Lodge.

After coffee, hot chocolate, or a treat at either Timberline Lodge or Wy'east Day Lodge, spin around for the glide down.

 ## 4 Palmer Glacier and Triangle Moraine

Start Point	Timberline Lodge, 6000 feet
High Point	Crater Rock, 10,500 feet
Trail Distance	6 miles
Trail Time	5 hours
Skill Level	Intermediate
Best Season	Spring
Map	USGS Mount Hood South

The Palmer Glacier and its lower snowfield are great spots for intermediate backcountry riders and skiers to test their gear or get in a few laps on a sunny day. Because this route is in the Timberline Lodge Ski Area, it is best hiked when the resort is closed or early mornings during ski season. Always check with ski patrol first. If there are in-area skiers, stay well clear of them, usually to climber's right.

If time permits and weather is good, skiing farther up Triangle Moraine yields more turns, usually on open snowfields. Be advised, this is an exposed area of the mountain, prone to foul weather. Pick a clear day if you are going to ski all the way up to Crater Rock. And on descent, beware of the Mount Hood Triangle (see the area overview, Special Notes).

GETTING THERE. From Portland, drive east on US 26 about 60 miles to Government Camp. Just past Government Camp, turn left on Timberline Road (see Route 3 map). After 6 miles winding up the hill, you'll reach Timberline Lodge Ski Area. Park in the Climber's Lot or the main lot adjacent to Wy'east Day Lodge. If you are climbing above 9000 feet into the wilderness area, get your wilderness and climbing permit at Wy'east Day Lodge.

THE ROUTE. Begin on the snowfield at Timberline Lodge and head more or less straight up the mountain. Stay to the right of the Magic Mile chairlift. The slope is

Freezing temps, blistering wind, poor visibility—quintessential conditions on Triangle Moraine

a wide-open, low-angle grade. After 1 mile you reach Silcox Hut at 7016 feet. Continue up the mountain, staying to the right of the Palmer chairlift. The top terminus of the chairlift is at 8540 feet.

You can continue up Triangle Moraine, the V-shaped steep, rocky pitch that lies between the White River and Zigzag glaciers. This takes you to Crater Rock, at 10,560 feet one of the most popular destinations on Hood's south side for non-summit skiers and snowboarders.

As an alternative to climbing, snowboarders and skiers who want to shave time and catch better snow up high can ride the Palmer chairlift and hike to Crater Rock to make this a super-quick trip. If snow is good, yo-yo a few laps between 8000 and 10,000 feet. It's a great way to scout the summit route for later in the season.

The ride down heads back along the climbing route. For much of the year, even well into summer, you should be able to make tracks all the way to Timberline Lodge. Below Crater Rock, use caution if the weather or visibility is poor. As noted in the area overview, be wary of the Mount Hood Triangle. If you follow the fall line below

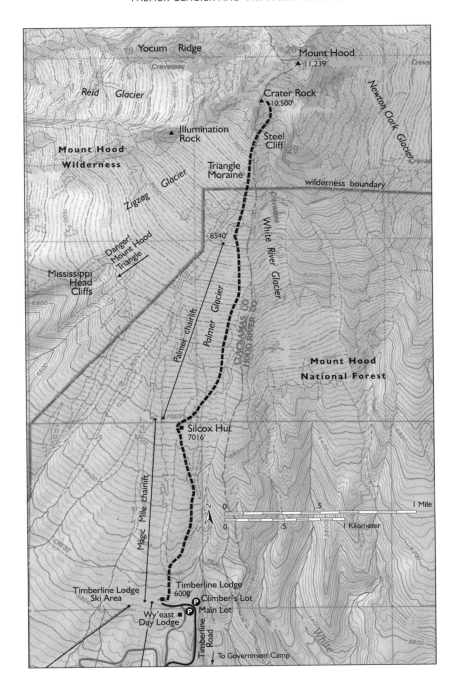

Crater Rock, you ride away from Timberline and down the Zigzag Glacier to the Mississippi Head Cliffs. The correct route down is a slight traverse to the rider's left that generally follows magnetic south on your compass.

5 Illumination Saddle and Upper Zigzag Glacier

Start Point	Timberline Lodge, 6000 feet
High Point	Zigzag Glacier, 9800 feet
Trail Distance	6 miles
Trail Time	4 hours
Skill Level	Advanced
Best Season	Spring
Map	USGS Mount Hood South

Illumination Rock is a second tour above Timberline's Palmer chairlift, similar to the Crater Rock route. Many people skin over to Illumination Rock to get away from the crowded South Climb and Crater Rock routes. Oftentimes here you can find fresh tracks when the slopes below Crater Rock and Triangle Moraine are tracked up.

It's a slightly longer tour, and takes some traversing to get over the Illumination Rock saddle. And, you have to be wary of the Mount Hood Triangle, as noted in the area overview. Continuing down the Zigzag Glacier, the natural fall line ends in the Mississippi Head Cliffs. But to get away from crowds, this is a great spot for wide-open slopes of midwinter pow or spring corn. Just make sure you go on a clear day in good weather; foul weather up here makes getting down difficult.

GETTING THERE. From Portland, drive east on US 26 about 60 miles to Government Camp. Just past Government Camp, turn left on Timberline Road. After 6 miles winding up the hill, you'll reach Timberline Lodge Ski Area. Park in the Climber's Lot or the Wy'east Day Lodge lot. Get your wilderness and climbing permit at Wy'east Day Lodge.

THE ROUTE. Begin on the snowfield at Timberline Lodge and head more or less straight up the mountain. Stay to the right (east) of the Magic Mile chairlift. The slope is a wide-open and low-angle grade. After a mile you reach Silcox Hut at 7016 feet. From here, continue up the mountain on a steeper slope, staying to the right of the Palmer chairlift. In another mile you reach the top of the Palmer lift at 8540 feet. From here traverse north, or to climber's left. Illumination Rock should be visible to the north another mile away.

The slopes above the rock offer the best turns, on the upper Zigzag Glacier, between 8000 and 9000 feet. The saddle right at the base of the rock leads to advanced ski

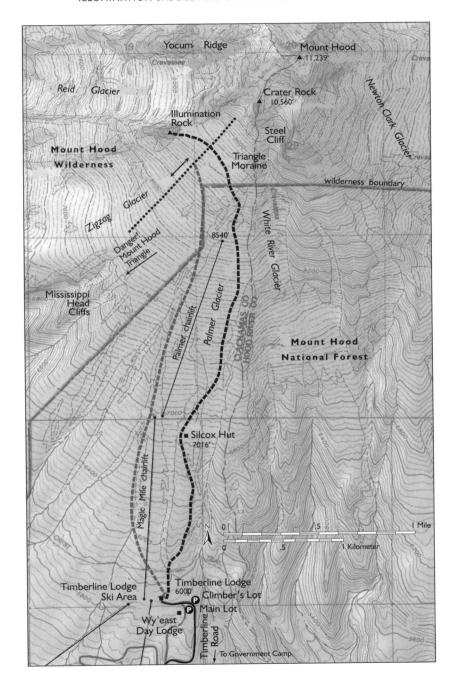

Clear day destination: Illumination Rock and upper Zigzag Glacier

routes of the Reid Glacier and one of the most difficult summit climbs on the mountain, the famed Leuthold Couloir.

The ride down heads back along the hiking route or, alternatively, on skier's right of the Palmer and Magic Mile chairlifts. On a clear day you should be able to see the whole route, all the way back to Timberline Lodge. In foul weather, make sure you have a GPS or compass to make the traverse back to the top terminus of the Palmer chairlift. For most of the year, there should be enough snow that you can ski or snowboard all the way back to Timberline Lodge, even through late summer.

6 South Climb, Hogsback Ridge

Start Point : Timberline Lodge, 6000 feet
High Point : Mount Hood summit, 11,239 feet
Trail Distance : 7 miles
Trail Time : 8 hours
Skill Level : Expert
Best Season : Spring
Map : USGS Mount Hood South

The South Climb is one of the most popular mountaineering routes in Oregon, if not the entire nation and world, rivaled probably only by Mount Fuji in Japan. Some

10,000 climbers attempt it annually. Its proximity to the metropolitan area of Portland, with drivable access up to 6000 feet, makes a summit bid doable in a day. One caution, though: the weather on Mount Hood is some of the worst in the world. Storms hit hard and fast, bringing snow, wind, rain, sleet, and avalanches. And, because the entire route is above timberline, there are very few areas where you can hunker down and safely wait out the weather. If foul weather sets in, your only respite is usually to build a snow cave.

That said, this is a spectacular descent. A summit climb followed by a ski is something unique to many of the Cascade volcanoes. If the weather and snow cooperate, it can be a superb 5000-foot descent.

Be advised, this route is for expert skiers and snowboarders only. There are several additional hazards on the summit pitch beyond Crater Rock: a steep, icy chute called the Pearly Gates, significant quantity of ice and rock fall in spring and summer, and the bergschrund—the crevasse at the top of the glacier. The summit pitch should be ridden only in spring when the bergschrund is closed, avalanche danger is at a minimum, and snow conditions are firm without ice. Otherwise, a more common practice is to leave your glissé gear at Hogsback Ridge, bootpack with crampons to

The descent is why we ascend—smooth spring corn on South Climb

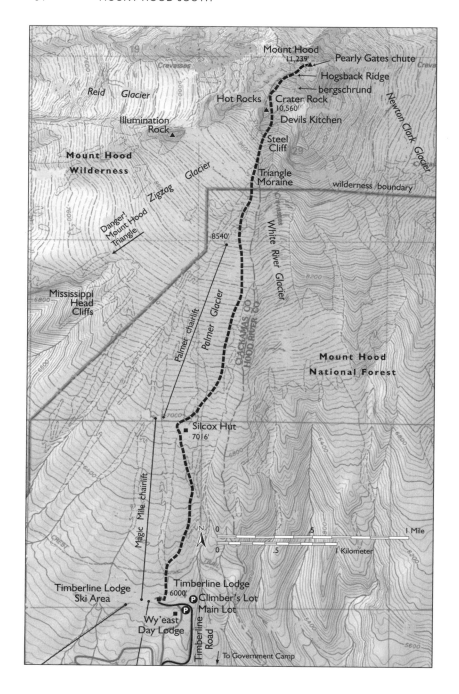

the summit and back, then ski or snowboard from Hogsback Ridge down the route. If you attempt the summit, be prepared to bring crampons, helmet, ice ax, rope, and pickets. Know how to use a running anchored belay for safety. Be cautious of crowds in the Pearly Gates chute.

GETTING THERE. From Portland, drive east on US 26 about 60 miles to Government Camp. Just past Government Camp, turn left on Timberline Road. After 6 miles winding up the hill, you'll reach Timberline Lodge Ski Area. Park in either the Wy'east Day Lodge lot or the Climber's Lot. Get your wilderness and climbing permits at Wy'east Day Lodge.

THE ROUTE. Begin on the snowfield at Timberline Lodge and head more or less straight up the mountain. Stay to the right of the Magic Mile chairlift. The slope is a wide-open, low-angle grade. After a mile you reach Silcox Hut at 7016 feet. From here, continue up the mountain on a steeper slope, staying to the right of the Palmer chairlift. In another mile you reach the top of the Palmer chairlift at 8540 feet. Continue 0.3 mile up the Palmer Glacier, up Triangle Moraine, to Crater Rock, the large rock at the base of summit.

At Crater Rock skirt around the base to the east, or climber's right, and gain the snow-covered Hogsback Ridge. Some parties rope up at this point. Hike along Hogsback Ridge to the final chute called the Pearly Gates. If the bergschrund is closed, it may be easy to cross. If it is open, you will need to detour a few hundred feet to the east, climber's right, close to the rock wall of the Steel Cliff. At this point, watch attentively for rock and ice fall, especially in the warm days of spring and summer. When climbing the final chute, be careful of falling on the final steep pitch through the Pearly Gates. Use an ice ax and crampons. If you are roped, consider using a running belay for safety. There have been several parties roped up, but not belayed, who have fallen and dragged their whole rope team down into the bergschrund. Because this chute gets crowded with a bottleneck of climbers in the late spring and summer, especially on weekends, try to avoid climbing when multiple parties are ascending or descending—more than once a group of climbers have fallen, and taken out other groups below them.

The ride down heads through the steep, narrow Pearly Gates chute, about a 40-degree slope, to Devils Kitchen bowl. Watch for climbers coming up the chute, and be careful of the bergschrund. You will want to descend with an ice ax or self-arrest grip poles. If you choose to stash your gear at Hogsback Ridge, hike down the way you came up.

The ride down from Hogsback Ridge and Crater Rock heads back along the climbing route. On a clear day you should be able to see the whole route, all the way back to the lodge. For untracked snow, the best bet is to ride down the slopes, staying just to the skier's right, or north, of the Palmer and Magic Mile lifts. For most of the year, you should be able to make tracks all the way back to Timberline Lodge, at least through midsummer.

Below Crater Rock, use caution if the weather or visibility is poor. As noted in the area overview, be wary of the Mount Hood Triangle. If you follow the fall line below Crater Rock, you ride away from Timberline and down the Zigzag Glacier to the Mississippi Head Cliffs. The correct route down is a slight traverse to the rider's left that generally follows magnetic south on your compass.

7   South Climb, West Crater Rim

Start Point : Timberline Lodge, 6000 feet
High Point : Mount Hood summit, 11,239 feet
Trail Distance : 7 miles
Trail Time : 8 hours
Skill Level : Expert
Best Season : Spring
Map : USGS Mount Hood South

The West Crater Rim route to the summit is less popular among climbers and glissé mountaineers. It is one step more difficult than the South Climb via Hogsback Ridge, and probably one of the more difficult and dangerous routes in this book. The summit pitch is marked by a bergschrund and steep avalanche-prone slope. If the final summit pitch is questionable for a safe ascent or descent, you can always turn around at Crater Rock and tackle the summit another day.

Like the South Climb via Hogsback Ridge and the Pearly Gates (Route 6), this summit route is for expert skiers and snowboarders only. There are several additional hazards on the summit pitch beyond Crater Rock: a steep chute, ice- and rockfall, and the bergschrund. The summit pitch should be ridden only in spring when the bergschrund is closed and avalanche danger is at a minimum. If you attempt the summit, be prepared to bring crampons, helmet, ice ax, rope, and pickets. Know how to use a running belay. Despite these cautions, this route can be a better ski than the South Climb via Hogsback Ridge, and can also be much less crowded.

GETTING THERE. From Portland, drive east on US 26 about 60 miles to Government Camp. Just past Government Camp, turn left on Timberline Road. After 6 miles winding up the hill, you'll reach Timberline Lodge Ski Area. Park in the Wy'east Day Lodge lot or the Climber's Lot.

THE ROUTE. Begin on the snowfield at Timberline Lodge and head more or less straight up the mountain. Stay to the right of the Magic Mile chairlift. The slope is a wide-open, low-angle grade. After a mile you reach Silcox Hut at 7016 feet. From here, continue up the mountain on a steeper slope, staying to the right of the Palmer chairlift. In another mile you reach the top of the Palmer lift at 8540 feet. Continue 0.3 mile up the Palmer Glacier toward Crater Rock, the large rock at the base of the summit.

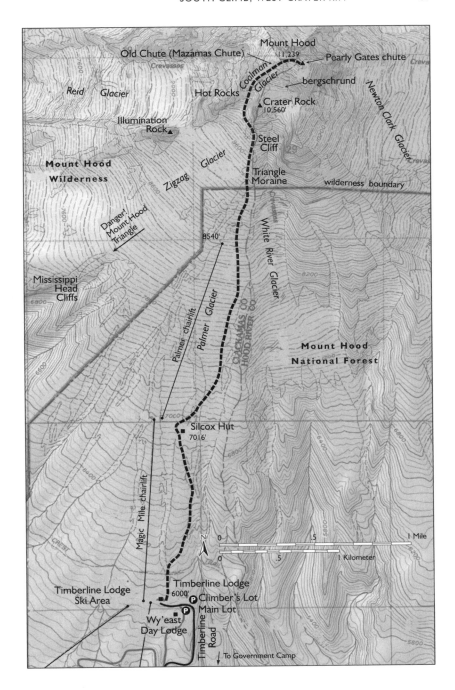

Forging a midwinter skintrack on Mount Hood

Below Crater Rock skirt around to the west, climber's left, climb past Hot Rocks, and continue up the steep face to the summit. Nearing the top you will gain a flat shelf on the Coalman Glacier. Depending on the time of year, you will probably hike over or around the bergschrund at the top of the glacier. You may have to skirt around it to the west, climber's left. The final few hundred feet climb through Old Chute (aka Mazamas Chute). When climbing this final pitch, be careful of a fall, avalanches, and rock or ice fall. Most parties rope up, and you should consider using a running belay. Usually crampons and an ice ax are necessary.

The ride down starts from the summit through the 40-degree Old Chute. Watch for climbers coming up the chute, and be careful of a fall. You may want to descend with an ice ax or self-arrest grip poles. If in doubt, hike down and put on your skis at 10,500 feet at the bench on the Coalman Glacier.

The ride down from Crater Rock heads back along the climbing route. On a clear day you should be able to see the whole route, all the way back to the lodge. For untracked snow, the best bet is to ride down the slopes, staying just to rider's right, or north, of Palmer and Magic Mile chairlifts. For most of the year, you should be able to make tracks all the way back to Timberline Lodge.

Below Crater Rock, use caution if the weather or visibility is poor. As noted in the area overview and in Route 6, be wary of the Mount Hood Triangle.

8 Salmon River Canyon

Start Point : Timberline Lodge, 6000 feet
High Point : Silcox Hut, 7016 feet
Trail Distance : 2 miles
Trail Time : 2 hours
Skill Level : Intermediate
Best Season : Winter
Map : USGS Mount Hood South

Salmon River Canyon is a popular short route in winter, especially when the snow is poor at lower elevation, the weather is lousy high up, and you are short on time. If you've tackled the Glade and Alpine trails (Routes 2 and 3), and you want some experience above timberline, this is a good place to start. The canyon terrain is not steep, so it best ridden with fresh dry snow or spring corn. It is close to the ski area and

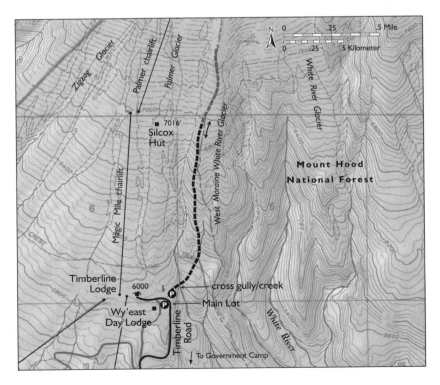

No, it's not cheating. Catch a ride up Palmer chairlift to jumpstart a summit bid.

has mellow terrain. You can bail out of the canyon to the ski area if needed. Although avalanche danger is low, watch for slides from cornices and small terrain traps like the creek crossing in the gully right at the parking lot. This route is one step harder than a beginner route, but not as difficult as most intermediate routes in this book—a good choice if you are looking for better snow above 6000 feet but not ready for the routes higher on the mountain.

GETTING THERE. From Portland, drive east on US 26 about 60 miles to Government Camp. Just past Government Camp, turn left on Timberline Road. After 6 miles winding up the hill, you'll reach Timberline Lodge Ski Area. Park in the Climber's Lot.

THE ROUTE. Unlike most routes that start from Timberline Lodge, the Salmon River Canyon route begins a few hundred feet down the road from Wy'east Day Lodge, at the backcountry parking lot. From the lot, cross the Salmon River gully with caution, making sure there is adequate snow coverage over the stream. You will have to climb down a hundred feet from the parking lot into the drainage, then back up the other side to gain the west ridge of the Salmon River Canyon. Ascend the ridge; after a few hundred feet in the trees, the slope opens with shallow gullies on both sides. Follow the drainage up to its terminus at about 7000 feet near Silcox Hut, the small shelter at the edge of the ski area.

You can continue higher up on the West Moraine of the White River Glacier. This moraine heads north up the mountain among sparse trees on a gentle slope. Be cautious of the steep slopes that fall away to the east to the huge deep chasm of the glacier and headwaters of White River. At least one party, caught after dark in a storm, has fallen off this ridge into the glacier below. The views into the canyon can be spectacular, so take in the scenery.

The descent follows the route up, on the flat open slopes below Silcox Hut. About halfway down, the slope narrows to a few gullies, then scattered trees. During most of the winter and spring you should be able to ride back down to the parking lot.

Once down near tree line, watch for the traverse back to the parking lot at 6000 feet. You will need to hike down to the small canyon, then back up to the parking lot.

9 Barlow Butte

Start Point	Barlow Pass Sno-Park, 4160 feet
High Point	Barlow Butte, 5069 feet
Trail Distance	5 miles
Trail Time	3 hours
Skill Level	Intermediate
Best Season	Winter
Map	USGS Mount Hood South

For someone looking to get away from the south-side crowds around Timberline, Barlow Butte is worth checking out. For those cramped for time, this small tree-covered knoll with easy access is another excellent intermediate spot close to civilization. It provides opportunity to hone skills with new gear or new partners, or simply to avoid the exposed slopes of the upper mountain. Keep in mind that although this is a popular cross-country ski area, the treed butte itself will see little traffic, and the trail will likely not be well marked—so routefinding skills are important.

GETTING THERE. From Portland, drive east on US 26 about 60 miles to Government Camp. About 3 miles past Government Camp, exit US 26 to follow OR-35 (Mount Hood Highway) toward Hood River. Once on OR-35, drive 2 miles and park at Barlow Pass Sno-Park, on the right.

THE ROUTE. The tour begins on Barlow Road (Forest Road 3530); snow-covered and unplowed in the winter, this is a popular cross-country ski trail leading to Devils Half Acre Meadow. Follow the road a few hundred feet down a gentle slope, then detour left to Barlow Butte/Mineral Jane Ski Trail 230, marked by a sign. If you miss this turn, you'll descend to Devils Half Acre. Follow the Barlow Butte/Mineral Jane Ski Trail for a half mile to another sign that marks Barlow Butte Trail 670. Take a right and follow the zigzags up the north-facing, tree-covered slope of the butte. Whereas Barlow Road and the Mineral Jane Trail are marked by blue cross-country ski blazes, the Barlow Butte Trail is not, since it is more of a summer hiking trail than a cross-country ski route. The trees are thick, so keep track of your position.

The summit is the site of an old lookout, with some steeper cliff chutes on the south- and east-facing slopes and tight tree skiing to the north. If you head off the south or east sides, you'll need to skin back up to return on the north side. If the snow is good, yo-yo a few laps in the tight trees before skinning back to your car on the approach trail.

Corn becoming slush in the high alpine (Nick Pope)

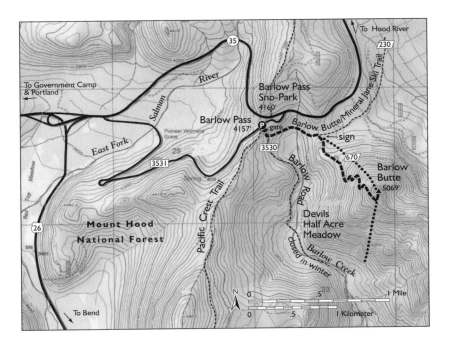

10   Boy Scout Ridge

Start Point : White River West Sno-Park, 4200 feet
High Point : Boy Scout Ridge, 6000 feet
Trail Distance : 5 miles
Trail Time : 2 hours
Skill Level : Intermediate
Best Season : Winter
Map : USGS Mount Hood South

Boy Scout Ridge is the lower section of the West Moraine of the White River. The upper moraine is accessed by the Salmon River Canyon route (Route 8). This is another excellent beginner–intermediate route that starts at the White River Sno-Park and goes to Timberline. Lower White River Canyon is popular among cross-country skiers, snowshoers, and sledders mostly because it is incredibly beautiful and accessible. Don't expect to find big, bold lines or steep chutes. But the scenery makes up for the lack of vertical.

GETTING THERE. From Portland, drive east on US 26 about 60 miles to Government Camp. About 3 miles past Government Camp, exit US 26 to follow OR-35 (Mount Hood Highway) toward Hood River. Once on OR-35, drive 5 miles and park

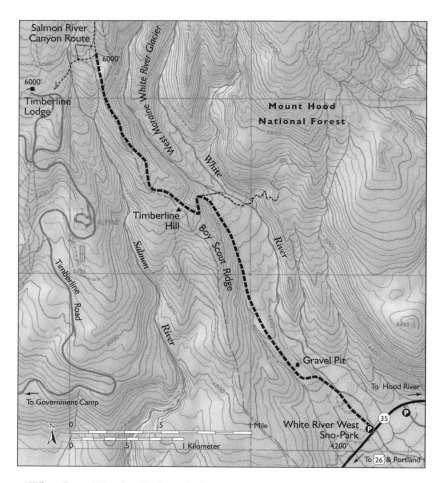

at White River West Sno-Park on the left. If the lot is full, there's another parking lot on the south side of the road after the bridge.

THE ROUTE. From the far end of the parking lot, start north along the river bottom on a cross-country and snowshoe ski trail; stay to skier's left of the canyon floor. In a half mile, you come to a small open slope called the Bowl or Gravel Pit. Climb the small slope to the bench above the river, then continue on the broad gentle slope through the trees.

At about 5000 feet you will come to tree line. Ascend the short but steep slope to the left to continue up Boy Scout Ridge. Once up on the broad, open ridge, you will see Timberline Lodge off to the left. Be cautious of the steep slopes that fall away to the east. For a longer tour, continue up the West Moraine of the White River Glacier (see Route 8).

All trails lead to the backcountry

For descent, follow the gentle slope you hiked up. Once down near tree line, watch for the trail you climbed up. You can reach the White River by descending back down the steep slope to 5000 feet. If you drop down to the floor, you may need to cross and recross the braided channel of the river, which may or may not be covered by snowbridges.

II   White River Canyon

Start Point	White River West Sno-Park, 4200 feet
High Point	White River Glacier, 8200 feet
Trail Distance	8 miles
Trail Time	6 hours
Skill Level	Intermediate
Best Season	Winter
Map	USGS Mount Hood South

White River Canyon, the huge drainage between Timberline Lodge and Mount Hood Meadows ski areas, is flanked by Boy Scout Ridge and the West Moraine on one side (Routes 8 and 10) and Vista Ridge on the other (Routes 17 and 21). The glacier and canyon are part of a large and incredibly beautiful glacier drainage. Its breathtaking

Carving south side turns on sun-drenched glaciers

view of Mount Hood and the spectacular moraines make this an awe-inspiring tour. Because of the large area, there is something for everyone, from low angle to steeps. On a clear day, the canyon can be in the sun all day, so the corn is often excellent riding here when slopes are bulletproof and windblown higher on the mountain. On the same note, pow is prevalent here when it is all tracked up in the resorts. Keep in mind, it's a long approach—1.5 miles on flat terrain—before you reach slopes steep enough to climb and ski.

The main risks of this area are threefold: the creek, avalanches, and crevasses. The creek may or may not be covered by snowbridges; these may or may not be stable, posing the risk of falling through into the creek. Getting soaked with freezing water can cause hypothermia; moreover, it can be difficult to climb out of the creek. Use caution when crossing, and if in doubt, find a better place to cross or stick to one side of the canyon or the other. In addition to the risk of avalanches frequenting the steep upper slopes, in this drainage avalanches can come from up high on the mountain and travel into the basin. Finally, you will need to watch for and avoid crevasses that mark the beginning of the White River Glacier at the head of the canyon.

GETTING THERE. From Portland, drive east on US 26 about 60 miles to Government Camp. About 3 miles past Government Camp, exit US 26 to follow OR-35

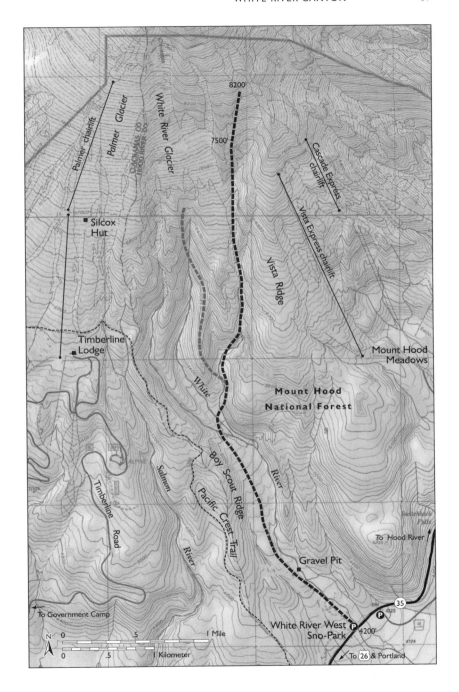

Palmer chairlift

Palmer Glacier

White River Glacier

CLACKAMAS CO
HOOD RIVER CO

8200

7500'

Cascade Express
chairlift

Vista Express chairlift

Silcox
Hut

Vista Ridge

Timberline
Lodge

Mount Hood
Meadows

White

Mount Hood

National Forest

Salmon

River

Boy Scout Ridge

Pacific Crest Trail

Timberline
Road

River

Switchback
Falls

To Hood River

Gravel Pit

35

To Government Camp

White River West
Sno-Park

P

P

4200'

N

0   .5   1 Mile

0   .5   1 Kilometer

To 26 & Portland

(Mount Hood Highway) toward Hood River. Once on OR-35, drive 5 miles and park at White River West Sno-Park on the left. There's another parking lot on the east side of the canyon, south side of the road.

THE ROUTE. From the far end of the parking lot, start north along the river bottom on a ski trail; stay to climber's left to avoid as much of the braided river channel as possible. In a half mile, you come to a small open slope called the Gravel Pit. Continue another mile up the river to tree line. From here you will see the huge west, east, and central moraines and numerous options for skiing.

Most people hike up the east side of the canyon, a steep slope that continues up to Vista Ridge at Mount Hood Meadows. It has a great fall line and faces south, so it can be good corn snow on spring mornings and turn to slush later in the day. Another option is the large moraine in the center of the canyon. On the center moraine, usually the east- or south-facing slopes have the best snow. The west side can be hard and windblown in winter.

On the way out, head down the way you came in, making tracks down the moraine, then skiing or snowboarding out the flats for the last mile. Again, watch the snowbridges.

⑫ Frog Lake Buttes

Start Point	Frog Lake Sno-Park, 3800 feet
High Point	Frog Lake Buttes summit, 5294 feet
Trail Distance	3 miles
Trail Time	3 hours
Skill Level	Intermediate
Best Season	Winter
Map	USGS Wapintia Pass

Like Barlow Butte (Route 9), Frog Lake Buttes are not a primary destination but a good alternative when you're looking for protection in the trees and want to avoid the crowds and foul weather at Timberline and White River. On the east side of Mount Hood, you may find better turns on Bennett Pass for a few extra miles, but Frog Lake Buttes are worthy of a short jaunt if you're looking for something different.

Because of the lower elevation, you'll want to hit this tour with fresh snow in midwinter. Like many of Oregon's foothills that linger around the snow–rain zone, these twin buttes can suffer from lower-elevation weather conditions: less snow than the higher elevations and rain, when snow level is high.

GETTING THERE. From Portland, drive east on US 26 about 60 miles to Government Camp. About 3 miles past Government Camp, continue south on US 26 toward Bend to Wapinitia Pass. In 4 miles, turn left (east) onto Forest Road 2610.

Navigating the wonderland of alpine fir and alpenglow.

In less than a half mile, park at Frog Lake Sno-Park on the right. The road is only plowed to the sno-park.

THE ROUTE. There's no formal winter trail here but many cross-country and snowmobile tracks. From the sno-park, continue on snow-covered Forest Road 2610 around the east side of Frog Lake. In a half mile or so, head east through the thick trees on Trail 530. In 1.5 miles, Trail 530 meets Trail 484. At the junction turn right, and continue on Trail 530 southeast toward the summit of the south butte. The trail will approach the summit from the west.

Alternatively, at the junction of Trails 530 and 484, you can head east-northeast toward the summit of the north butte. Neither route will likely be marked with blazes, so you'll have to find your way through the thick trees, perhaps without a trail.

Ski the glades of the buttes, and yo-yo a few laps to get in some vertical before skinning back out to your car.

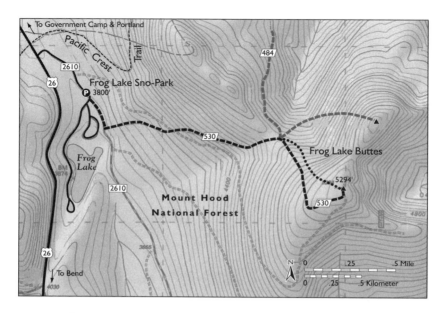

13 Mount Hood Circumnavigation

Start Point : Timberline Lodge, 6000 feet
High Point : 9000 feet, multiple glaciers
Trail Distance : 12 miles
Trail Time : 1 day
Skill Level : Expert
Best Season : Spring
Maps : USGS Mount Hood South, Mount Hood North

The Mount Hood Circumnavigation is an expert ski mountaineering objective. The 12-mile trip, which gains 6000 to 8000 feet, is for expert mountaineers only. Although not completed by this author, it's worth mentioning as an excellent way to get to know the mountain and, sooner or later, a route the ski mountaineers either complete or at least have on their tick list. More burly and dangerous than the South Side summit routes (see Routes 6 and 7), this takes more planning, preparation, and guidance than listed here.

There are several starting points, but a round trip from Timberline Lodge is the most common. Most skiers head clockwise and stick between the 6000- and 9000-foot elevations.

GETTING THERE. From Portland, drive east on US 26 about 60 miles to Government Camp. Just past Government Camp, turn left on Timberline Road. After 6 miles winding up the hill, you'll reach Timberline Lodge Ski Area. Park at either the Wy'east Day Lodge lot or the Climber's Lot. Get a wilderness and climbing permit at Wy'east Day Lodge.

THE ROUTE. Although not a detailed description, this gives mountaineers a general idea of the route points and the bailouts.

- Ski up Timberline Lodge Ski Area to Illumination Saddle.
- Cross the Reid Glacier to Yocum Ridge via the "terrible traverse."
- Cross the Sandy Glacier under the headwall to Cathedral Ridge.
- Cross the Ladd Glacier above Barrett Spur.
- Cross the Coe Glacier to Snowdome.
- Cross the Eliot Glacier to Cooper Spur.
- The first emergency bailout is down the Tilly Jane Trail to Tilly Jane Sno-Park.
- Cross the Newton Clark Glacier to Gnarl Ridge, Pea Gravel Ridge, and then Superbowl to Mount Hood Meadows Sno-Park.
- The second bailout is down the Heather Canyon Ski Trail to Hood River Meadows Sno-Park.
- Cross the White River Glacier back to Timberline Lodge Ski Area.

High pressure clarity in the high alpine

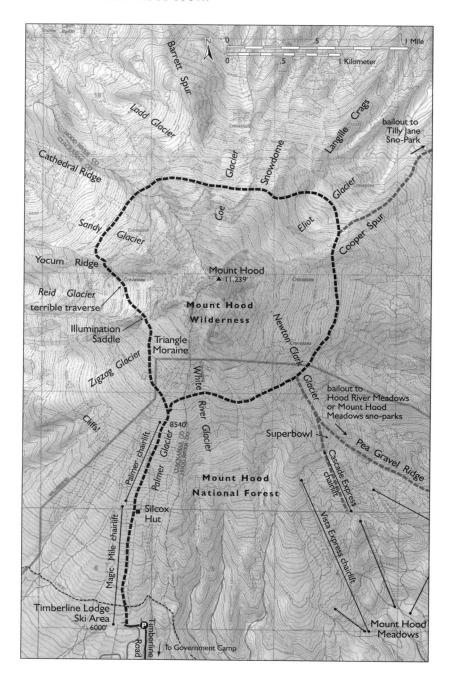

Opposite: Time to call in sick: It's a powder day.

MOUNT HOOD EAST

THE SOUTHEAST AND EAST SIDE OF MOUNT HOOD can be some of the best winter backcountry snow riding in northern Oregon. Compared to the south side, the snow here stays a bit drier and the sky is a bit sunnier. This corner of the mountain is dominated by Mount Hood Meadows Ski Resort and includes a large area. The Cascade Express chairlift and snowcat skiing take resort snow riders to 8000 feet. Heather and Clark canyons extend to 7000 feet and offer good terrain for both downhillers and cross-country skiers.

Winter access is via two main resort sno-parks: Mount Hood Meadows and Hood River Meadows. Many of the tours on this side are partially or entirely within the ski area. These routes provide some early-winter riding before the resort opens, or riding through the spring after the resort shuts down for the season. Although the rules fluctuate from year to year, at the time of this writing lift-access backcountry touring is not allowed, nor is inbounds uphill traffic during resort operations. You can hike above the Cascade Express chairlift, inbounds, to Superbowl when the patrol allows access above the lift.

Uphill traffic is allowed only via two routes, out of bounds, on the north and west borders of the ski area, as described below. In midwinter, it may be crowded here, especially when competing with lift-access downhill skiers and snowboarders for Superbowl or with Nordic skiers in lower Heather Canyon.

This is a good bet for early-season pow; I've skied as early as October on these routes. Spring skiing also can be great here, especially in April and May when the snow is still plentiful. The approach up the ski resort is easy and crowd-free when the resort is closed on weekdays in spring. This is a good place to tour to avoid the southside crowds and when Cooper Spur Road is still closed on the north side.

MOUNT HOOD EAST MAPS

The single best map for an overview of the area is the Geo-Graphics Mount Hood Wilderness Map, a 1:30,000-scale map with 40-foot contours and 2000-meter UTM Grid. If you're a map junkie, here's the complete list.

USFS Mount Hood National Forest
USFS Hood River Ranger District
USFS Mount Hood Wilderness
USFS Mount Hood National Forest North
Geo-Graphics Mount Hood Wilderness
National Geographic Trails Illustrated Mount Hood
Cross-Country Ski and Snowshoe Trails, Mount Hood, Oregon
Green Trails Mount Hood No. 462
Green Trails Mount Hood Climbing No. 462S

PRIMARY INFORMATION CENTERS/RANGER DISTRICTS

- Mount Hood National Forest Headquarters, Portland, OR: (503) 668-1700, www.fs.fed.us/r6/mthood
- Hood River Ranger District: (541) 622-3191

AVALANCHE/WEATHER/ROAD CONDITIONS

- Northwest Weather and Avalanche Center: (503) 808-2400, www.nwac.us
- Mount Hood Meadows Avalanche Reduction Operations: www.skihood.com/The-Mountain/Safety/Avalanche-Reduction-Operations (This website lists the current status of avalanche control for Heather and Clark canyons. You can also call (503) 337-2222, ext. 1705. Check this before heading into Heather Canyon or Clark Canyon.)
- Oregon DOT Trip Check: (800) 977-6368, www.tripcheck.com

SKI AREA SNOW REPORTS

- Mount Hood Meadows: (503) 227-7669, www.skihood.com. (The links to the web-cams and weather data from the "conditions" page are especially useful.)

PERMITS

- Wilderness permits are required for climbing in the Mount Hood Wilderness, which on the east side is above about 9000 feet. For the most part this includes only the Wy'east Face and upper Newton Creek drainage. These self-issued permits are available at the ranger stations or at Timberline Wy'east Day Lodge, but not at either of the sno-parks at Mount Hood Meadows.
- A Sno-Park Pass is required from November 1 to April 30.

SPECIAL NOTES

Since most of these runs are partially or entirely within the Mount Hood Meadows Ski Resort, they are best ridden before the resort is open for the season or when it is closed in spring. Lift-access riding (at the time of this writing) is not allowed, even during preseason grooming and maintenance operations. The exception is for those routes entirely in-area such as Superbowl and Heather Canyon, for which the patrol opens terrain for hiking above the Cascade Express chairlift. They require avalanche safety equipment for hiking. If you hike during the season from the parking lot to access the routes out of bounds, there are two uphill routes:

North Boundary. From Hood River Meadows Sno-Park, turn right at the first Heather Canyon Runout sign, exiting the ski area permit area, and head to the Newton Creek drainage. This can be a long trek up through Newton Canyon through brambles and downed timber.

South Boundary. From Mount Hood Meadows Sno-Park, start up the Mitchell Creek drainage, out of bounds in the trees to climber's left of the Buttercup and Vista Express chairlifts. The route is just out of bounds along the south rope line.

Make sure you check the Mount Hood Meadows Avalanche Reduction Operations; www.skihood.com/The-Mountain/Safety/Avalanche-Reduction-Operations lists the current status of avalanche control. If the ski patrol is doing control work in Heather and Clark canyons, you don't want to be touring on these routes. You can also call (503) 337-2222, ext. 1705.

14 Bennett Pass

Start Point	Bennett Pass Sno-Park, 4600 feet
High Point	Bennett Ridge, 4800 feet
Trail Distance	3 miles
Trail Time	2 hours
Skill Level	Intermediate
Best Season	Winter
Map	USGS Mount Hood South

Bennett Pass is a popular cross-country area along with Teacup Lake, which lies below the ridge along OR-35. The cross-country trails provide easy access to 600 feet of vertical on gentle, treed slopes—perfect for a short beginner–intermediate back-country tour, with plenty of opportunity to yo-yo if the snow is good. Keep this route in mind when the upper mountain routes are crowded or blasted by wind and snow. Because Bennett Pass is at a lower elevation, you may want to catch this route a few days after a storm. As long as temperatures are below freezing, snow will stay good in the pass. But in rising temperatures or full sun, it can get slushy and turn to cement.

GETTING THERE. From Hood River, drive south on OR-35 (Mount Hood Highway) for 32 miles to Bennett Pass Sno-Park.

THE ROUTE. From the sno-park, head up the Bennett Ridge Ski Trail, which follows the old Bennett Pass Road, Trail 3550. In 1.5 miles, you'll pass the trail to the White River overlook on the right, although it may not be well marked. There are so many hikers, snowshoers, and skiers here, you may find tracks leading in multiple

The solace of a skintrack (Jennifer Donnelly)

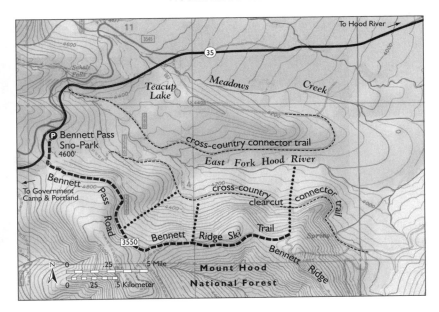

directions on and off the trail, so be careful to stay on the road. Bennett Pass Road follows the contour at 4800 feet, through thick forest, and wraps around to the north along Bennett Ridge.

You can descend the northwest-facing slopes through the trees at almost any spot along the ridge. Some slopes are steeper; most are treed, but the big conifers are spaced widely enough for great turns. Continue about 1.5 miles from the parking lot to a wide-open clearcut, another great spot to descend. At the bottom of the slope, near the Teacup Lake Nordic trails, you will hit one of several connector cross-country ski trails. Here's a good spot, when the slope flattens out, to skin back up for another lap.

When your day is ending, skin back up and schuss back out the Bennett Pass Road to your car.

15 Mount Hood Meadows Bowls

Start Point	Mount Hood Meadows Sno-Park, 5360 feet
High Point	One Bowl, 6400 feet
Trail Distance	2 miles
Trail Time	1 hour
Skill Level	Intermediate
Best Season	Early winter
Map	USGS Mount Hood South

This short, fairly straightforward run is another good place for beginner–intermediates to start. Because it is in the Mount Hood Meadows Ski Resort, the Bowls route is

Preseason inbounds touring: a short junket for early winter turns

perhaps at its best in early winter, the week before the resort opens for the season. Lately, the resort has been enforcing the no-uphill-traffic policy preseason, because of snowcat and snowmobile work. In spring you will find a lot of snow, but it will likely be hard-packed or crud from the resort skiers and snowboarders. Once in a while, though, you can get a good preseason or postseason run here.

Depending on the snow, choose this route as early as October, to catch preseason powder, or as late in May, after the resort has closed. Because this is a popular early-season route, it may be fairly crowded with people hiking, snowshoeing, or skinning, and inexperienced backcountry skiers and riders.

There are five bowls: Five Bowl is the closest to the lodge, and One Bowl is at the top. All the bowls are avalanche prone, and during the ski season the patrol does control work to make them safer. This is not so during pre- and postseason, so be careful.

GETTING THERE. From Hood River, drive south on OR-35 (Mount Hood Highway) for 35 miles. At Bennett Pass, exit and turn right up the Mount Hood Meadows Access Road to Mount Hood Meadows Sno-Park.

THE ROUTE. From Mount Hood Meadows parking lot, head up the Daisy chairlift line and ski run. Once you reach the bottom of the Cascade Express chairlift, head

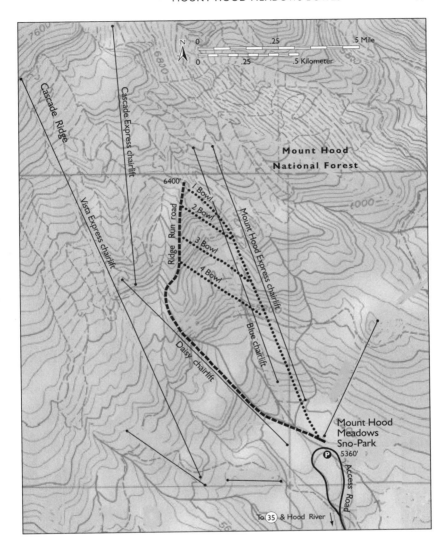

right up the Ridge Run road; this brings you to the top of the bowls on your right. Pass Four Bowl, Three Bowl, and Two Bowl. You'll have to leave the Ridge Run road to continue up to One Bowl.

You can hit any of the bowls, and take the runout back to the lodge. In deep snow, the runout won't be packed from inbounds skiers, so it could be slow, especially for snowboarders.

Beware of avalanche danger in the early season; all four bowls are steep avalanche-prone slopes. If there are many people snowshoeing and skinning, especially inexperienced ones, watch that someone above you doesn't kick a slide down.

16 Mitchell Creek Bowl and Iron Canyon

Start Point	Mount Hood Meadows Sno-Park, 5360 feet
High Point	Mitchell Creek headwaters, 6200 feet
Trail Distance	1 mile
Trail Time	1 hour
Skill level	Intermediate
Best season	Winter
Map	USGS Mount Hood South

When Mount Hood Meadows put the kibosh on uphill traffic inbounds, I had to search for another way to get a little exercise when I was working or had dropped my family off to spin on the lifts. There's a hidden bowl, just out of bounds, that gives about 500 feet of turns. It's short, and only takes about 20 minutes to ski to the top, so you can make several laps. This is a nice junket when the above-timberline routes are socked in with fog and wind, and the Heather Canyon runs are off-limits due to avalanche danger and control work.

GETTING THERE. From Hood River, drive south on OR-35 (Mount Hood Highway) for 35 miles. At Bennett Pass, exit and turn right up the Mount Hood Meadows Access Road to Mount Hood Meadows Sno-Park.

THE ROUTE. From the main parking lot, walk below the Buttercup chairlift bottom lift station to the maintenance building. Right at the nondescript aluminum shed, skin up the rope line along the Mitchell Creek drainage. You'll skin through the trees alongside the Vista Express chairlift. At some point, you cross Mitchell Creek. Be careful of snowbridges; at some spots the creek

Drop the kids at the resort, then skin the out-of-bounds stash in Mitchell Creek Bowl.

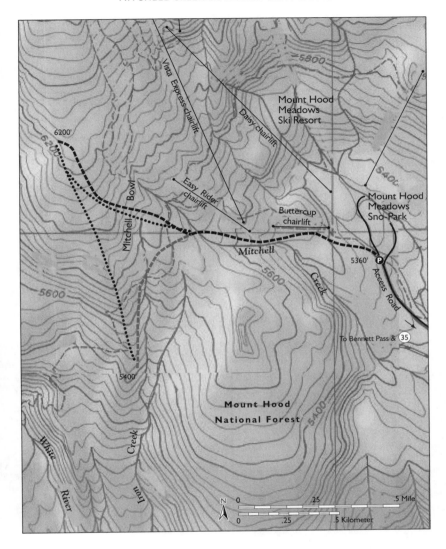

may not be covered by snow. In a few minutes you'll see the Mitchell Creek bowl on skier's left, just out of bounds. Skin up the broad, flat ridge to 6200 feet, the top of the bowl.

The shortest run is to ski the bowl back down to the creek, cross the creek, and skin back to the maintenance shed. If time permits, make a couple laps.

Alternatively, you can ski below the bowl, into a broad ridge. You will drop into the upper section of North Fork Iron Creek, which eventually drops you on OR-35, or into the White River canyon, both a long skin back to your car—or you can hitch-hike back.

17 Vista Ridge

Start Point : Mount Hood Meadows Sno-Park, 5360 feet
High Point : Vista Ridge, 7800 feet
Trail Distance : 4 miles
Trail Time : 2 hours
Skill Level : Intermediate
Best Season : Winter
Map : USGS Mount Hood South

Vista Ridge is a long, low-angle route that is great for those just getting to know the east side of the mountain and who want a longer tour than the Mitchell Creek bowl (Route 16). Offering spectacular scenic vistas of the White River, the ridge is the east moraine of the giant White River Glacier. This is a good route for winter well into spring, but the turns are not super-steep. There's a safety factor, too: the ski resort runs offer an easy escape to safety. Route 21 offers a longer ascent up Vista Ridge to Superbowl.

South boundary uphill access to Vista Ridge and points beyond

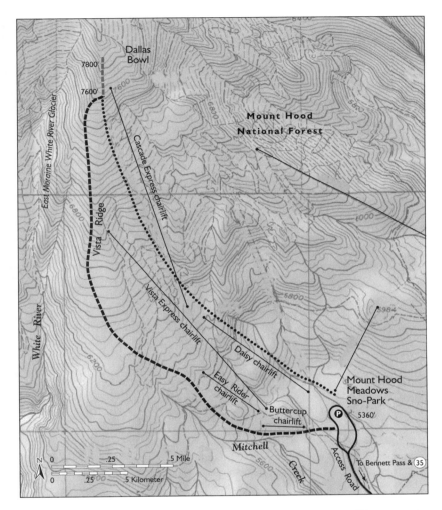

Because of the exposed nature of the ridge, there's often good windblown powder and pockets of dense, dry, wind-compacted snow. At the same time, coverage can be sparse. A storm that drops a few feet elsewhere on the east side may only dump a few inches on Vista Ridge, because the wind blows the snow into the canyons to the north.

As this has become a popular uphill route, there's a good chance you'll find a skin track here.

GETTING THERE. From Hood River, drive south on OR-35 (Mount Hood Highway) for 35 miles. At Bennett Pass, exit and turn right up the Mount Hood Meadows Access Road to Mount Hood Meadows Sno-Park.

THE ROUTE. From Mount Hood Meadows Sno-Park, follow the South Boundary for uphill traffic as described in the area overview for Mount Hood East. You start up the Mitchell Creek drainage, just out of bounds in the trees along the rope line, climber's left of the Buttercup and Vista Express chairlifts. Once near tree line, you will come out on the broad Vista Ridge. Initially trees are sparse, then nonexistent. Stay just out of bounds; there's a rope line here during the resort season. Around 7000 feet, the ridge gets rocky, and at one spot you may have to take off your skis and hike across a rock band. At the top of the Cascade Express chairlift, you can spin around. Or, continue up the ridgeline to top out at 7800 feet—the top of a bowl above the Cascade chairlift called Dallas Bowl. To descend, head down the ridge you hiked up. Alternatively, you can ski down the resort slope.

18   Lower Heather Canyon

Start Point	Hood River Meadows Sno-Park, 4520 feet
High Point	Heather Canyon, 6000 feet
Trail Distance	3 miles
Trail Time	2 hours
Skill Level	Intermediate
Best Season	Winter
Map	USGS Mount Hood South

Lower Heather Canyon is a good intermediate trip that can be skied again and again with many different slopes. Be advised that due to the low elevation, you may find sparse coverage and rotten snow outside of winter. It is best attempted in midwinter or early spring.

Because it is part of Mount Hood Meadows Ski Resort, check access rules before heading up the canyon. At the time of this writing, Heather Canyon is only accessible if you buy a lift ticket and if the patrol has opened it. Otherwise, go pre- or postseason when the resort is closed—although of late, the ski resort has prohibited uphill traffic before the season, too, because of snowcat and maintenance operations.

Although the lower canyon is accessible, there are two big hazards here. First, the slopes are steep, and thus avalanche prone. If the patrol is doing control work, make sure you check the uphill travel policy and also the ski resort website for avalanche control work. The other big hazard is the streams. In early or late season, the streams may not be snow covered and are difficult to cross if the snowbridges are not intact; without them, exiting the canyon is extremely difficult. Moreover, the creeks may be hidden under snow that can't support you. One fall in the creek, and you may need technical extrication with a rope to be rescued. The ski patrol yanks people out of the creeks almost every season here, and there's been at least one inbounds avalanche that has caught a skier here. So be careful in Lower Heather Canyon.

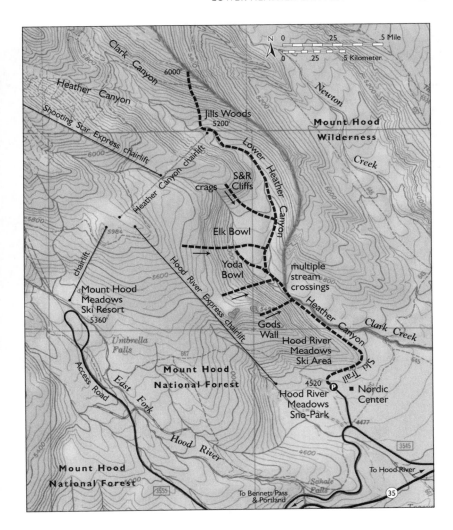

GETTING THERE. From Hood River, drive south on OR-35 (Mount Hood Highway) for 32 miles. A mile before Bennett Pass, turn right up the Hood River Meadows Access Road to Hood River Meadows Sno-Park.

THE ROUTE. From the Hood River Meadows parking lot, take the Heather Canyon Ski Trail, following the Clark Creek drainage. Follow the trail about 2 miles until the canyon opens up at about 5500 feet. From here you can ride any of many shots of the lower bowl. The first shot is Gods Wall, a very steep, advance, avalanche-prone chute to climber's left. The most accessible is wide-open Yoda Bowl. Then, on climber's left, you will find Elk Bowl, followed by S&R Cliffs. On climber's right, the

Preseason inbounds uphill traffic in search of October powder

north side of the canyon, also inbounds, is a nice treed section called Jills Woods, which has south-facing fall lines down the canyon floor.

When you are finished yo-yoing, head back out the ski trail.

19 Upper Heather and Clark Canyons

Start Point	Hood River Meadows Sno-Park, 4520 feet
High Point	Heather or Clark canyons, 7000 feet
Trail Distance	5 miles
Trail Time	2 hours
Skill Level	Advanced
Best Season	Spring
Map	USGS Mount Hood South

Upper Heather and Clark canyons are within the permit area of Mount Hood Meadows Ski Resort. So, at the time of this writing, these canyons are only accessible if you buy a lift ticket and if the patrol has opened the route. Otherwise, go

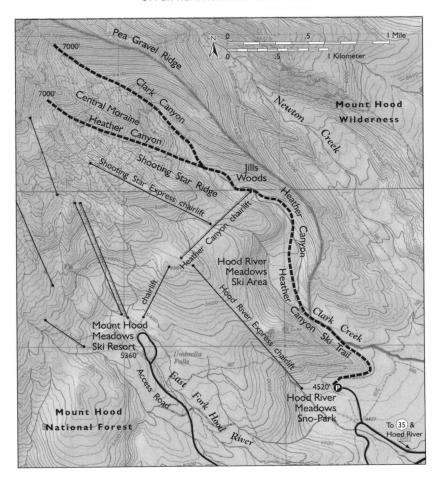

pre- or postseason when the resort is closed—although, as mentioned above (see Route 18), of late the resort has closed uphill traffic before the season, too.

In early season, you'll find better coverage in upper slopes of Clark and Heather canyons. But skiing, or hiking, up the Heather Canyon Runout Trail may be difficult because the snowbridges may not cover the tortuous stream. Or worse, they may cover the stream but not be strong enough for you to walk over. Many snow riders have fallen in the creek here and required rope extrication. Better, hit the upper slopes of the twin canyons in spring, after the resort is closed. You'll find spring corn here, along with easy access up the trail.

GETTING THERE. From Hood River, drive south on OR-35 (Mount Hood Highway) for 32 miles. A mile before Bennett Pass, turn right up the Hood River Meadows Access Road to Hood River Meadows Sno-Park.

Summer tracks high above tree line on Mount Hood

THE ROUTE. Skin up the Heather Canyon Ski Trail. When you reach tree line, there's a large central moraine. To climber's left is Heather Canyon; to climber's right is Clark Canyon. Skin up the bottom of either canyon or up the central moraine. You'll find a multitude of slopes to ski in this huge twin drainage. You can continue farther up the canyon and ski any of the shots within the ski resort boundary, given the restrictions noted above. The best lines in spring are the south-facing slopes of Pea Gravel Ridge, when the sun has warmed them to corn (see also Route 20).

In early winter, you may find better snow on the north-facing slopes. Try the shots from Shooting Star Ridge into Heather Canyon.

20 Newton Canyon

Start Point	Hood River Meadows Sno-Park, 4520 feet
High Point	Pea Gravel Ridge Creek Canyon, 5500 feet
Trail Distance	4 miles
Trail Time	3 hours
Skill Level	Advanced
Best season	Winter
Map	USGS Mount Hood South

Newton Creek is a huge drainage between Heather Canyon and Cooper Spur, becoming more popular with backcountry aficionados since Mount Hood Meadows limited their uphill traffic. It's accessible and has many slopes for turns. The canyon is framed by Pea Gravel Ridge to the south and Gnarl Ridge to the north. Pea Gravel offers turns with safer slopes. Gnarl Ridge has many steeps and is avalanche prone.

GETTING THERE. From Hood River, drive south on OR-35 (Mount Hood Highway) for 32 miles. A mile before Bennett Pass, turn right up the Hood River Meadows Access Road to Hood River Meadows Sno-Park.

THE ROUTE. From the Hood River Meadows parking lot, take the North Boundary uphill traffic route as described in the area overview at the beginning of this

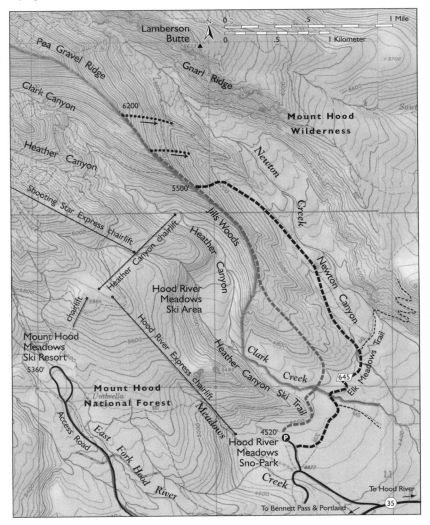

Drop-knee turns, well into summer (Nick Pope)

section. Start up the Heather Canyon Runout Trail. At the first sign exit the ski area permit area and head up the south aspect of the Pea Gravel Ridge.

Another way to get up Newton Canyon is to follow the Newton Creek Ski Trail 645, a half mile from the parking lot to the canyon. The trail forks at the creek, and you follow Trail 645 up Newton Canyon. Near the tree line, ascend the north aspect of Pea Gravel Ridge through the trees on climber's left. There's a good chance you'll find lots of thick trees and brambles in the lower canyon.

Alternatively, from the parking lot of Hood River Meadows Sno-Park, you can ski directly up to Pea Gravel Ridge along the Heather Canyon Ski Trail and follow the ridgeline to the upper canyon. But you either need to be just out of bounds, or make sure that the ski resort allows uphill traffic, and that there's no avalanche control work going on.

Once on Pea Gravel Ridge, descend one of multiple slopes into Newton Canyon. If the snow is good, the closest turns are right at 5500 feet. From Pea Gravel Ridge, drop right down into the Newton Creek. Depending on the conditions, skin higher up Pea Gravel or all the way to the wide-open upper basin.

For a burly ski in the spring, check out the chutes of south-facing Gnarl Ridge.

To return, the best option is to skin back to Pea Gravel Ridge, descend the southwest slope into Clark and Heather canyons, then ski back out the Heather Canyon Ski Trail. If you decide to ski all the way out Newton Canyon, you'll find thick brush and flat slopes—barely worth the slog.

21   Superbowl via Vista Ridge

Start Point	Mount Hood Meadows Sno-Park, 5360 feet
High Point	Superbowl, 8400 feet
Trail Distance	5 miles
Trail Time	3 hours
Skill Level	Advanced
Best Season	Spring
Map	USGS Mount Hood South

Superbowl is an outrageous ride when the weather and snow cooperate. This route is known for exceptionally high avalanche danger most of the winter, for slabs during and after storms, and well into spring, for wet slides. More than once, Superbowl has slid all the way to Heather Canyon chairlift. Thus, choose your day wisely to attempt this route. Route 17 offers lower, safer terrain up Vista Ridge.

Although there is no lift access to the top, this route is also within Mount Hood Meadows Ski Area. In winter in-area skiers access Superbowl by hiking above the Cascade Express lift or sometimes via a snowcat service, when permitted by the ski patrol. When the route is open, the patrol requires avalanche gear.

The best combination of snow and weather, not to mention avoiding lift-access skiers and snowboarders, is in April or May, when the resort is closed on weekdays. Go for those clear sunny days of spring corn. There are so many variations from the top of Superbowl, you can make several trips a season and still it will be different every time. Because access is significantly different from the two sno-parks, two separate approaches and descents are described.

GETTING THERE. From Hood River, drive south on OR-35 (Mount Hood Highway) for 35 miles. At Bennett Pass, exit and turn right up the Mount Hood Meadows Access Road to Mount Hood Meadows Sno-Park.

THE ROUTE. From Mount Hood Meadows Sno-Park, follow the South Boundary for uphill traffic. Start up the Mitchell Creek drainage, just out of bounds in the trees along the rope line, climber's left of the Buttercup and Vista Express chairlifts. Once near tree line, you will come out on Vista Ridge. Stay just out of bounds; there's a rope line here during the resort season. At the top of the Cascade Express chairlift, continue up the ridgeline where the slope steepens. About 500 feet above the lift you will be at the top of the slope called Dallas Bowl. Continue up a ridge and small gully to about 8400 feet. You can drop in anywhere along the ridge.

Burly inbounds descent in Dallas Bowl.

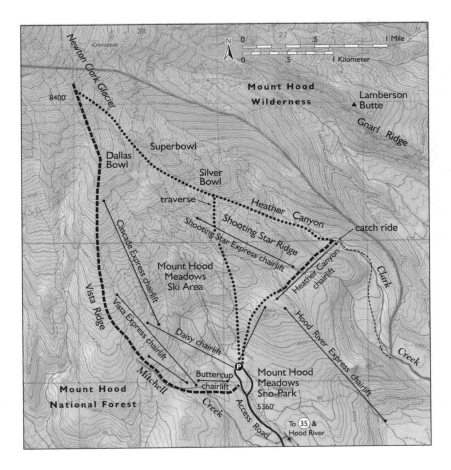

If you ride the Cascade Express chairlift and the ski patrol has opened the hiking route, catch the snowcat road from the top of the chairlift, which takes you to Dallas Bowl and beyond, as described above. The ridge between 7000 and 8000 feet has some cliff bands, so hike well above these before starting your descent.

To descend, head down the huge, wide bowl, taking any one of several lines starting at 8000 feet. Some are steep; there is one section down the middle that is the obvious easy way down. Once down into Heather Canyon, make turns down to about 6000 feet. From here there are three options back to the parking lot: You can drop to the canyon bottom and skin back up to Shooting Star Ridge, which then has ski trails back to the parking lot. Alternatively, traverse across Silver Bowl to Shooting Star Ridge to avoid climbing back out of Heather Canyon. A third option, if you have a lift pass and if the Heather Canyon chairlift is running, is to catch a lift ride back out.

The Wy'east Face—one of the classic but most dangerous descents on Hood

22   Superbowl via Heather Canyon

Start Point : Hood River Meadows Sno-Park, 4520 feet
High Point : Superbowl, 8400 feet
Trail Distance : 6 miles
Trail Time : 4 hours
Skill Level : Advanced
Best Season : Spring
Map : USGS Mount Hood South

Compared to the Vista Ridge approach (Route 21), the route to Superbowl via Heather Canyon is longer. The big advantage is that you can ski all the way back to

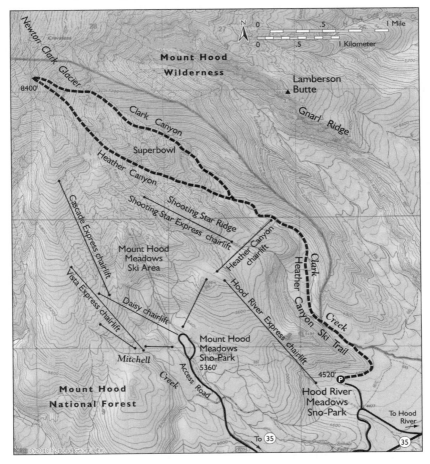

your car without traversing or catching a ride. However, the approach across the flat bottom of the Heather Canyon Runout Trail can add extra time. As with the Heather and Clark canyon routes above, Superbowl is in the ski area and uphill traffic is not allowed inbounds. At the time of this writing, this approach via Heather Canyon is only accessible if you buy a lift ticket and if the patrol has opened it. Otherwise, go pre- or postseason when the resort is closed. It is an extension of Route 19 to reach higher snowfields.

GETTING THERE. From Hood River, drive south on OR-35 (Mount Hood Highway) for 32 miles. A mile before Bennett Pass, turn right up the Hood River Meadows Access Road to Hood River Meadows Sno-Park.

THE ROUTE. From the Hood River Meadows parking lot, if the resort is closed, take the Heather Canyon Ski Trail, but be mindful of the creek crossings and the snowbridges. Follow the trail 2 miles until the canyon opens up at about 5500 feet. From here you can take Clark Creek drainage to the climber's right or the Heather Canyon drainage to climber's left, which is probably easier. Skin all the way to 8400 feet up the bowl, but pay attention to avalanche danger.

Descend the wide, broad slopes of Superbowl down to the Heather Canyon Ski Trail. Schuss back out the ski trail to the car. Be careful in late or early spring when the creek may not be covered with snow.

23 Wy'east Face

Start Point	Hood River Meadows Sno-Park, 4520 feet
High Point	Wy'east Face, 10,500 feet
Trail Distance	6 miles
Trail Time	6 hours
Skill Level	Expert
Best Season	Spring
Map	USGS Mount Hood South

Wy'east Face is the smooth, steep, expansive snowfield above Heather and Clark canyons, directly above Superbowl. It is sometimes called Newton Clark Headwall. Although it's really an extension of the Superbowl route, it deserves its own place in these routes because it's a spectacular mountaineering objective, not a routine backcountry ski. It is a classic late-spring or early-summer descent with a beautiful fall line that can rack up over 5000 feet of vertical. The route is capped by spectacular views, excellent south-facing snow, and few crowds. Be advised, the face can be dangerous. This is an expert ski and snowboard mountaineering route.

The best time to ride is in spring corn, early in the day to minimize avalanche danger. The risk can be high in winter, making this route something many ski and

The climb to Wy'east in early morning sun and on early season powder

snowboard mountaineers save until spring. Avalanche danger is paramount: the face has slides during storms as well as during the clear, hot spring days. Wet slides have run all the way down Heather and Clark canyons to nearly the bottom of the Heather Canyon chairlift.

There are two routes to Wy'east Face, the same two that ascend to Superbowl. One is via Heather Canyon, the other via Vista Ridge. Some have traversed from Timberline Lodge Ski Area or skied up White River Canyon to get to the Wy'east. The most direct route is up Heather Canyon, but the shortest route is via Vista Ridge.

GETTING THERE. From Hood River, drive south on OR-35 (Mount Hood Highway) for 32 miles. For the Heather Canyon approach, turn right up the Hood River Meadows Access Road to Hood River Meadows Sno-Park. For the Vista Ridge approach, exit at Bennett Pass, and turn right up the Mount Hood Meadows Access Road to Mount Hood Meadows Sno-Park.

THE ROUTE. Once you attain the top of Superbowl at 8000 feet via either the Vista Ridge or Heather Canyon route (see Routes 21 and 22), continue directly up the Wy'east Face. At 8400 feet, you will have an excellent view of the routes and the ability to check conditions. Climb to above 10,000 feet. If you are making a summit climb, the top 800 feet is a technical climb not described here. Watch for avalanche hazards. There are no islands of safety, and if you fall it's a long, dangerous slide.

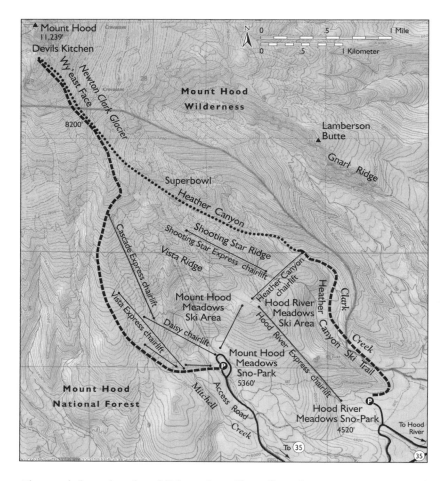

Also watch for rock and ice fall from above. You will need crampons, an ice ax, and a helmet.

The descent is a long, continuous run: down the steep Wy'east Face, left to descend into Superbowl, then down either the Clark or Heather canyon drainage back to Hood River Meadows Sno-Park; in spring, watch for sparse covering of the snowbridges on the Heather Canyon Ski Trail. Or, if you started from Mount Hood Meadows Sno-Park, return as described in Route 21 (Superbowl via Vista Ridge).

24 Gunsight Ridge

Start Point	Pocket Creek Sno-Park, 3800 feet
High Point	Gunsight Ridge, 5800 feet
Trail Distance	3 miles
Trail Time	2 hours
Skill Level	Advanced
Best Season	Winter
Map	USGS Badger Lake

Gunsight Ridge is the closest turns to Hood River, unless the local hills are skiable. The Pocket Creek cross-country ski area provides access to Gunsight Ridge and Badger Lake. A clearcut visible from the road and from Mount Hood Meadows provides an open slope for turns. It's a clean fall line over a rocky scree slope, so you'll want to make sure there's plenty of snow coverage. This route can suffer from lack of snow, due to its low elevation, and needs a fair bit of base to cover the stumps and boulders. Nonetheless, with a half day to spare, this two-hour workout yields great turns.

Don't rule out a jaunt to the glades of Gunsight Ridge and maybe a dip to Badger Lake.

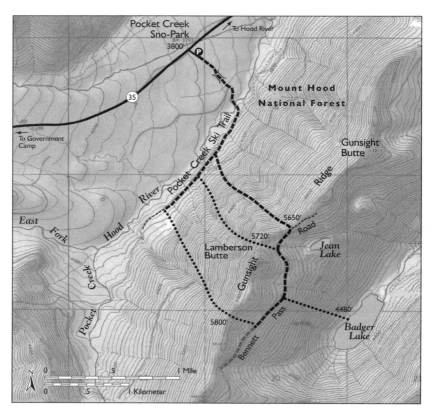

GETTING THERE. From Hood River, drive south on OR-35 (Mount Hood Highway) for about 30 miles. Turn left into the Pocket Creek Sno-Park, 1 mile below Bennett Pass.

THE ROUTE. From the sno-park, follow the Pocket Creek Ski Trail, a summertime Forest Road 3540. It meanders through the woods and across the bridge. At the base of the ridge, the trail turns southwest along the base. After about a mile, look for the wide cleared swath that leads to Gunsight Ridge. Ascend on climber's left or right, using the trees for safety. Realistically, you can ascend at several points along the ridge through the trees.

Once atop the ridge, you'll be on Bennett Pass Road, a few miles north of Bennett Pass (encountered in Route 14). From the road, descend the slopes through the trees or along the clearcut back to your car.

The adventurous can make a lap down the east side of Gunsight Ridge to Badger Lake, in the Badger Creek Wilderness, on a steep, thickly wooded hillside. Then skin back out to the ridge and Bennett Pass Road.

Opposite: Skiing into the wild, uncrowded north side

MOUNT HOOD NORTH

THE NORTH SIDE IS PROBABLY THE LEAST VISITED and most spectacular area of Mount Hood. Year-round snow and dazzling vistas of the huge Eliot Glacier and its headwall make this a worthy trip nearly any time of year. Not only can the snow be excellent and untracked, but also the north side has a wide variety of tours from beginner to expert. Most of the routes are accessed from Cloud Cap Road and the Tilly Jane Historic Area.

In winter, the north-side trailhead is the Tilly Jane Sno-Park, near Cooper Spur Ski Area. Cloud Cap Road is gated here. The tours head through the woods and up Pollalie Ridge to the Tilly Jane Historic Area. At Tilly Jane, there are several buildings, some of which you can camp in. An A-frame shelter is generally available on a first-come, first-served basis, but may be reserved; the Tilly Jane guard station is booked with a reservation. Both are managed by the Oregon Nordic Club. There are two cookhouses, an amphitheater, and a primitive campground as well, all part of an American Legion camp from yesteryear.

In summer, a 9-mile road from the sno-park is cleared of snow and debris, allowing access for vehicles. Sometimes in the spring, you can drive to a second gate at Inspiration Point; later in July, you can drive all the way to Cloud Cap Saddle. In addition to another primitive campground, there are two privately run buildings at Cloud Cap. The historic Cloud Cap Inn, built in 1889, is now used as the rescue base for Hood River's Crag Rats Mountain Rescue team. The Snowshoe Club has another building, constructed in 1910. If you are in the area in summer, knock on the door of Cloud Cap Inn; if there are Crag Rats around, ask for a tour. The Forest Service also runs tours of the inn, usually one weekend a summer.

The uncrowded north side dazzles.

MOUNT HOOD NORTH MAPS

As with the south and east sides, the best map for an overview of the area is the Geo-Graphics Mount Hood Wilderness Map, a 1:30,000-scale map with 40-foot contours and 2000-meter UTM Grid. For those who collect maps, here is the complete list.

USFS Mount Hood National Forest
USFS Zigzag Ranger District
USFS Mount Hood Wilderness
USFS Mount Hood National Forest North
Geo-Graphics Mount Hood Wilderness
National Geographic Trails Illustrated Mount Hood
Cross-Country Ski and Snowshoe Trails, Mount Hood, Oregon
Green Trails Mount Hood No. 462
Green Trails Mount Hood Climbing No. 462S

PRIMARY INFORMATION CENTERS/RANGER DISTRICTS

- Mount Hood National Forest Headquarters, Portland, OR: (503) 668-1700, www.fs.fed.us/r6/mthood
- Hood River Ranger District: (541) 352-6002

AVALANCHE/WEATHER/ROAD CONDITIONS

- Northwest Weather and Avalanche Center: (503) 808-2400, www.nwac.us
- Oregon DOT Trip Check: (800) 977-6368, www.tripcheck.com

SKI AREA SNOW REPORTS

- Cooper Spur Mountain Resort: (503) 230-2084, www.cooperspur.com

OVERNIGHT SHELTERS

- Tilly Jane A-frame and Guard Station, Oregon Nordic Club, Portland and Columbia Gorge Chapters: (541) 296-4837, www.onc.org

PERMITS

- Wilderness permits are required for climbing in the Mount Hood Wilderness, which includes all routes that are above Cloud Cap Saddle. Free, self-issued permits are available at the climbing register at the Cloud Cap Saddle Campground.
- A Sno-Park Pass is required from November 1 to April 30 at the Tilly Jane Sno-Park.
- A Northwest Forest Pass is required for Cloud Cap Saddle and Elk Cove trailheads.

SPECIAL NOTE

Call the Hood River Ranger District to check if Cloud Cap Road is open for routes starting from Cloud Cap; it opens in June or July in most years.

25 Tilly Jane Trail

Start Point : Tilly Jane Sno-Park, 3800 feet
High Point : Tilly Jane Creek, 6600 feet
Trail Distance : 6 miles
Trail Time : 3 hours
Skill Level : Beginner
Best Season : Winter
Maps : USGS Mount Hood North, Dog River

Tilly Jane is a fun beginner trail akin to the south side's Alpine Trail (Route 3), only slightly steeper. Favored by cross-country skiers and snowshoers, it can get crowded on nice weekends in the winter. It is close to Hood River and an excellent way to get to know the north side. The lower trail, in trees and low angle, is safe from avalanches and storms. The upper basin is exposed above the timberline, but due to its low elevation you can find almost any type of snow, from light powder to thin slush with roots and rocks poking through the snow. The Gnarl Ridge fire from 2009 has created an eerily beautiful tour among burned snags.

Cruising up the Tilly Jane Trail, through the eerie Gnarl Ridge burn

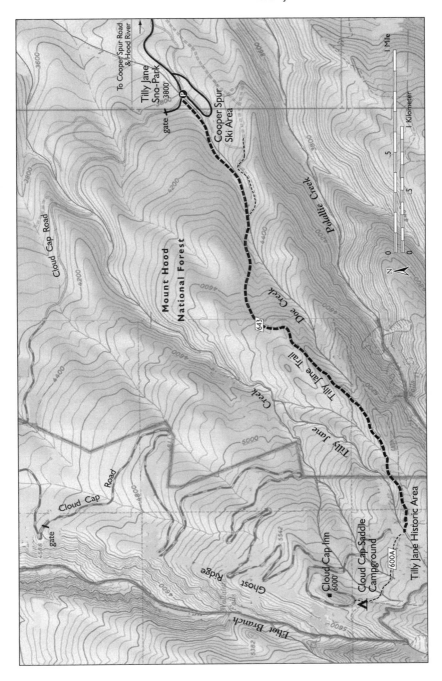

To Cooper Spur Road & Hood River

Tilly Jane Sno-Park
3800'

gate

Cooper Spur Ski Area

Mount Hood National Forest

Cloud Cap Road

643

Doe Creek

Polallie Creek

Tilly Jane Trail

Tilly Jane Creek

Cloud Cap Road

gate
4486'

Cloud Cap

Ghost Ridge

Eliot Branch

Cloud Cap Inn
6000'

Cloud Cap Saddle Campground

600A

Tilly Jane Historic Area

5542'

5600'

5382'

N

1 Mile

1 Kilometer

GETTING THERE. From Hood River, drive south on OR-35 (Mount Hood Highway) for 23 miles to Cooper Spur Road. Turn right and follow Cooper Spur Road for 2 miles, then turn left on Cloud Cap Road (Forest Road 3512). Follow this 1 mile farther to Tilly Jane Sno-Park.

THE ROUTE. Head southwest on Tilly Jane Trail 643, through thick woods. In a half mile, the trail meets up with a connector trail from Cooper Spur Ski Area. At this fork, follow the Tilly Jane Trail up the hill to the right; the trail follows a ridge through the Gnarl Ridge burn for 2 miles to the Tilly Jane Historic Area.

At Tilly Jane, you'll find the A-frame shelter, an American Legion cookhouse, an amphitheater, and the Guard Station. Both the A-frame and Guard Station are available for rent.

Adventurous skiers looking for more exercise, but not turns, can take a spur to Cloud Cap Saddle. From the Tilly Jane Historic Area, follow Trail 600A, which winds through the woods for another half mile to Cloud Cap Saddle Campground, the Snowshoe Club hut, and the historic Cloud Cap Inn.

Another option is to ski the woods above the A-frame, to the southwest. Skin up another half mile until you come to a nice bowl. If you want to ski all the way up to the Tilly Jane headwaters or Cooper Spur, see Route 28 (Cooper Spur and Upper Tilly Jane). This makes for a long day, but excellent turns are likely the higher you skin up Tilly Jane Creek.

The descent follows the climbing route. Be careful if you skin above Tilly Jane A-frame: the thick woods can make finding your way back difficult, and you can end up in the wrong drainage. Keep a map, compass, and GPS handy. There will be a multitude of ski tracks here on a nice winter weekend, so don't count on following tracks. If you miss the Tilly Jane Trail, you'll end up eventually on Cloud Cap Road, and you can skin back to the car on the road.

26 Polallie Canyon

Start Point	Tilly Jane Sno-Park, 3800 feet
High Point	Polallie Ridge, 5000 feet
Trail Distance	4 miles
Trail Time	4 hours
Skill Level	Advanced
Best Season	Winter
Maps	USGS Mount Hood North, Dog River

Pollalie Canyon is a steep, glacially carved canyon, prone to avalanches due to steep shots and lack of thick tree covers. But, with the right conditions, it offers some of the most technical and advanced skiing on all of Mount Hood. There is a cliff band at 6300 feet and waterfalls at 5000 feet, so exercise caution when exploring the canyon.

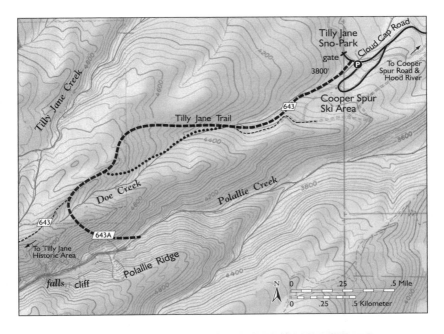

Big canyon, big risk: on the rim of Polallie Canyon

GETTING THERE. From Hood River, drive south on OR-35 (Mount Hood Highway) for 23 miles to Cooper Spur Road. Turn right and follow Cooper Spur Road for 2 miles, then turn left on Cloud Cap Road (Forest Road 3512). Follow this 1 mile farther to Tilly Jane Sno-Park.

THE ROUTE. Ski up Tilly Jane Trail 643, which starts just up and across the road from the sno-park. Head southwest as the trail climbs through thick woods. In a half mile, the trail meets up with another from the Cooper Spur Ski Area and continues up the hill to the right. At around 5000 feet, ski through the burned trees from the Gnarl Ridge fire and leave the Tilly Jane Trail. Head south and cross the Doe Creek drainage to Polallie Ridge. The trail is marked as 643A on some maps but won't be visible or marked with blazes in winter.

The best place to drop in is in the trees, below 5000 feet. Be watchful of cliffs and trees. After a lap or two, skin back up to Polallie Ridge and back to the Tilly Jane Trail. As an alternative on descent, you can ski the burned tree slopes adjacent to the Tilly Jane Trail, between 5000 and 4500 feet, if there are no signs prohibiting it.

27 Old Wagon Road and Ghost Ridge

Start Point	Tilly Jane Sno-Park, 3800 feet
High Point	Cloud Cap Saddle, 6000 feet
Trail Distance	9 miles
Trail Time	6 hours
Skill Level	Intermediate
Best Season	Winter
Maps	USGS Mount Hood North, Dog River

Old Wagon Road and Ghost Ridge are two fun beginner–intermediate routes on the north side that have a long approach on a snowmobile trail. The historic wagon road was first built in 1889, allowing horse-drawn carts to transport people from the Columbia River to the Cloud Cap Inn. It was cleared for skiers in 1989. Although the ski trail is steeper than Tilly Jane, the approach is mostly flat on Cloud Cap Road. Ghost Ridge parallels the road and offers an alternative if the wagon road is packed with blowdowns or is rough with snowcat or snowmobile tracks.

GETTING THERE. From Hood River, drive south on OR-35 (Mount Hood Highway) for 23 miles to Cooper Spur Road. Turn right and follow Cooper Spur Road for 2 miles, then turn left on Cloud Cap Road (Forest Road 3512). Follow this 1 mile farther to Tilly Jane Sno-Park.

THE ROUTE. From Tilly Jane Sno-Park, ski west on Cloud Cap Road past the gate; the road is open to skiers and snowmobilers in the winter. Follow the road 2.5

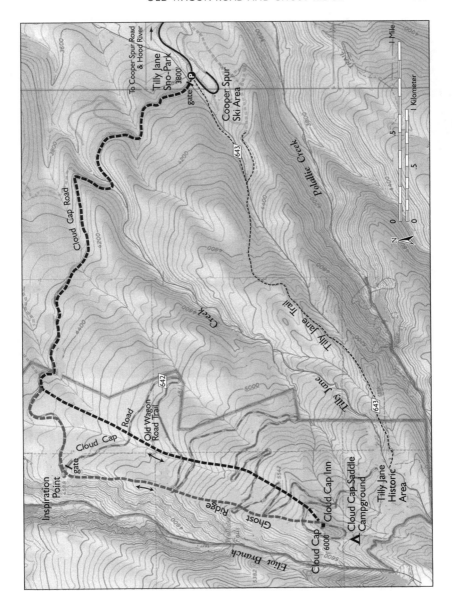

miles to the Old Wagon Road Trail 642. This narrow trail climbs 1500 feet directly up to Cloud Cap through thick woods. At several spots the trail crosses Cloud Cap Road, the 9-mile zigzag that is only open in summer and fall. Near the top, the trail steepens, then ends at the Cloud Cap Inn and Snowshoe Club hut.

The descent heads back down the trail. Keep your turns tight, as it gets narrow in places. Watch for debris under the snow, especially in light snow years. Watch for

Yoyoing the wind-protected glades of Ghost Ridge

people hiking up, and use caution crossing the road, because of the drainage ditches and snowmobilers.

Alternatively, ski Ghost Ridge down to Inspiration Point. You'll probably find less downed timber, fewer snowmobile tracks, and drier snow on the ridge, compared to Old Wagon Road. Keep in mind that the flat 2.5-mile return back to your car requires extra time. Snowboarders will probably need to convert their splitboard back to ski mode or put on snowshoes. Skiers may have to skin back, unless you can find a ski track to schuss with help from lots of poling.

28 Cooper Spur and Upper Tilly Jane

Start Point	Cloud Cap Saddle, 6000 feet
High Point	Cooper Spur, 8500 feet
Trail Distance	4 miles
Trail Time	4 hours
Skill Level	Advanced
Best Season	Spring
Map	USGS Mount Hood North

Cooper Spur is a large snowfield with great snow and weather in the spring, early summer, and even in fall, with an early-season snowfall. When Cloud Cap Road is open to Cloud Cap Saddle, this can be a great day trip. If the road is still closed, it can be an easy overnight for those just venturing into multiday trips; book the A-frame shelter or the Tilly Jane Guard Station. You can also make this a long day trip from Tilly Jane Sno-Park. Most skiers and snowboarders ascend to well under Tie-In Rock at 8500 feet; they ski and ride the snowfield back to the Timberline Trail. Climbing to the summit above 8500 feet is technical and one of the more dangerous summit routes on the mountain.

GETTING THERE. From Hood River, drive south on OR-35 (Mount Hood Highway) for 23 miles to Cooper Spur Road. Turn right and follow Cooper Spur Road for 2 miles, then turn left on Cloud Cap Road (Forest Road 3512). Follow this 1 mile farther to Tilly Jane Sno-Park. If the road is closed, start your long day tour from here. If the road is open, continue another 9 miles on gravel and dirt to Cloud Cap Saddle Campground. The road is rough and takes at least 30 minutes to drive. The road is open in June or early July most years. It may be that the road is only open to Inspiration Point, where there's a second gate. Call the Hood River Ranger District in advance to check on road status. This isn't the best road for a car with low clearance

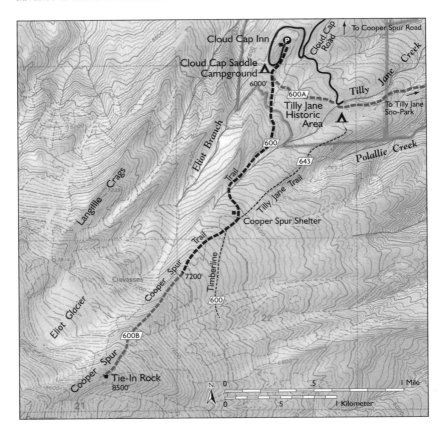

Onward to Tie-In Rock, upper Cooper Spur

and without sturdy tires. This road is best suited for four-wheel-drive, high-clearance vehicles with traction tires.

THE ROUTE. From Cloud Cap Saddle, hike Timberline Trail 600 south for a mile, and then ski up the Tilly Jane Creek headwaters, a wide-open basin. Gain the ridge to the west of the Tilly Jane basin and find a rock shelter at 6600 feet. Here the route follows Cooper Spur Trail 600B. Climb south up to the expansive snowfields of Cooper Spur, the east moraine of the huge Eliot Glacier. The views are spectacular. This lower section of the climber's trail may be marked with posts. The lower snowfield is a gentle slope with steeper sections between 7000 and 8000 feet. For those with less experience, consider stopping at 7000 feet. If you want to continue, you can climb all the way to Tie-In Rock at 8500 feet. Don't continue beyond 8500 feet; it's a technical summit climb.

On descent, follow any of many fingers of the expansive snowfield. The snow may be so good you'll want to make a couple of laps. The snowfield terminates in the Polallie Canyon cliff at 6300 feet, so you'll want to traverse back to the Tilly Jane drainage and Trail 600 well above this cliff. A good place to traverse back is just below the Cooper Spur Shelter around 6600 feet. Use extreme caution in storms or whiteout fog, which can occur any time on the exposed snowfield, even on clear days of midsummer sun.

From the shelter, drop down into the Tilly Jane drainage, which has fabulous turns also. From here, depending on where you parked, you will make two descents. If you parked at Cloud Cap Saddle, at the bottom of the Tilly Jane basin, right at tree line, traverse back to Cloud Cap Saddle following the trail you came up on, 600, which follows the east moraine of the Eliot Glacier back to the trailhead. If you accidentally end up at the Tilly Jane Historic Area, take the connector trail, 600A, back to your car.

If you've hiked all the way up from Tilly Jane Sno-Park because Cloud Cap Road was closed, ski the Tilly Jane drainage back to the historic area, and follow the Tilly Jane Trail back to your car, as described in Route 25.

29 Snowdome

Start Point	Cloud Cap, 6000 feet
High Point	Snowdome, 9600 feet
Trail Distance	5 miles
Trail Time	5 hours
Skill Level	Advanced
Best Season	Summer
Map	USGS Mount Hood North

Snowdome is a sister route to Cooper Spur, located west across the large Eliot Glacier and perhaps one of the best ski and snowboard descents on Mount Hood. It can be combined with Route 30 for a long, spectacular day of great turns. Like Cooper Spur, it gets north sun, so the mornings are best in summer. The slope can be slushy in the afternoon but firms up when the sun dogs behind the west ridge, so you can make an evening descent if you are camping here. Snowdome is an excellent overnight trip. Often good snow is found here late summer into fall.

GETTING THERE. From Hood River, drive south on OR-35 (Mount Hood Highway) for 23 miles to Cooper Spur Road. Turn right and follow Cooper Spur Road for 2 miles, then turn left on Cloud Cap Road (Forest Road 3512). Follow this 1 mile farther to Tilly Jane Sno-Park. If the road is closed, start your long day tour from here. If the road is open, continue another 9 miles on gravel and dirt to Cloud Cap Saddle Campground. The road is rough and takes at least 30 minutes to drive. The road is open in June or early July most years. It may be that the road is only open to Inspiration Point, so call ahead to check first.

THE ROUTE. Hike Timberline Trail 600 south from Cloud Cap for 1 mile up the Tilly Jane Creek headwaters, a wide-open basin. You cannot cross the Eliot Branch of

Crossing Eliot Glacier en route to Snowdome—the best stash of north side snow

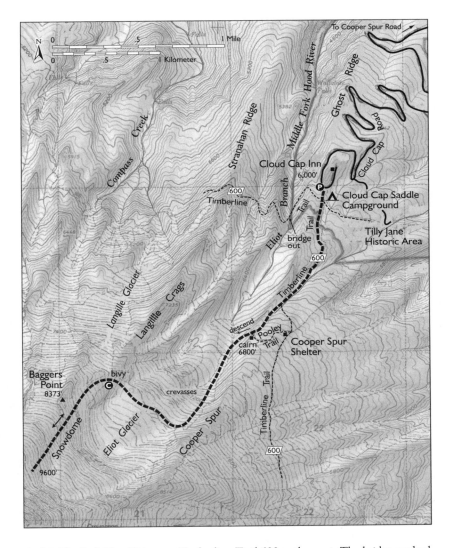

the Middle Fork Hood River on Timberline Trail 600 to the west. The bridge washed out a few years ago, and this section of the Timberline Trail is closed at the time of publication. The creek is raging here and the west slope of the Eliot Branch is steep and dangerous.

Ski to the top of the Tilly Jane headwaters. At 6800 feet, on the east moraine of Eliot Glacier, just below Cooper Spur, you'll see a large cairn. This marks the Pooley Trail, named after famed Crag Rat and founder of Mountain Rescue Association, Dick Pooley. The trail now descends a few hundred feet to the Eliot Glacier. Once down into the glacier, ski up the climber's left of the glacier, watching for crevasses.

Cross at the 7600-foot bench. Be advised, you'll find glide cracks and crevasses here. There are massive crevasses and seracs both above this bench and below. This is the only reasonable place to cross the Eliot Glacier safely on skis. Once across the glacier, Snowdome is the 2000-foot snowfield on the west side of the glacier, just above the rock bands of the Langille Crags.

A good camping spot exists at the base of Snowdome at about 7700 feet. You'll find a few rock bivy windbreaks just to the west of a cone marked as 7814 feet on the USGS Mount Hood North map.

Ski up the snowfield to the top at 9600 feet; along the way you'll pass a large rocky ridge that terminates in a pile of rocks. This is called Baggers Point, at 8373 feet. You'll know you're at the top because you'll stop at the large crevasse and seracs of the headwall ascending to Cathedral Ridge and the summit climb called the Sunshine Route.

The descent is right down Snowdome. If the weather or visibility is poor, make sure you descend to skier's right of Baggers Point; the left puts you down into the dangerous crevasses of the Coe Glacier. Head back across the Eliot Glacier, ski down to 7000 feet, make the short climb back up the Pooley Trail, and ski down the Tilly Jane headwaters. Don't follow Tilly Jane draining into the woods, or you will miss Cloud Cap Saddle and end up at the Tilly Jane Historic Area. Traverse back to Cloud Cap at the 6000-foot contour, marked as Trail 600.

30   Langille Bowls

Start Point	Cloud Cap, 6000 feet
High Point	Langille Glacier, 7700 feet
Trail Distance	6 miles
Trail Time	5 hours
Skill Level	Advanced
Best Season	Summer
Map	USGS Mount Hood North

Just below and to the northwest of Snowdome, the bowls of the Langille Glacier are another excellent uncrowded spot on the north side. You can combine this bowl with Route 29 for an epic day at 3500 feet of ski descent. Since most of the snowfields are steep but crevasse free, they make excellent runs when the snowpack is stable such as in the summer. And because most are lower than Snowdome, they can be combined with a Snowdome run for a long descent or skied when the higher elevations have hard snow or otherwise poor conditions. There are several snowfields and aspects to choose from, giving you a whole day of riding and hiking.

Because the bridge is washed out at the Eliot Branch of the Middle Fork Hood River on the Timberline Trail 600 to the west, the route is longer than in years past. The creek is very fast here and the west slope is steep and dangerous; this section of

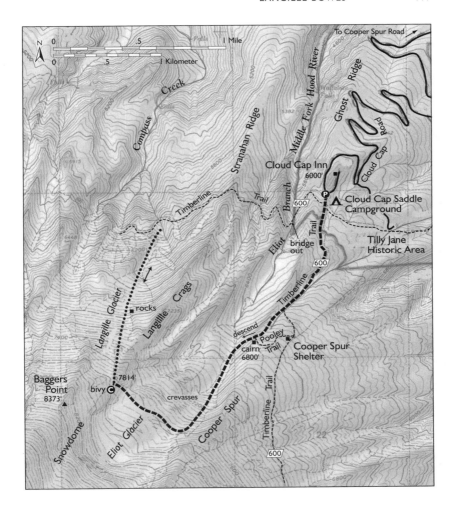

trail is closed by the Forest Service. So you have to access the Langille Bowls via the Eliot Glacier.

GETTING THERE. From Hood River, drive south on OR-35 (Mount Hood Highway) for 23 miles to Cooper Spur Road. Turn right and follow Cooper Spur Road for 2 miles, then turn left on Cloud Cap Road (Forest Road 3512). Follow this 1 mile farther to Tilly Jane Sno-Park. If the road is closed, start your long day tour from here. If the road is open, continue another 9 miles on gravel and dirt to Cloud Cap Saddle Campground. The road is rough and takes at least 30 minutes to drive. The road is open in June or early July on most years. It may be that the road is only open to Inspiration Point, so call ahead to check first.

Homeward bound up the Pooley Trail after a long tour

THE ROUTE. Hike the Timberline Trail 600 south from Cloud Cap for 1 mile up to the top of the Tilly Jane Creek headwaters, a wide-open basin.

At 6800 feet, on the east moraine of Eliot Glacier, just below Cooper Spur, you'll see a large cairn. This marks the Pooley Trail, named after famed Crag Rat and founder of Mountain Rescue Association, Dick Pooley. The trail descends a few hundred feet to the Eliot Glacier. Ski up the climber's left of the glacier, watching for crevasses, and cross at the 7600-foot bench. Be advised, you'll find glide cracks and crevasses here. There are massive crevasses and seracs both above this bench and below. This is the only reasonable place to cross the Eliot Glacier safely on skis. Once across the glacier, skin up to the base of Snowdome at about 7700 feet. You'll find a few rock bivy windbreaks just to the west of a cone marked as 7814 feet on most topo maps.

From here, you can rip up turns in the bowls of the Langille Glacier directly below and to the north. You'll find plenty of clean fall lines and moderately steep slopes. You may have to stop in a few spots to cross rock bands between bowls at about 7700 and 6400 feet. Most years, through midsummer, you can ski all the way to tree line at 6000 feet, where you'll find the Timberline Trail.

Because the Eliot Branch bridge is washed out on the Timberline Trail, make sure you allow plenty of time to get home. You'll have to skin back up to 7800 feet, recross the Elliot Glacier, climb back up the Pooley Trail, and ski down the Tilly Jane headwaters back to your car. Don't follow Tilly Jane draining into the woods, or you will miss Cloud Cap Saddle and end up at Tilly Jane Historic District. Traverse back to Cloud Cap at the 6000-foot contour, marked as Trail 600.

Scoping out lines on Snowdome in July

Corn turning to slush on a perfect summer ski

31 Barrett Spur

Start Point : Elk Cove Trail, 4400 feet
High Point : Barrett Spur, 7600 feet
Trail Distance : 8 miles
Trail Time : 6 hours
Skill Level : Advanced
Best Season : Spring
Map : USGS Mount Hood North

Barrett Spur is one of the more remote descents on Mount Hood, and one of the few on the northwest flank. The roads are not plowed to the trailhead, so access in winter

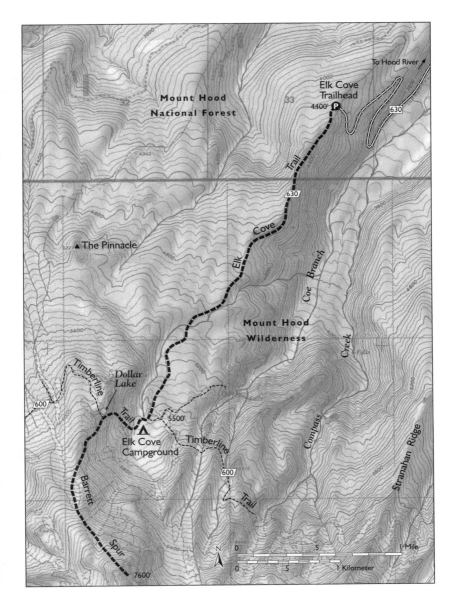

and spring can be long. Some use snowmobiles. Timing in late spring or early summer is critical. The best time is when the roads and trails are clear but there is still snow above 6000 feet. Some years you'll have a big window, six to eight weeks. In summer, you'll want to go early to be skiing by mid- to late morning; otherwise, the sun can turn the corn to slush.

GETTING THERE. From Hood River, head south on OR-35 (Mount Hood Highway) 15 miles west to Baseline Drive, then left on Clear Creek Road, which turns into Forest Road 2840. You may get stopped by snow here—if you don't have a snowmobile, it will be a long ski in. Follow it 5 miles to Forest Road 630. Head north 3 miles to the trailhead at the road's terminus.

THE ROUTE. Follow the Elk Cove Trail 630 and climb gently north for 3 miles through the woods to Elk Cove, a spectacular mountain meadow campground at the junction of the Elk Cove Trail and the Round-the-Mountain Trail. For an overnight trip, Elk Cove is a fantastic place to camp.

At tree line, take the Timberline Trail 600 west for a few minutes until you wrap around to Dollar Lake, another great campsite. From there, find a spot to climb up the ridge to Barrett Spur. Once on the spur, continue due south up the wide snowfield to the summit.

The route down follows the route up, for the easiest, safest turns. The northwest-facing spur is moderate slopes. The northeast-facing slopes, facing Elk Cove, are steeper. You can make turns on the steeper pitches, if conditions are favorable and safe, down to Elk Cove. You will have to hike back out the approach trail unless it is snow covered and free from blowdowns, in which case you can ski the trail back to your car.

Opposite: Traversing under a basalt spire in search of fresh tracks (Pete Keane)

SANTIAM PASS TO MCKENZIE PASS

SANTIAM PASS, located in the Willamette National Forest, is a frequent destination for Eugene and Salem skiers and snowboarders, inbounds and backcountry. It offers a wide variety of routes, from cross-country trails to some of the more challenging mountaineering ascents in this book. Plan well for these routes; by the time some of the approach roads open, you may only have a short window for good snow.

Mount Jefferson is one of the more rugged and remote Cascade volcanoes. Sans winter resorts, it is one of the most spectacular mountain peaks on the Pacific Crest. Second in height in Oregon to only Mount Hood, Jefferson rises 10,497 feet high. The first ascent was in 1888 by Ray Farmer and E. C. Cross. Although many climbed to the base of the 500-foot summit pinnacle, Farmer and Cross were the first to reach the top. Like several of the volcanoes in this book, Jefferson can't be skied or snowboarded from the summit because of its pinnacle of loose volcanic rock, ice, and snow. The highest an expert can reasonably ski or snowboard from is around 9500 feet.

For multiday trips, Jefferson Park makes a beautiful camp in the spring and summer. In fact, it may be crowded with backpackers and mountaineers. Some have said this is one of the loveliest spots on the entire Pacific Crest Trail, which stretches from Mexico to Canada via California, Oregon, and Washington.

Mount Washington, punching up at 7794 feet, is a shorter approach and a much shorter peak, but equally rugged. It makes a great spring or early-summer descent for those who don't have time for a full weekend. Like Jefferson, Washington can't be skied or snowboarded from the apex because of the rocky summit pyramid. The first ascent was probably by a Bend group in 1923 including Ervin McNeal, Phil Philbrook, Armin Furrer, Wilbur Watkins, Leo Harryman, and Ronald Seller.

There are a few other craggy peaks in this section of Oregon, like Three Fingered Jack. And this landscape is dominated by many smaller cinder cones, knolls, and domes worthy of a half day of making tracks if snow conditions are good. Snow quality may be suspect and variable on these lower objectives, however, depending on snow cover, temperature, blown-down trees, and low-elevation weather.

SANTIAM PASS TO MCKENZIE PASS MAPS

The best overview maps are the Geo-Graphics wilderness maps, of Mount Jefferson and Mount Washington. The Mount Washington map includes Hoodoo Butte, Hayrick Butte, Potato Hill and Cache Mountain, and Belknap Crater. The Mount Jefferson map has a small inset map of Three Fingered Jack. The Three Sisters map covers the McKenzie Pass routes.

USFS Willamette National Forest
Imus Geo-Graphics Santiam Pass Winter Recreation
Geo-Graphics Mount Jefferson Wilderness
Geo-Graphics Mount Washington Wilderness
Geo-Graphics Three Sisters Wilderness
Green Trails Mount Jefferson No. 557, Three Fingered Jack No. 589, Sisters No. 590

PRIMARY INFORMATION CENTERS/RANGER DISTRICTS

- Willamette National Forest Headquarters, Eugene, OR: (541) 465-6521, www.fs.fed.us/r6/willamette
- Detroit Ranger District: (503) 854-3366
- McKenzie Ranger District: (541) 822-3381

AVALANCHE/WEATHER/ROAD CONDITIONS

- Northwest Weather and Avalanche Center: (503) 808-2400, www.nwac.us
- Oregon DOT Trip Check: (800) 977-6368, www.tripcheck.com

SKI AREA SNOW REPORTS

- Hoodoo Mountain Resort: (541) 822-3337, www.hoodoo.com

PERMITS

- Wilderness permits are required for climbing in the Mount Jefferson and Mount Washington wildernesses. Free, self-issued permits are available at the climbing register at the trailhead.
- A Northwest Forest Pass is required for trailheads.
- A Sno-Park Pass is required for these routes between November 1 and April 30.

SPECIAL NOTES

Call ahead to make sure the road is open to the Mount Jefferson trailhead; usually this is sometime in June. If heading to the McKenzie Pass routes, Black Crater and Belknap Crater, call to see if the gate on OR-242 is open and the road is clear.

32 Mount Jefferson, Jefferson Park Glacier

Start Point : Whitewater Creek trailhead, 4100 feet
High Point : Jefferson Park Glacier, 9000 feet
Trail Distance : 14 miles
Trail Time : 10 hours
Skill Level : Advanced
Best Season : Summer
Map : USGS Mount Jefferson

This is one of the most scenic routes in the book, if not on the entire Pacific Crest. Don't have your sights set on the summit unless you are an expert mountaineer and rock climber; the headwall, knife-edge ridge, and summit pinnacle are technical glacier and rock climbing. For the best combination of good turns but easy approach, go in summer when the snow is melted from the approach trail and Jefferson Park area.

Telemarking the summer slush back to camp after turning around shy of the summit on Jefferson Park Glacier

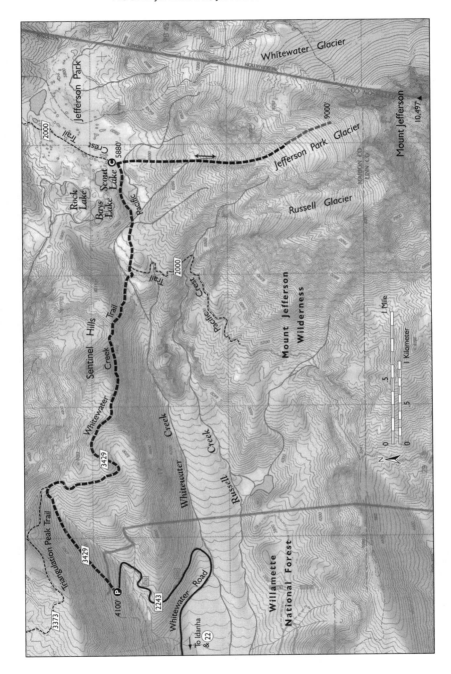

Because of the long approach and the long, steady climb up the glacier, this is best done as an overnight. You can sleep at the trailhead and make it halfway up the snow-field and back in a day—but it's a long trip. The descent will likely be in afternoon slush, and you will miss the beauty of camping at Jefferson Park. Better to plan two days, and camp at Jefferson Park. You can ski all three routes included here (Routes 32–34) in a long weekend and explore the area.

GETTING THERE. From Salem, drive east on OR-22 (North Santiam Highway) for 55 miles to Idanha. About 6 miles past Idanha, turn left on Whitewater Road (Forest Road 2243). Follow FR 2243 about 8 miles to its terminus at the Whitewater Creek trailhead.

THE ROUTE. Follow Whitewater Creek Trail 3429. At 1.5 miles, continue right after the junction with Triangulation Peak Trail 3373. In 4 miles the trail crosses Whitewater Creek, then in another half mile meets Pacific Crest Trail 2000. From this junction, follow the Pacific Crest Trail north about a mile to the Jefferson Park area. Find a suitable campsite near Scout Lake if you are planning a multiday trip. You will need to purify water or maybe even melt snow, if early in the season.

The climber's trail heads due south from Jefferson Park, directly up the snowfields below the glacier and the east moraine, staying on climber's left of the snowfields. After about a mile, you will reach the glacier, around 7500 feet. If you are inexperienced in glacier travel, spin around here. With basic mountaineering equipment, you can continue higher: stay on the climber's left, near the east moraine, to avoid crevasses. You can climb up to about 9000 feet before you hit the technical section of climbing.

The descent goes directly down the way you came up. Watch for crevasses if you hiked high on the glacier. Once you pack up your camp at Jefferson Park, you'll most likely be hiking, not skiing, back down the Whitewater Creek Trail if you've planned a midsummer trip.

33 Mount Jefferson, Russell Glacier

Start Point : Whitewater Creek trailhead, 4100 feet
High Point : Russell Glacier, 8000 feet
Trail Distance : 12 miles
Trail Time : 10 hours
Skill Level : Advanced
Best Season : Summer
Map : USGS Mount Jefferson

If you have more time and are looking for another ride on Jefferson, Russell Glacier is an option. The approach is a bit shorter but a bit more difficult than Jefferson Park. This is still an overnight trip or a long day.

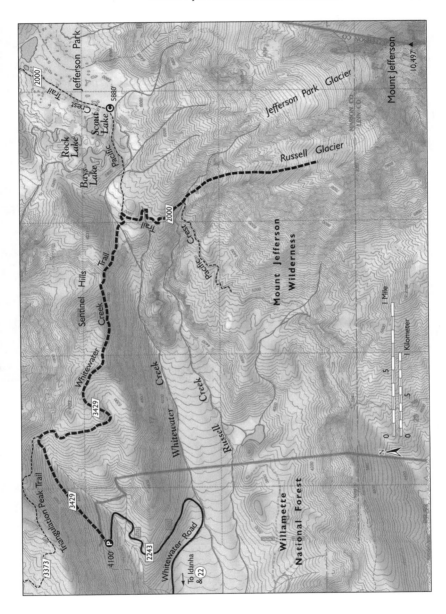

GETTING THERE. From Salem, drive east on OR-22 (North Santiam Highway) for 55 miles to Idanha. About 6 miles past Idanha, turn left on Whitewater Road (Forest Road 2243). Follow FR 2243 about 8 miles to its terminus at the Whitewater Creek trailhead.

Big, bold, remote Mount Jefferson

THE ROUTE. Follow Whitewater Creek Trail 3429. In 1.5 miles, turn right at the junction with Triangulation Peak Trail 3373. In 4 miles the trail crosses Whitewater Creek, then in another half mile meets Pacific Crest Trail 2000. If you are camping at Jefferson Park, continue another mile east to find a bivy around Scout Lake. Otherwise, follow the Pacific Crest Trail south about a mile. In another half mile, cross the headwaters of Russell Creek, a potentially difficult crossing, with likely no bridge. Then take the climber's trail southeast up the lower snowfields of the Russell Glacier. Stay on the west moraine, as the drainage here is steep and narrow. Unless you have crevasse rescue and glacier travel skills and equipment, stay on the lower snowfields, below 8000 feet.

On the way down, be careful of getting low in the drainage, as there is a waterfall and a narrow slot. Ride the west moraine the way you hiked up, but use caution; this is not a fall-line descent but involves some traversing.

34 Mount Jefferson, Park Butte

Start Point : Whitewater Creek trailhead, 4100 feet
High Point : Park Butte summit, 6851 feet
Trail Distance : 14 miles
Trail Time : 10 hours
Skill Level : Advanced
Best Season : Summer
Map : USGS Mount Jefferson

If you are planning a Jefferson Park Glacier trip, remember you can always bop over to Park Butte and get some more turns. It's not worth the long hike in to Jefferson Park just to ski the butte, plus its south-facing slopes usually soften more readily, especially in the summer. So make this an early-morning or late-evening ride, combined with a Jefferson Park Glacier trip (Routes 32–33). If for some reason Jefferson Park Glacier is too steep, icy, or difficult, this offers a good backup route.

GETTING THERE. From Salem, drive east on OR-22 (North Santiam Highway) for 55 miles to Idanha. About 6 miles past Idanha, turn left on Whitewater Road (Forest Road 2243). Follow FR 2243 about 8 miles to its terminus at the Whitewater Creek trailhead.

Dropping into spring cornfield (Pete Keane)

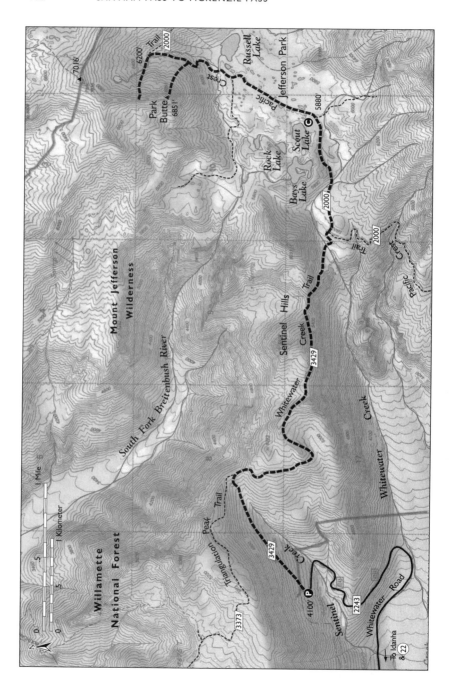

THE ROUTE. Follow Whitewater Creek Trail 3429. At 1.5 miles it meets up with Triangulation Peak Trail 3373. In 4 miles the trail crosses Whitewater Creek, then in another half mile meets Pacific Crest Trail 2000. From this junction, follow the Pacific Crest Trail north about a mile to the Jefferson Park area, 5 miles in. Find a suitable campsite here if making an overnight trip, probably around Scout Lake.

From Jefferson Park, Park Butte is easily identified at the north end of the lake area. Cross the meadows near Russell Lake, following the Pacific Crest Trail. On the east flank, leave the trail and climb one of the snowfields on the east side to the Park Butte summit. Continue to the peak at 6851 feet. Descend the way you climbed up.

35 Potato Hill

Start Point : Potato Hill Sno-Park, 4100 feet
High Point : Potato Hill, 5207 feet
Trail Distance : 4 miles
Trail Time : 2 hours
Skill Level : Beginner
Best Season : Winter
Map : USGS Three Fingered Jack

Potato Hill is primarily a cross-country area, but the ridge gives 600–800 feet of downhill turns. The north side, facing the road, is cliff-strewn. The west- and southwest-facing flanks of the hill are the best spots for skinning and skiing. It's a short trip, so it can be combined with Hoodoo and Hayrick buttes tours (Route 36). Or if you just want a few turns and you're short on time, make a few laps up Potato Hill.

Storm skiing—a Pacific Northwest classic

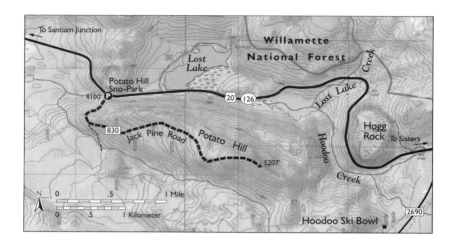

GETTING THERE. From Salem, drive east on OR-22 (North Santiam Highway) for 85 miles to Santiam Junction. Then continue east on US 20/OR-126 for about 1 mile to Santiam Pass. Potato Hill Sno-Park will be on the right (south) side of the road, about 3 miles before Hoodoo Sno-Park.

THE ROUTE. From the sno-park, there is an unplowed road that leads nearly to the summit. Follow the trail south from the sno-park for a half mile. Take the left fork, Forest Road 830 (Jack Pine Road), heading east up a broad slope toward the top. For the last half mile, you can hike through the trees to the summit.

The best tracks for descent are the east and southeast sides of the hill. Be careful of the steep cliffs to the north, right above the road.

36 Hoodoo Butte and Hayrick Butte

Start Point	Hoodoo Sno-Park, 4820 feet
High Point	Hoodoo Butte; 5600 feet; Hayrick Butte, 5500 feet
Trail Distance	2 miles; 2 miles
Trail Time	2 hours
Skill Level	Intermediate
Best Season	Winter
Map	USGS Three Fingered Jack

Santiam Pass, with a huge network of cross-country ski trails, is a popular and busy destination for central Willamette Valley Nordic skiers. Hoodoo Ski Bowl, a small two-chair resort, is one of the oldest resorts in Oregon. Although Hoodoo can suffer

Over the snow and through the woods to high county snow we go

from warm-weather drizzle and thin snowpack at times, it can also have excellent midwinter snow. Plus Hoodoo and Hayrick buttes are one of the quickest jaunts for powder turns. These twin buttes offer short but reasonably steep shots close to the highway, avoiding the long approaches of the big volcanoes.

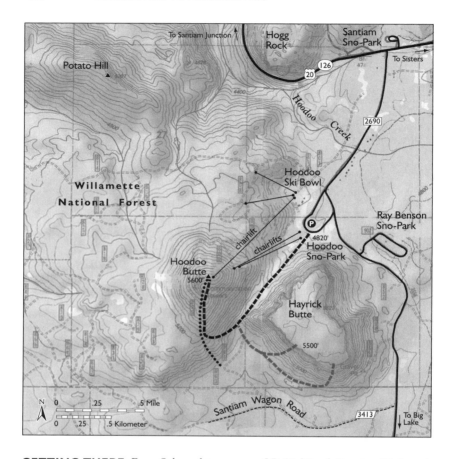

GETTING THERE. From Salem, drive east on OR-22 (North Santiam Highway) for 85 miles to Santiam Junction. Drive 5 miles farther east on US 20/OR-126, through Santiam Pass, to the turnoff for Hoodoo, on the right side of the road. Park at Hoodoo Sno-Park at the Nordic center or at the Ray Benson Sno-Park.

THE ROUTE. Follow the cross-country trail from Hoodoo Sno-Park south for a half mile to the pass between the two buttes, Hoodoo and Hayrick. An old road leads to the summit of Hoodoo Butte, which is part of the inbounds area of the resort. Ski the back (south) side of Hoodoo Butte from the summit down through an old burn.

Alternatively, ascend Hayrick Butte and lay tracks on the south side. The north has avalanche-prone slopes that are steep and cliff ridden. On the summit of either butte, the views of Mount Washington and Big Lake are spectacular. If you ski down into the flats south of the buttes, you'll reach the Santiam Wagon Road, Trail 3413.

37 Mount Washington, Northwest Bowl

Start Point	Big Lake West Campground, 4680 feet
High Point	Northwest Bowl, 7000 feet
Trail Distance	10 miles
Trail Time	8 hours
Skill Level	Advanced
Best season	Spring
Maps	USGS Mount Washington, Three Fingered Jack

Mount Washington's Northwest Bowl is a common mountaineering route for Eugene and Salem locals. It can be skied in a day, excluding the summit pinnacle. This route is shorter than a Mount Jefferson trip but more involved than a quick winter jaunt to Hayrick and Hoodoo buttes (Route 36). Drive early, start hiking by daybreak, and you can be making turns by noon. Use caution, though, as this route is not well marked. Serious routefinding may be needed, and you may need to mark your route with wands (thin bamboo sticks with flags used by mountaineers).

GETTING THERE. From Salem, drive east on OR-22 (North Santiam Highway) for 85 miles to Santiam Junction. Continue east on US 20/OR-126 for 4 miles, over

The sun-kissed Northwest Bowl of Mount Washington (Dave Waag)

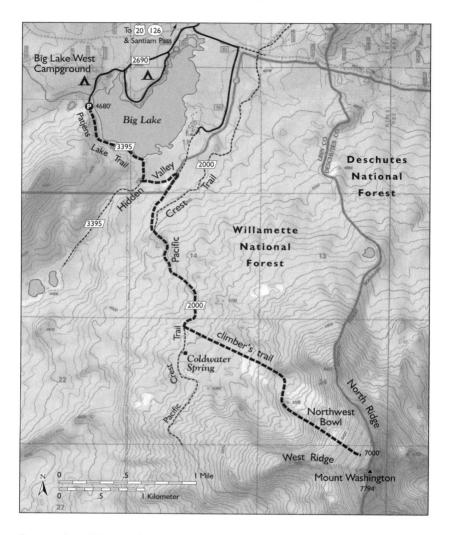

Santiam Pass. Turn south on Forest Road 2690 and drive 4 miles to Big Lake West Campground.

THE ROUTE. From the campground, start around the south end of Big Lake on Patjens Lake Trail 3395. After the trail leaves the lake, follow a series of trails about a mile east to Pacific Crest Trail 2000. Hike south on the Pacific Crest Trail for 2 miles, at which point you will find the climber's trail heading up the mountain to the east. Once on the climber's trail, follow the right fork to the Northwest Bowl.

After climbing through thick woods and some meadows, you come to the bottom of the Northwest Bowl and the north side of West Ridge. Hike up the snow to about 7000 feet, the base of the summit pinnacle, and on to the saddle on North Ridge at 7500 feet. From here it's a fifth-class rock climb to the summit for skilled mountaineers.

Ski the Northwest Bowl from 7000 feet down to the climber's trail at timberline. Be careful you don't get off track, as routefinding is difficult and there are several drainages.

38 Cache Mountain

Start Point : Corbett Sno-Park, 4200 feet
High Point : Cache Mountain summit, 5579 feet
Trail Distance : 10 miles
Trail Time : 8 hours
Skill Level : Intermediate
Best Season : Winter
Map : USGS Three Fingered Jack

Cache Mountain is another roadside cinder cone with a millennium of vertical. Down the road from Hoodoo Ski Resort, it offers fewer crowds. But, like Black Butte

Powder farming, Oregon style (Pete Keane)

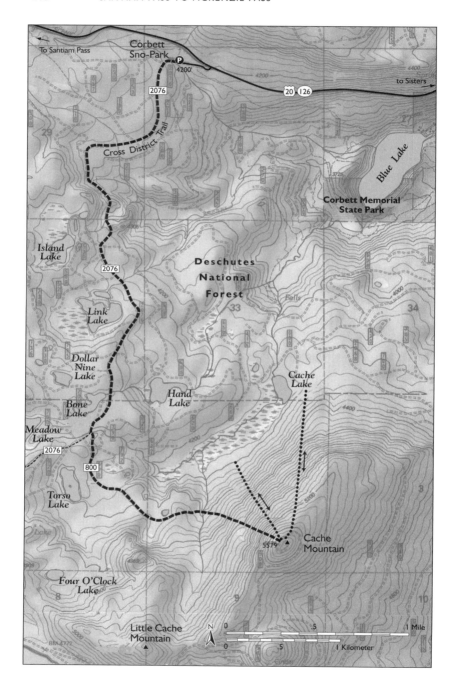

(Route 40), it is a long, flat skin in. And you may hear the buzz and drone of snowmobiles in the area. In fact, some ride a snowmobile to the base, or even to the summit, to make yo-yoing easier. If you want a motor-free backcountry experience, you might want to pick another spot.

GETTING THERE. From Salem, drive east on OR-22 (North Santiam Highway) for 85 miles to Santiam Junction. Continue east on US 20/OR-126 for 7 miles, over Santiam Pass, to Corbett Sno-Park, on the right (south) side of the road.

THE ROUTE. The skin route (or snowmobile ride) follows Forest Road 2076 (also called the Cross District Trail), closed in winter to cars and widely used by snowmobilers. The road heads south through a lake and marsh area. After 3 miles, take a left on Forest Road 800. Head east up the road toward the summit. After a mile, Forest Road 800 ends. Continue up the west side of Cache Mountain, through a clearcut, another mile to the summit. Be advised, snowmobilers may continue via Forest Road 2076, a long loop around to the south side, to reach the summit.

The north and northwest flanks have good skiing in the thin trees; you'll find good visibility, as there was a burn years ago. The mountain is skiable down to 4200 feet. Ski to Cache Lake at 4200 feet, on the north side of the cinder cone. Skin back up the summit to make a few laps, but don't forget about the long trek out on flat road back to your car.

(39) Three Fingered Jack

Start Point	Jack Lake, 5145 feet
High Point	Northeast Bowl, 6000 feet
Trail Distance	6 miles
Trail Time	6 hours
Skill Level	Advanced
Best Season	Spring
Maps	USGS Three Fingered Jack, Marion Lake

Three Fingered Jack is a remote and rugged tour. If you've conquered all the other peaks in the Mount Washington and Mount Jefferson area, it may be worth a jaunt to check out this craggy, beautiful, less-traveled peak. Expect a long approach, and some serious routefinding. But if you are up for an adventure, consider heading into Three Fingered Jack's Northeast Bowl. Like many of the central Oregon volcanoes, you will find the trifecta of thickly wooded slopes on the approach, wide-open bowls and glaciers above timberline, and a craggy summit that requires technical rock climbing. For Three Fingered Jack, like Mount Washington, the ski objective is to make turns on the lower slopes. Combine your tour with a summit bid only if you have technical rock climbing skills and equipment.

The elusive Three Fingered Jack in midwinter (Dudley Chelton)

GETTING THERE. From Salem, drive east on OR-22 (North Santiam Highway) for 85 miles to Santiam Junction. Continue east on US 20/OR-126 for 5 miles, over Santiam Pass, to Forest Road 12. Turn north to Jack Creek, then continue on Forest Road 1230, then Forest Road 1234 to Jack Lake.

THE ROUTE. From Jack Lake, follow Canyon Creek Trail 4010 west for 2 miles. Continue up the drainage to the Northeast Bowl at the headwaters of Canyon Creek. You can only ski up to about 6000 feet until you reach the craggy, jagged rock of Three Fingered Jack's 7841-foot peak.

Alternatively, you can follow Old Summit Trail 4014 south for a mile or two, then ski due west through an old burn up to the ridge at 6000 feet or a bit higher.

In either case, make turns on the open slopes, then follow either approach trail back to the trailhead.

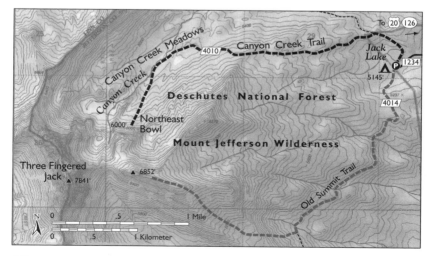

40 Black Butte

Start Point	Forest Road 1110, 3700 feet
High Point	Black Butte summit, 6436 feet
Trail Distance	2 miles
Trail Time	2 hours
Skill Level	Intermediate
Best Season	Winter
Maps	USGS Black Crater, Black Butte

Black Butte is another roadside cinder cone, in proximity to Black Butte Ranch, and near Sisters. Thick forests on this near-perfect cone can protect the snow from wind and sun. It's worth a quick exploration if the conditions are good. However, like several of the Santiam Pass tours on cinder cones and buttes, Black Butte can also suffer from low elevation; midseason rain or warm temperatures can turn this to slush. So pick a powder day. The snow will stay good for several days after a storm if the temperatures are cold.

GETTING THERE. From Salem, drive east on OR-22 (North Santiam Highway) for 85 miles to Santiam Junction. Continue east on US 20/OR-126, over Santiam

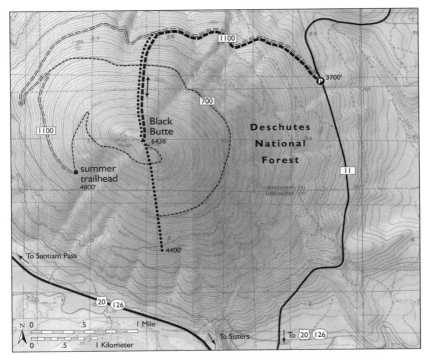

Pass, 20 miles toward Sisters. At Indian Ford Junction, turn left and head north on Forest Road 11 for 3 miles. At Forest Road 1110, turn left and find a place to park.

THE ROUTE. Ski up the road 1.5 miles to the north-facing trees of the cone. Ski due south, up the north slope to the summit of Black Butte. Alternatively, ski up to the end of Forest Road 1110 which traverses the north and west sides of Black Butte, where there's a summer trailhead. After a mile, you can skin directly up the north side of the butte.

Depending on the weather and season, the best snow will likely be either the south and southwest glades or the north-facing treed slopes. On descent, catch the road back to your car.

Popping out of the trees en route to high vistas

41 Black Crater

Start Point	Black Crater trailhead, 4900 feet
High Point	Black Crater summit, 7251 feet
Trail Distance	8 miles
Trail Time	4 hours
Skill Level	Intermediate
Best Season	Winter
Maps	USGS Black Crater, Mount Washington

Black Crater and Belknap Crater (Route 42) are two McKenzie Pass gems, one on either side of the highway. Lying on the south side of the road, with less than a thousand feet of skiable vertical, Black Crater offers a change of pace from the Santiam Pass crowds.

OR-242 through McKenzie Pass is closed in winter, but you can drive south on OR-242 from Sisters as far as the gate closing the road; from there, it is a 3-mile skin up the road to the Black Crater trailhead. Some skiers and snowboarders use snowmobiles. Otherwise, it is a long approach for a thousand feet of turns. It's better to leave

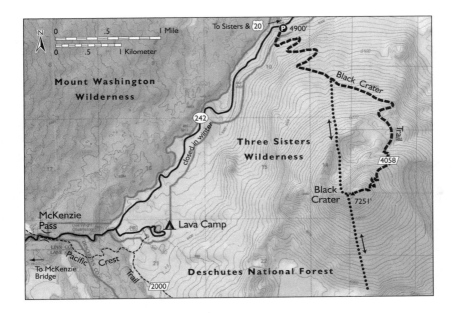

this route until the road is open in the spring, when you can drive to the trailhead. But you will have a short window for spring corn. You'll want to catch Black Crater with plenty of snow on the cone, so go right after the road opens. You can reach Black Crater from McKenzie Pass also, a shorter trip for Eugene riders and skiers. The road is closed at Alder Springs. Just call ahead to see if the road is open, unless you plan to use a snowmobile. Note: Road is open to bikes several weeks before it is open to cars.

GETTING THERE. From Salem, drive east on OR-22 (North Santiam Highway) for 85 miles to Santiam Junction. Continue east on US 20/OR-126, over Santiam Pass, to Sisters. In Sisters, turn right and head west on OR-242 (McKenzie Highway). In 8.5 miles you'll reach the gate. If the gate is open, continue 3 more miles to the Black Crater trailhead on the left side, 12 miles from Sisters. From the west, drive 52 miles from Eugene to McKenzie Bridge on OR-126. In 4 miles, turn right on OR-242. Continue 15 miles to McKenzie Pass, if the road is open.

THE ROUTE. From the Black Crater trailhead, follow Trail 4058 south. It meanders up the north side of the crater before wrapping around to approach the summit from the east. This is primarily a summer hiking trail, so don't expect signs or blazes. The northwest aspect has several couloirs called the Black Cauldron. Descend with caution; the trees are few up high and the chutes steep and avalanche prone.

Alternatively, you can ski the southeast aspect in the trees. You may get a longer run, 1200 feet. If you ski the east trees, you have to skin back up to the summit to retrace your route back to the car.

Belknap Crater's distinctive cinder cone

42 Belknap Crater

Start Point : McKenzie Pass, 5324 feet
High Point : Belknap Crater summit, 6872 feet
Trail Distance : 6 miles
Trail Time : 4 hours
Skill Level : Intermediate
Best Season : Winter
Map : USGS Mount Washington

The second McKenzie Pass cinder cone is Belknap Crater, on the north side of the road, opposite Black Crater (Route 41). The trailhead leaves right from McKenzie Pass. But, like the Black Crater route, it's a long approach. However, it's shorter than Black Crater by 2 miles.

OR-242 through McKenzie Pass is closed in winter, but you can drive south from Sisters as far as the gate closing the road; from there, it's a 6-mile road skin to the trailhead, probably too far for a day tour unless you start at dawn and plan to be back just before nightfall. Some snowmobile up the road to the trailhead. Better to leave this route until the road is open in the spring. But, you will have a short window for spring corn. You'll want to catch Belknap Crater with plenty of snow on the cone, so go right after the road opens. You can reach Belknap Crater from McKenzie Pass also, a shorter trip for Eugene riders and skiers. The road is closed at Alder Springs. Just call ahead to see if the road is open, unless you plan to use a snowmobile. Note: Road is open to bikes several weeks before it is open to cars.

GETTING THERE. From Salem, drive east on OR-22 (North Santiam Highway) for 85 miles to Santiam Junction. Continue east on US 20/OR-126, over Santiam Pass, to Sisters. From Sisters, head west on OR-242 (McKenzie Highway). In 8.5 miles you will reach the gate (see map for Route 41). If the gate is open, continue 6 miles to McKenzie Pass. The Belknap trailhead is right at McKenzie Pass on the right (north) side of the road, about 15 miles from Sisters. From the west, drive 52 miles from Eugene to McKenzie Bridge on OR-126. In 4 miles, turn right on OR-242. Continue 15 miles to McKenzie Pass, if the road is open.

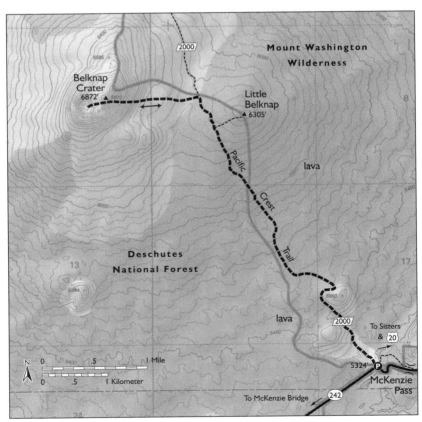

THE ROUTE. The Belknap Crater route follows the Pacific Crest Trail 2000, north and northwest from the pass through a lava flow. Ski up the trail, which should be marked with the Pacific Crest Trail blazes. In 2.4 miles, you will pass the trail to Little Belknap, a knoll to the right. In another quarter mile, you will reach some woods. Here, leave the trail and ascend the east flank of the crater. Descend by the same route.

Gaining the summit and gearing up for the schuss down, old school

Opposite: The wild high desert of Three Sisters Wilderness

THREE SISTERS WILDERNESS
AND BEND

THREE SISTERS WILDERNESS is some of the most spectacular and tranquil scenery in Oregon. This is the heart of where the Cascade volcanoes meet the high desert. In summer, scents of juniper and sage mark your camp. In winter, the snow is often lighter and drier than on the west slopes of the Cascades, and the weather is more often clear and sunny. This region includes five volcanoes clustered in an accessible area just outside of Bend: North Sister, Middle Sister, South Sister, Broken Top, and Mount Bachelor (although the latter is outside the wilderness area). Plus you will find a smattering of buttes, cinder cones, and volcanic remnants—like Tam McAurther Rim and Paulina Peak—worthy of 500–1000 feet of vertical on midwinter powder days.

Access to this area is from two main towns. The high desert town of Sisters is the entry point to North Sister and Middle Sister, from either the Pole Creek Spring or Obsidian trailheads. The city of Bend and the small hub of Mount Bachelor Ski Area, 20 miles west, is the entry to the southern end of the wilderness with many options for making tracks, both midwinter powder shots and spring-corn descents.

South Sister is a classic ride and a good first summit descent for intermediate riders looking for a big-mountain experience. It is an annual ritual for Bend and Eugene skiers and boarders. The Middle Sister's Southeast Ridge is one of the cleanest 3000-foot fall-line descents in Oregon. Mount Bachelor has some beginner sidecountry stashes, and Tumalo Mountain is a short jaunt from town. Basically, there is something for everyone here, in all seasons too.

Ascending the frozen glacial waves of Three Sisters (Pete Keane)

THREE SISTERS WILDERNESS–BEND MAPS

The best overview map is the Geo-Graphics Three Sisters Wilderness, updated more recently than others. The full list is below.

USFS Deschutes National Forest

USFS Newberry Crater National Volcano Monument

Adventure Maps Mountain Biking and Cross-Country Skiing Central Oregon

Geo-Graphics Three Sisters Wilderness

Pacific Northwest Recreation Map Series Willamette Cascades

Green Trails Three Sisters No. 621, Broken Top No. 622

PRIMARY INFORMATION CENTERS/RANGER DISTRICTS

- Deschutes National Forest Headquarters, Bend, OR: (541) 383-5300, www.fs.fed.us/r6/deschutes
- Bend–Fort Rock Ranger District: (541) 383-4000
- Sisters Ranger District: (541) 549-2111

AVALANCHE/WEATHER/ROAD CONDITIONS

- Northwest Weather and Avalanche Center: (503) 808-2400, www.nwac.us
- Oregon Avalanche Institute: www.oravalanche.org (a new organization run by Three Sisters Backcountry)
- Oregon DOT Trip Check: (800) 977-6368, www.tripcheck.com

SKI AREA SNOW REPORTS

- Mount Bachelor: (541) 382-7888, www.mtbachelor.com

GUIDES

- Three Sisters Backcountry: (541) 549-8101, www.threesistersbackcountry.com

OVERNIGHT SHELTERS

- Kwohl Butte Shelter, Deschutes National Forest: (541) 383-5300, www.fs.fed.us/r6/deschutes
- Jeff View Shelter, Deschutes National Forest: (541) 383-5300, www.fs.fed.us/r6/deschutes

BEACON PARKS

- Mount Bachelor: (541) 382-7888, www.mtbachelor.com

PERMITS

- Wilderness permits are required for climbing in the Three Sisters Wilderness. Free, self-issued permits are available at most trailheads.
- A Northwest Forest Pass is required for most trailheads in Three Sisters Wilderness.
- A Sno-Park Pass is required for these routes between November 1 and April 30.

SPECIAL NOTE

Call ahead to check road access to trailheads, especially Cascade Lakes Highway, which is gated and not plowed in winter beyond Mount Bachelor Ski Resort.

43 North Sister, Southeast Ridge

Start Point : Pole Creek Spring, 5520 feet
High Point : Southeast Ridge, 9600 feet
Trail Distance : 10 miles
Trail Time : 8 hours
Skill Level : Expert
Best Season : Summer
Maps : USGS North Sister, Trout Creek

North Sister is a craggy, remote peak, not skiable from the summit because of the gnarly crags at the apex—like Mounts Jefferson, Thielsen, and Washington. In fact, it is one of the most technical and dangerous climbs in the Cascades because of the steep summit pyramid laced with loose, scrappy basalt. Middle and South Sisters offer primo skiing in safer conditions. But, for the more adventurous, and for those who need to ski all three, the best route for skiing is North Sister's Southeast Ridge, well below the summit.

Because of the long approach and the long trek up the mountainside, this is best done in one long summer day, or with an overnight camp.

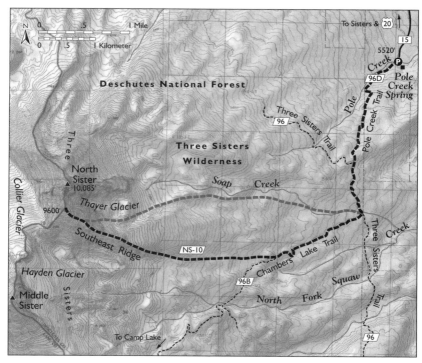

Fording Soap Creek, en route to Camp Lake

GETTING THERE. From Sisters, head west on OR-242 (McKenzie Highway). After 1 mile, turn south on Forest Road 15, Pole Creek Road. Follow FR 15 about 10 miles; it ends at the Pole Creek Spring trailhead.

THE ROUTE. From Pole Creek Spring, follow Pole Creek Trail 96D south about 1.5 miles to the junction with Three Sisters Trail 96. Continue south on Trail 96 about another 0.5 mile to Soap Creek. Just after the trail crosses Soap Creek, leave Trail 96 and take Chambers Lake Trail 96B west toward Camp Lake. In a mile you reach the ridge trail NS-10, leading right up the Southeast Ridge. The trail follows the ridge up to a slew of craggy gendarmes at 9000 feet. Alternatively, you can track right up Soap Creek for a more direct route to the ridge; but this route will be unmarked and overland, through brush and woods.

For descent, ski the ridge and snowfields next to the Thayer Glacier, but that will drop you into the Soap Creek drainage and routefinding back to the trail may be difficult. Ski out Soap Creek or traverse back to NS-10.

44 Middle Sister, Southeast Ridge

Start Point : Pole Creek Spring, 5520 feet
High Point : Middle Sister summit, 10,053 feet
Trail Distance : 14 miles
Trail Time : 8 hours
Skill Level : Advanced
Best Season : Summer
Maps : USGS Trout Creek, North Sister

Middle Sister's Southeast Ridge is one of the best descents in this book, a clean 3000-foot fall line among beautiful volcanic scenery. Akin to the Southwest Chute on Mount Adams, it is a must-do—an excellent nontechnical route. It makes a fabulous overnight trip because of the scenic camp spot and beautiful approach trail. The approach is quite long but well worth the ride if the snow is good, and especially if you hike in early enough to make some evening turns in the slopes above camp and then summit the next morning. The route follows a snowfield that is free of crevasses.

Dawn patrol: crossing the firm summer firn for a summit bid on Middle Sister

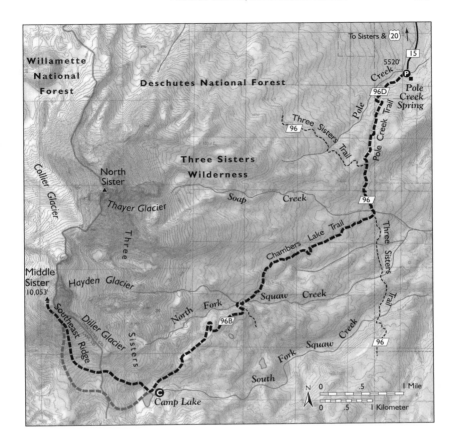

GETTING THERE. From Sisters, head west on OR-242 (McKenzie Highway). After 1 mile, turn south on Forest Road 15 (Pole Creek Road). Follow FR 15 about 10 miles; it ends at Pole Creek Spring.

THE ROUTE. From Pole Creek Spring, follow Pole Creek Trail 96D south about 1.5 miles to the junction with Three Sisters Trail 96. Continue south on Trail 96 about another 0.5 mile to Soap Creek. Just after the trail crosses Soap Creek, leave Trail 96 and take Chambers Lake Trail 96B west toward Camp Lake. At 5.5 miles reach Camp Lake, where you will find plenty of spots to camp.

From Camp Lake, climb north around a small cliff band to gain Middle Sister's Southeast Ridge. Follow the ridge all the way to the summit. Depending on the season and snowpack, you may find some scree slopes to cross between the snowfields.

Descent follows the snowfields adjacent to the rocky-ridge climbing route. Alternatively, you can take one of the slopes or gullies to the east.

45 Middle Sister, Hayden Glacier

Start Point : Pole Creek Spring, 5520 feet
High Point : Middle Sister summit, 10,053 feet
Trail Distance : 10 miles
Trail Time : 8 hours
Skill Level : Expert
Best Season : Summer
Maps : USGS Trout Creek, North Sister

A shorter but more difficult route than Middle Sister's Southeast Ridge (Route 44), the north face via Hayden Glacier is for experts. Simply put, you need to ascend and descend on the crevassed glacier. You will need crampons, ice ax, and full glacier travel gear. But if you are looking for a more technical route and one that is a bit shorter, consider this trip. Route 46 approaches the same point, but from the west side.

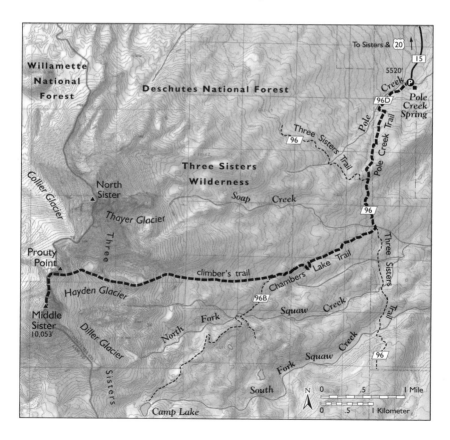

Getting ready for an alpine start in Three Sisters Wilderness

GETTING THERE. From Sisters, head west on OR-242 (McKenzie Highway). After 1 mile, turn south on Forest Road 15 (Pole Creek Road). Follow FR 15 about 10 miles; it ends at Pole Creek Spring.

THE ROUTE. From Pole Creek Spring, follow Pole Creek Trail 96D south about 1.5 miles to the junction with Three Sisters Trail 96. Continue south on Trail 96 about another 0.5 mile to Soap Creek. Just after the trail crosses Soap Creek, leave Trail 96 and take Chambers Lake Trail 96B west toward Camp Lake. After a mile, hike past the primitive climber's trail that heads due west to the North Sister. In another half mile, take the second climber's trail to the Hayden Glacier and the prominent rock between North and Middle Sister called Prouty Point.

Follow the climber's trail west to timberline, the lower snowfields of the glacier, and then Hayden Glacier. Head for the saddle just south of Prouty Point. There are many crevasses here, so consider staying on the lower snowfield between the glacier and timberline. From Prouty Point, head due south up the North Ridge to the summit of Middle Sister.

The descent follows the north-face snowfield down to Prouty Point and back across the glacier to the approach trail.

46 Middle Sister, Collier Glacier

Start Point : Obsidian trailhead, 4749 feet
High Point : Middle Sister summit, 10,053 feet
Trail Distance : 16 miles
Trail Time : 10 hours
Skill Level : Expert
Best Season : Summer
Maps : USGS Trout Creek, North Sister

The approach to Middle Sister and North Sister from the west could be left until the other routes in this area have been done. It is a long two-day ascent on the Obsidian Trail, includes some glacier travel, and does not have the long, continuous descent of Middle Sister's Southeast Ridge (Route 44). But if you have done Middle Sister from Pole Creek and have a few days, this is a challenging climb and descent. And it is incredibly beautiful. Part of the route travels on the Collier Glacier, so it requires expert ski/snowboard mountaineering ability, including well-refined glacier travel skills. Take one day to hike in, set up camp, and make some evening turns on the lower glacier; a second day will give you time to summit, ski, and hike back to the trailhead. Go in summer, when the days are long, the snow is firm, and the crevasses are open and visible.

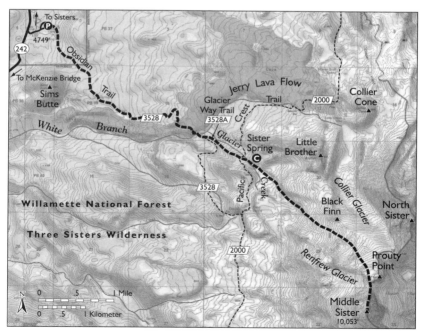

Exiting the route on dirt, back to the car

GETTING THERE. From Sisters, head west on OR-242 (McKenzie Highway) for 17 miles. Park at the Obsidian trailhead on the left side of the road. Keep in mind, the McKenzie Pass Road is closed in winter, so call in advance to make sure the gate is open and the road is clear from snow.

THE ROUTE. Head southeast on Obsidian Trail 3528 for 4 miles through the woods and across Jerry Lava Flow. At the first junction, head east (toward Pacific Crest Trail 2000); the Obsidian Trail is renamed Glacier Way Trail 3528A for the next mile along Glacier Creek. Once you reach the PCT, you'll reach a beautiful spot to camp near Scott Spring and Obsidian Falls. But it may be heavily used in the summer.

Continue east on the mountaineering trail that you can find at the junction of the Glacier Way and Pacific Crest trails. The trail leads past the Black Finn rock formation and up the ridge between the Renfrew Glacier to the south and the Collier Glacier to the north. Head up the snowfield to the south arm of the Collier Glacier at about 8500 feet.

Cross the Collier Glacier, using extreme caution for crevasses. Head southwest on the edge of the glacier toward the small saddle just south of the prominent Prouty Point, 9312 feet. If you head east across the glacier, you will end up at the col between North Sister and Middle Sister, at 8840 feet. From here you can ride some of the slopes flanking North Sister, but you will have to traverse south to get to Middle Sister. From Prouty Point, head due south up the North Ridge to the summit.

The descent follows the north-face snowfield down to Prouty Point and down to the Obsidian Trail.

47 South Sister, Green Lakes

Start Point : Green Lakes trailhead, 5450 feet
High Point : South Sister summit, 10,358 feet
Trail Distance : 14 miles
Trail Time : 8 hours
Skill Level : Advanced
Best Season : Summer
Maps : USGS South Sister, Broken Top

South Sister is one of the most accessible mountains in Oregon. Of the two main approaches, the Green Lakes route is less crowded and slightly longer. Several east-facing slopes can be ridden, and it gives good access to Broken Top; hence it is perhaps a better choice for a multiday or multipeak trip.

In the winter, the road ends at the ski area, so you should plan to skin or snowshoe the last 4 miles to the trailhead, adding an extra half day. Or with so many other great winter tours closer by, wait until the road opens to tackle South Sister.

GETTING THERE. From Bend, drive west on OR-46 (Cascade Lakes Highway) for 21 miles to Mount Bachelor Ski Area. Four miles past the ski area, you'll reach the Green Lakes trailhead on the right side of the road.

THE ROUTE. Follow Green Lakes Trail 17 along Fall Creek north for 4 miles. It is well traveled in the summer and probably still snow covered in spring. The last 2

Climbing the basalt stairway on South Sister, earning every turn

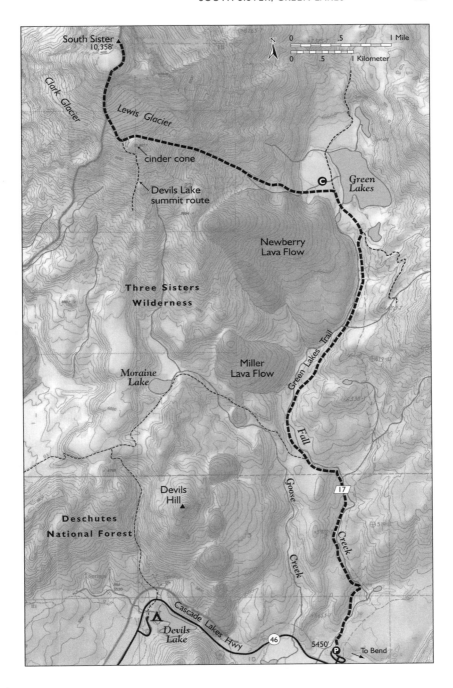

South Sister
10,358'

Clark Glacier

Lewis Glacier

cinder cone

Devils Lake
summit route

Green
Lakes

Newberry
Lava Flow

Three Sisters
Wilderness

Green Lakes Trail

Miller
Lava Flow

Moraine
Lake

Fall

Goose

17

Devils
Hill

Creek

Deschutes
National Forest

Creek

Cascade Lakes Hwy

Devils
Lake

46

5450'

To Bend

0   .5   1 Mile

0   .5   1 Kilometer

N

miles will be along the Miller and Newberry lava flows, vast expanses of rock with little vegetation. At Green Lakes, set up camp if you are staying overnight.

The summit route follows a deep drainage from the south end of the lake, up a bowl, to top of the snowfield. The route then winds between the Lewis Glacier and a cinder cone marked as 9017 feet on the topo maps. You will meet up with the Devils Lake route and follow the ridge to the summit.

Descend the climbing route.

48 South Sister, Moraine Lake

Start Point	Devils Lake Campground, 5450 feet
High Point	South Sister summit, 10,358 feet
Trail Distance	7 miles
Trail Time	5 hours
Skill Level	Advanced
Best Season	Summer
Map	USGS South Sister

One of the most popular routes in all of Oregon, this trip can be crowded in summer and spring but quite peaceful in the winter. Many make this an annual climb. In spring and summer, timing is tricky: you'll want the road to be open, but enough snow on the lower trail so you can ski all the way to the car. For an overnight two-day trip, many camp at scenic Moraine Lake.

Because the approach road (OR-46) is closed in winter, if you're willing to skin a few extra miles (or catch a snowmobile ride), you can be rewarded with great turns. But that makes for a long day. In the winter, the road is kept open as far as Mount Bachelor Ski Area, so you should plan an extra half day to ski the last 6 miles to the Devils Lake trailhead.

GETTING THERE. From Bend, drive west on OR-46 (Cascade Lakes Highway) for 21 miles to Mount Bachelor Ski Area. Six miles past the ski area, you'll reach the Devils Lake trailhead and parking area on the left.

THE ROUTE. Hike due north on the Devils Lake Trail 36. The steep trail winds along the Hell Creek drainage. This trail leads you between two hills, Kaleetan Butte and Devils Hill. At about 6680 feet you will pass the intersection with Moraine Lake Trail 17.1. In this broad, flat area, find a suitable campsite if you are planning a two-day trip.

To ascend the slopes of South Sister, continue north across the flats toward the summit, hike up the snowfield, and gain the main ridge, which leads to the summit. At 9000 feet the trail meets up with the Green Lakes Trail.

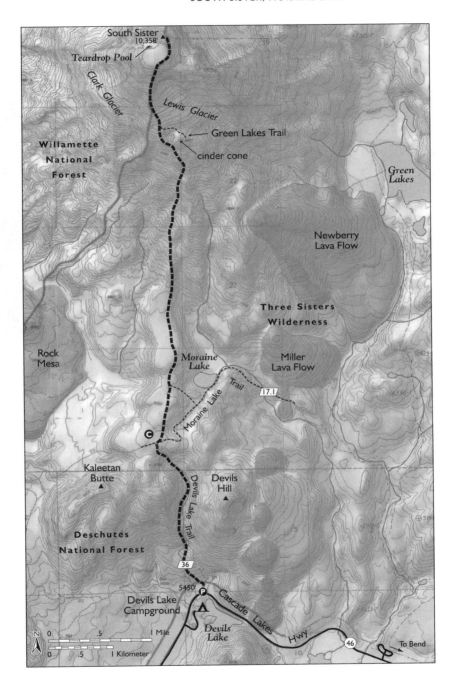

South Sister
10,358'

Teardrop Pool

Clark Glacier

Lewis Glacier

Green Lakes Trail

cinder cone

Green
Lakes

Willamette
National
Forest

Newberry
Lava Flow

Three Sisters
Wilderness

Rock
Mesa

Moraine
Lake

Miller
Lava Flow

Moraine Lake Trail

17A

Kaleetan
Butte

Devils
Hill

Devils Lake Trail

Deschutes
National Forest

36

5450'

P

Devils Lake
Campground

Cascade Lakes Hwy

Devils
Lake

46

To Bend

N

0   .5   1 Mile

0   .5   1 Kilometer

Evening at camp, Moraine Lake

The descent follows the snowfields adjacent to the ascent trail. With enough snow, and if you've timed it right, you should be able to ski all the way to your car.

49 Broken Top, Crater Bowl

Start Point	Dutchman Flat Sno-Park, 6400 feet; Forest Road 380, 7000 feet
High Point	Crater Bowl, 8500 feet
Trail Distance	12 miles; 4 miles
Trail Time	8 hours
Skill Level	Advanced
Best Season	Spring
Map	USGS Broken Top

Although the approach area is popular for cross-country skiers and snowmobilers, Broken Top is definitely an advanced trip for downhillers. In winter, you will likely need to break trail once beyond the Dutchman Flat area; you may need to do some serious routefinding in the thick woods. But if you've captured the Three Sisters or

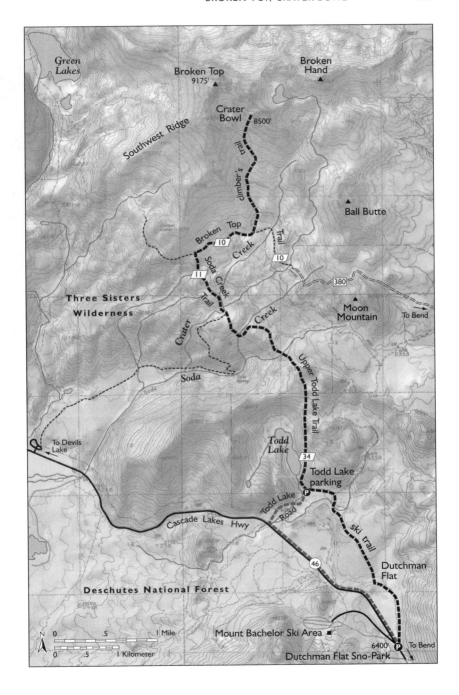

The craggy peaks of Broken Top and the smooth cone of South Sister

don't have time for the midwinter trek into South Sister or Middle Sister, Broken Top is worthy of turns.

GETTING THERE. From Bend, drive west on OR-46 (Cascade Lakes Highway) for 21 miles to Mount Bachelor Ski Area. In winter, follow signs to Dutchman Flat Sno-Park, across the road from the ski area. In spring you may be able to drive another 2 miles to Todd Lake, which saves the first 2 miles of skinning up the trail.

You can get much closer to Crater Bowl in summer. Drive to the Todd Lake parking area as described above. If the snow gate is open, take the primitive Forest Road 370 (Three Creek Lake Road) for 3 miles, where you turn left on Forest Road 380. Drive another mile to the Broken Top trailhead. Keep in mind, if the snow is melted sufficiently to get to the Broken Top trailhead, you may not find much on Crater Bowl.

THE ROUTE. In winter or spring, start from Dutchman Flat Sno-Park or Todd Lake, respectively. From Dutchman Flat, take the ski trail to Todd Lake to bypass the road. Continue north from Todd Lake, first on Upper Todd Lake Trail 34 through the woods for 2 miles, then on Soda Creek Trail 11 for 2 more miles. At mile 5, connect with Broken Top Trail 10 which heads east for a mile, then connects with the primitive climber's trail heading north to the bowl.

If you do take the summer route, follow the Broken Top Trail northwest for a mile to meet up with the primitive climber's trail heading north to the bowl.

From the foot of the south-facing bowl at 7000 feet, choose a line and hike to the top. Around 8500 feet, you will reach a rock band that continues upward to the Crook Glacier and the rocky summit. The summit is a climbing route that will require a rope and rock climbing protection if you want to stash your boards and get the full adventure.

Descend from 8500 feet down one of many lines to the bottom of the bowl.

50 Broken Top, Southwest Ridge

Start Point : Green Lakes trailhead, 5450 feet
High Point : Southwest Ridge, 8200 feet
Trail Distance : 14 miles
Trail Time : 8 hours
Skill Level : Advanced
Best Season : Spring
Map : USGS Broken Top

The Southwest Ridge is probably one of the more popular Broken Top routes because it can be combined with a South Sister trip via the Green Lakes Trail. Because of the fairly low elevation, it is best to go in spring or early summer before snow melts. For access, choose a summer weekend and climb both peaks.

Don't wait too long—the Southwest Ridge snow melts early.

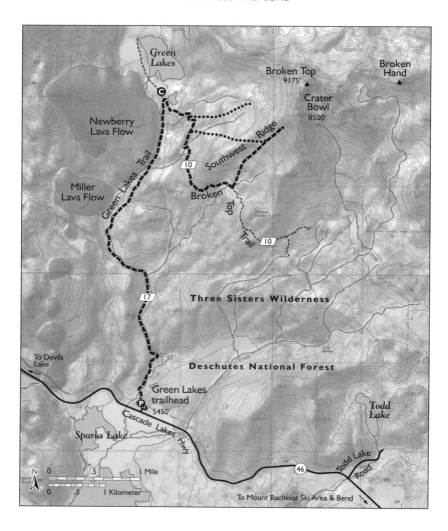

GETTING THERE. From Bend, drive west on OR-46 (Cascade Lakes Highway) for 21 miles to Mount Bachelor Ski Area and Dutchman Flat Sno-Park. Continue past the ski area for 4 miles to the Green Lakes trailhead. Keep in mind that in the winter, the road ends at the ski area, so you should plan to ski or snowshoe the last 4 miles to the trailhead, adding an extra half day. Or just wait until spring, when the gate opens and the road is clear.

THE ROUTE. From the Green Lakes trailhead, follow Green Lakes Trail 17 along Fall Creek north for 4 miles. It is well traveled in the summer and snow covered in winter and early spring. Skirt around the big Newberry and Miller lava flows and, if camping, find a spot to pitch your tent around the Green Lakes.

To ascend Broken Top's Southwest Ridge, head southeast from the Green Lakes on the Broken Top Trail 10. Use care crossing Fall Creek, especially if on a snow-bridge or downed tree. After 1.5 miles you will be at the foot of the ridge, a long, gentle slope.

Climb up to around 8200 feet on the Southwest Ridge. Descend down the broad ridge. Alternatively, ski the west-facing aprons.

51 Ball Butte

Start Point	Dutchman Flat Sno-Park, 6400 feet
High Point	Ball Butte summit, 8091 feet
Trail Distance	12 miles
Trail Time	6 hours
Skill Level	Intermediate
Best Season	Winter
Map	USGS Broken Top

Closer to the road than the Broken Top, South Sister, and Tam McArthur Rim mid-winter half-day trips, Ball Butte is ideal for a few laps when Tumalo Mountain (Route

Ascending an exposed ridge in search of freshies (Jennifer Donnelly)

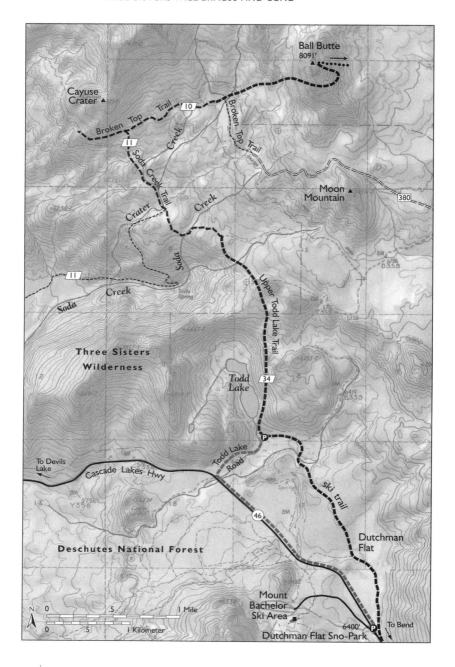

55) is tracked out or crowded. Also, Moon Mountain (Route 52) is nearby, so you may be able to ski both routes in a day.

GETTING THERE. From Bend, drive west on OR-46 (Cascade Lakes Highway) for 21 miles to Mount Bachelor Ski Area and Dutchman Flat Sno-Park. In spring you may be able to drive another 2 miles to Todd Lake, which saves the first 2 miles of skinning up the trail.

THE ROUTE. In winter or spring, start from Dutchman Flat Sno-Park or Todd Lake, respectively. From Dutchman Flat, take the ski trail to Todd Lake to bypass the road. Continue north from Todd Lake first on the Upper Todd Lake Trail 34 through the woods for 2 miles, then on Soda Creek Trail 11 for 2 more miles. Meet up with Broken Top Trail 10, which heads east. After a mile, skirt around the east side of Ball Butte, as the west-facing side is cliff. Skin to the summit.

Descend the way you came up on the east face.

52 Moon Mountain

Start Point	Dutchman Flat Sno-Park, 6400 feet
High Point	Moon Mountain summit, 7459 feet
Trail Distance	8 miles
Trail Time	4 hours
Skill Level	Intermediate
Best Season	Winter
Map	USGS Broken Top

Another short knob close to the road, like Ball Butte (Route 51) and Tumalo Mountain (Route 55), Moon Mountain is worthy of a few turns with a shorter approach route than Ball Butte. But it's probably the least thrilling of the trio that lie on the north side of Cascade Lakes Highway, accessible from Dutchman Flat. You can catch some turns on Moon Mountain in a half day, or combine it with a tour to Ball Butte.

GETTING THERE. From Bend, drive west on OR-46 (Cascade Lakes Highway) for 21 miles to Mount Bachelor Ski Area and Dutchman Flat Sno-Park. In spring you may be able to drive another two miles to Todd Lake, which saves the first 2 miles of skinning up the trail.

THE ROUTE. In winter or spring, start from Dutchman Flat Sno-Park or Todd Lake, respectively. From Dutchman Flat, take the ski trail to Todd Lake to bypass the

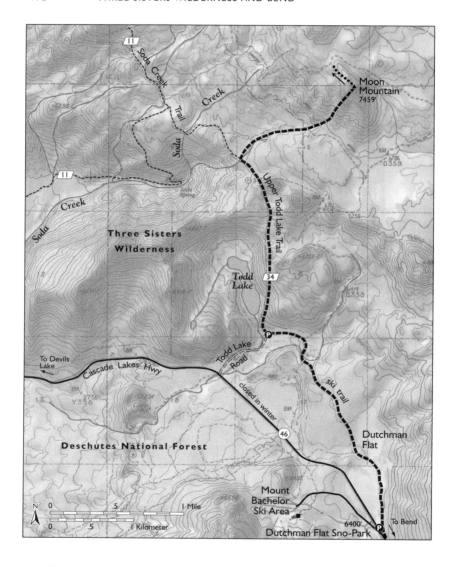

road. Continue north from Todd Lake, first on Upper Todd Lake Trail 34 through the woods for 2 miles, then on Soda Creek Trail 11. After a mile, head east up the Soda Creek drainage, where you may or may not find a trail, for a mile to Moon Mountain.

The best skiing is probably the north-facing treed slopes. Hit these for a few runs, then head back via the approach trail.

Powder smile! The descent is worth the ascent. (Pete Keane)

53 Todd Lake Rim

Start Point : Dutchman Flat Sno-Park, 6400 feet
High Point : Todd Lake rim, 6600 feet
Trail Distance : 6 miles
Trail Time : 3 hours
Skill Level : Intermediate
Best Season : Winter
Map : USGS Broken Top

The Todd Lake rim is worth a few turns if the snow is good and time is short. It's closer than Ball Butte and Moon Mountain (Routes 51 and 52), and can be accessed quickly by the cross-country trail from Dutchman Flat. Don't expect big lines, but the 500-foot slopes are worthy of powder turns after storms.

GETTING THERE. From Bend, drive west on OR-46 (Cascade Lakes Highway) for 21 miles to Mount Bachelor Ski Area and Dutchman Flat Sno-Park. In spring you may be able to drive another 2 miles to Todd Lake, which saves the first 2 miles of skinning up the trail.

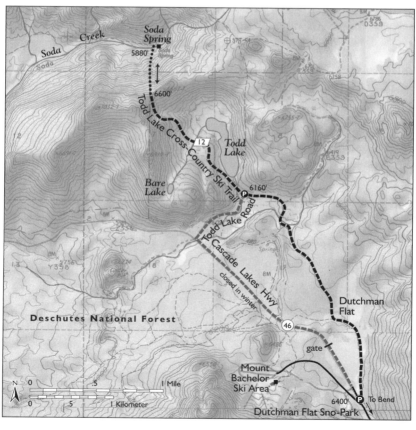

Opposite: Just up from Bend, a quick zip up Tumalo Mountain (Peter Van Tilburg)

THE ROUTE. Ski up the Dutchman Flat ski trail to Todd Lake. At Todd Lake, head northwest up Todd Lake Cross-Country Ski Trail 12 toward the rim on the northwest side of the lake, 1 mile.

Ski up the Todd Lake rim, choosing a safe route up this steep slope. You can ski to the 6600-foot crest of the rim. If time permits, ski down the back of the rim to Soda Spring, then skin back out. Make a short 500-foot run back to Todd Lake and head home.

54   Tam McArthur Rim

Start Point	Upper Three Creek Sno-Park, 5100 feet
High Point	Tam McArthur Rim, 7600 feet
Trail Distance	16 miles
Trail Time	10 hours
Skill Level	Advanced
Best Season	Winter
Maps	USGS Broken Top, Tumalo Falls, Trout Creek Butte

Tam McArthur Rim is a hidden local stash of midwinter pow. This is a long, long approach—probably too long for most day trips in winter. But for guided and snowmobile-assisted backcountry skiers and snowboarders, this is a classic adventure, with excellent skiing in open bowls and tight trees, and a spectacular view. The rocky crag is a 2-mile, 1500-foot escarpment on the eastern edge of Three Sisters Wilderness. One side drops into pine and hemlock forests of Three Creeks Lake, the other into Broken Hand and the craggy mess of Broken Top.

It was named after Lewis "Tam" McArthur, the Oregonian behind *Oregon Geographic Names*. Trips to the rim are guided by Three Sisters Backcountry, with yurts conveniently located at 6600 feet at Three Creek Lake. Also at the lake is the Jeff View Shelter, open to the public by reservation.

It's a long jaunt for a day trip, without a snowmobile. If you time it right, the road will open in the spring as far as the lake, and you'll still have skiable slopes on the rim bowls, which are northeast and east facing. Otherwise, consider booking a guided, catered weekend to enjoy exploring the craggy rim.

GETTING THERE. From Bend, drive north 2 miles on US 97, then exit on OR-20 and drive 20 miles northwest to Sisters. From Sisters, head south on Forest Road 16 (Three Creeks Road). In about 10 miles you'll pass the Lower Three Creek and Upper Three Creek Sno-Park where the plowed road ends.

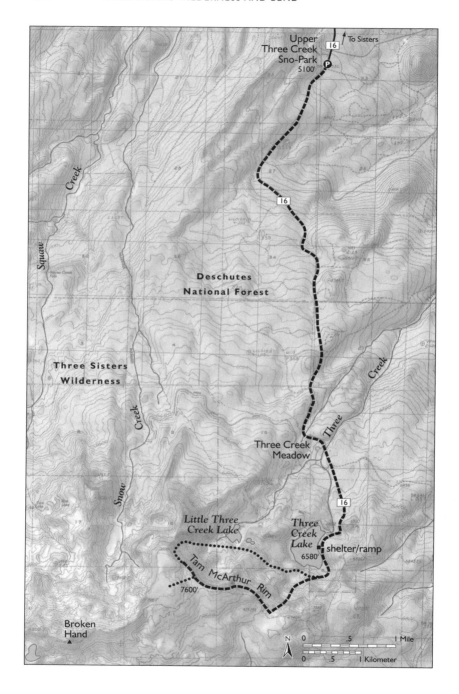

Upper
Three Creek
Sno-Park
5100'

16

To Sisters

16

Deschutes
National Forest

Three Sisters
Wilderness

Squaw

Creek

Creek

Snow

Creek

Three

Creek

Three Creek
Meadow

16

Little Three
Creek Lake

Three
Creek
Lake
6580'

shelter/ramp

Tam McArthur Rim

7600'

Broken
Hand
▲

N   0   .5   1 Mile
   0   .5   1 Kilometer

THE ROUTE. There are three ways to travel the 5-mile flat road to the bottom of the rim at Three Creek Lake. You can make the long skin in, which will take several hours. You can snowmobile in, which is how the guides get you in to the yurts run by Three Sisters Backcountry. Or, in spring when the road is clear of snow, you can drive in but this may mean little snow on the rim.

From the lake, ski up the slopes of the rim, sticking to woods or open slopes, depending on the conditions. The 1-mile route encounters crags and cliffs, thick woods, and many open low-angle bowls. The path of least resistance is east of the lake.

You can ski down to the lake on one of the many open, low-angle bowls, steeper chutes, or wooded glades. You can make a run to the west, too, off the rim, into the Broken Hand rock formation and Snow Creek.

Getting the beta from Three Sisters Backcountry guides (Jonas Tarlan)

55 Tumalo Mountain

Start Point	Dutchman Flat Sno-Park, 6400 feet
High Point	Tumalo Mountain summit, 7775 feet
Trail Distance	3 miles
Trail Time	2 hours
Skill Level	Intermediate
Best Season	Winter
Maps	USGS Broken Top, Bachelor Butte

One of the most accessible winter routes in this region, Tumalo Mountain is a good place to start for beginner–intermediates needing a challenging hike that is close to Bend locals. It's also great for those wanting to squeeze in a tour before or after work, or when the ski resort is packed. There was a fire lookout on the summit, long since dismantled. Tumalo is a popular backcountry destination for Bend locals because it's so close to the road; expect crowds on weekend powder days. Look for a skin track to make ascent easier.

GETTING THERE. From Bend, drive west on OR-46 (Cascade Lakes Highway) for 21 miles to Mount Bachelor Ski Area and park at Dutchman Flat Sno-Park.

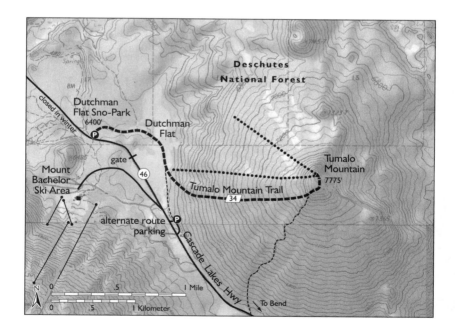

Up Tumalo Mountain, the closest turns to Bend (Peter Van Tilburg)

THE ROUTE. From Dutchman Flat, take the Tumalo Mountain Trail 34 to the summit. The trail heads east and east-northeast near the summit. The northwest-facing open country has some cliffs and good skiing but a longer skin back to your car. Ski west through the thickly wooded forest for the quickest way back.

There's also a summer primitive road and summit trail up the south side, directly from Cascade Lakes Highway.

56 Cinder Cone

Start Point : Mount Bachelor Sno-Park, 6400 feet
High Point : Cinder Cone, 7200 feet
Trail Distance : 1 mile
Trail Time : 1 hour
Skill Level : Beginner
Best Season : Winter
Map : USGS Bachelor Butte

Although the ski area covers the entire mountain, Mount Bachelor (aka Bachelor Butte) is still a sidecountry or backcountry destination for many skiers and riders year-round. It's a good spot for those looking for a workout and some excellent winter turns with easy access to the road. Of the two routes the ski resort had marked for uphill travel at the time of this writing, the Cinder Cone is allowed 24/7, so take a midnight full-moon tour if you like. It is a designated inbounds uphill hiking route. If you catch this in winter, get a dawn patrol session before the resort crowds track it up. For spring or summer corn, choose the summit route (Route 57) because the snow will be more plentiful up high.

This is one of the shortest routes in this book, and one of the easiest and safest tours, akin to the Glade and Alpine trails of Mount Hood (Routes 2 and 3). So if you are a beginner with new gear, this is your spot for a shakedown tour near Bend.

GETTING THERE. From Bend, drive west on OR-46 (Cascade Lakes Highway) for 21 miles to Mount Bachelor Ski Area. Park in the main parking lot.

THE ROUTE. In winter, the Cinder Cone route begins at the Red chairlift, climbs the Leeway ski run, and gives access to the Cinder Cone. You can yo-yo endlessly

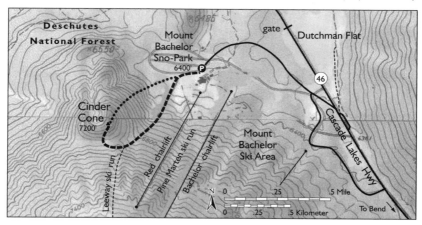

Cinder Cone and Mount Bachelor, from yonder on Tumalo Mountain
(Peter Van Tilburg)

on this open and gladed knob if the pow is fresh. It will give you nearly 800 feet of vertical descent. Don't skin directly up the Cinder Cone because of in-area and side-country skiers descending.

57   Mount Bachelor

Start Point	Mount Bachelor Sno-Park, 6400 feet
High Point	Mount Bachelor summit, 9065 feet
Trail Distance	4 miles
Trail Time	3 hours
Skill Level	Intermediate
Best Season	Spring
Map	USGS Bachelor Butte

Mount Bachelor (aka Bachelor Butte) has plenty of year-round backcountry for skiers and riders. It is accessible during most of the ski mountaineering season and is an easy short tour from Bend. The best time to ride these slopes for excellent spring and summer corn is when the resort closes during weekdays in late spring and for weeks after it closes for the season. Plus, it's a great workout and has a beautiful fall-line descent.

If you climb to Mount Bachelor's summit during hours of lift operation, check with ski patrol and stay well clear of runs; at the time of this writing uphill traffic is limited to two routes: the northeast summit route and the northwest Cinder Cone summit route. These may change from year to year. Access is limited during avalanche control and grooming, so check with the ski resort first. And both routes are closed when the summit chair is not running.

GETTING THERE. From Bend, drive west on OR-46 (Cascade Lakes Highway) for 21 miles to Mount Bachelor Ski Area. For the Cinder Cone summit route, park in the main lot (as for Route 56). For the northeast summit route, park at Sunrise Lodge.

THE ROUTE. For the Cinder Cone summit route, start at the main parking lot and main lodge. The Cinder Cone route begins at the Red chairlift, climbs the Leeway ski run, and ascends the West Village and Ed's Garden ski runs, sticking to the trees to the north. You can only continue to the summit if the Summit chairlift is operating, up the West Ridge ski run, overlooking the cirque, a large glacial remnant.

In the spring, start at Sunrise Lodge parking lot. The northeast summit route starts at the Rainbow chairlift, follows the Flying Dutchman and East Healy ski runs, then

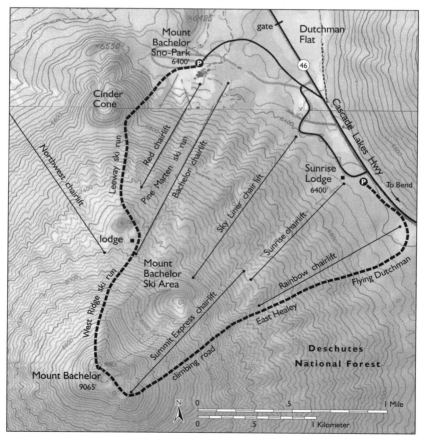

The view from atop Mount Bachelor, looking north toward Three Sisters

a climbing road on the northeast ridge. There are signs that mark the bottom and the midway points. Above timberline, follow the climbing road, which is generally marked.

58 Kwohl Butte

Start Point : Sunrise Lodge Sno-Park, 6400 feet;
: Edison Sno-Park, 5300 feet
High Point : Kwohl Butte, 7359 feet
Trail distance : 3 miles; 8 miles
Trail Time : 3 hours; 5 hours
Skill Level : Intermediate
Best season : Winter
Map : USGS Bachelor Butte

Kwohl Butte is a local powder stash just south of Mount Bachelor (aka Bachelor Butte). At the time of this writing, Mount Bachelor Ski Area allows backcountry access from the lifts. But that may change year to year and from day to day; access may be limited during avalanche control and grooming, so check with the ski patrol first. Alternatively, you can take a longer approach from Edison Sno-Park to catch turns on this knoll.

Be aware—a big avalanche on Mount Bachelor's cirque

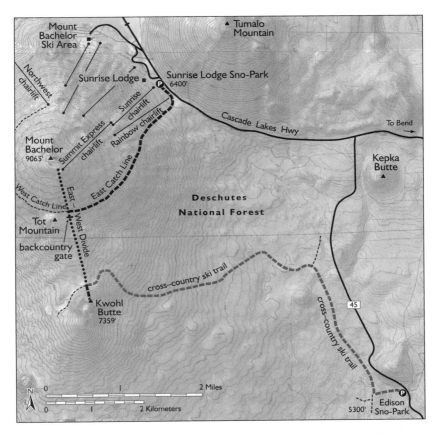

GETTING THERE. From Bend, drive west on OR-46 (Cascade Lakes Highway) for 21 miles to Mount Bachelor Ski Area. Park in the Sunrise Lodge lot.

Alternatively, head up OR-46 toward Mount Bachelor for 18 miles and turn left on Forest Road 45, the cutoff road to Sunriver. Head south for 4 miles to Edison Sno-Park.

THE ROUTE. From the ski resort, the backcountry access gate is at the bottom of Larry Valley, on the south side of the East Catch Line. You can skin up the East Catch Line from the Sunrise Lodge parking lot, or you can catch the Rainbow chairlift and the Summit Express chairlift if it's open, and then descend to the gate. Either way, make sure ski patrol allows backcountry access from inbounds.

Descend through the trees to 7000 feet and follow that contour around to the southeast side of Mount Bachelor. Then climb Kwohl Butte: the route is treeless and wide open for a few hundred vertical. There's a small shelter on the west side of the butte for those interested in winter camping. Allow time to skin back up to the East Catch Line to return to the ski resort parking lot.

Alternatively, from Edison Sno-Park, follow the cross-country ski trail that heads north, then west to Kwohl Butte. You'll meander through lava fields and ponderosa stands before reaching the base of the butte in 4 miles.

59 Paulina Peak

Start Point	Ten Mile Sno-Park, 5600 feet
High Point	Paulina Peak summit, 7984 feet
Trail Distance	10 miles
Trail Time	6 hours
Skill Level	Intermediate
Best Season	Winter
Map	USGS Paulina Peak

Paulina Peak is a massive shield volcano with a center crater, named after the Snake Indian chief who opposed settlers in this land. The crater has jagged peaks around the rim and lakes in the center. The surrounds were established as a National Volcano Monument in 1990. It might not have burly lines like the stratovolcanoes of the Three Sisters, but in midwinter Paulina Peak offers spectacular scenery with an easy approach. The sno-park is only 2 miles from the rim, so access is easy. Be advised, you'll find lots of snowmobilers and cross-country skiers here.

GETTING THERE. From Bend, drive south 23 miles on US 97. Turn left and head east on Forest Road 21 (Paulina East Lake Road). Drive 10 miles to Ten Mile Sno-Park.

THE ROUTE. From Ten Mile Sno-Park, follow Forest Road 21, also cross-country ski trail 1, to the rim of Newberry Crater overlooking Paulina Lake. If you are doing

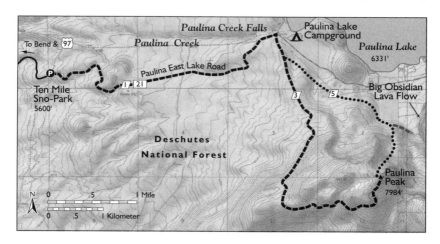

Dropping in a powder-filled gully on Paulina Peak (Pete Keane)

a winter overnight, you can camp here at Paulina Lake Campground. Don't walk or ski on the snow-covered lake; the ice may be thin. At the rim expect fantastic views.

Head south on cross-country trail 3 for 4 miles; the trail wraps around the south of Paulina Peak. Then ski up to the summit.

Descend the northeast bowl or the northwest chutes. The northeast bowls will put you down toward the Big Obsidian Lava Flow to the south of Paulina Lake. You can follow snowmobile/cross-country ski trail 5 back to Paulina Lake Campground and then out the road to your car.

Opposite: Way above the clouds
on remote Diamond Peak

WILLAMETTE PASS TO
DIAMOND LAKE

WILLAMETTE PASS IS A LOCAL HOTSPOT for middle Willamette Valley residents, especially snowriders from Eugene and Corvallis. Like its sister to the north, Santiam Pass, the Willamette Pass area has a plethora of cross-country ski trails and a small ski resort. If you search, you can find big peaks and small hills too. The backcountry options include Diamond Peak, a relatively remote but wide-open Cascade volcano, and a smattering of treed buttes and cinder cones.

Diamond Peak is fairly difficult to access. In winter, the nearest plowed road makes the north approach a super-long, super-flat skin, in which you will likely be breaking trail. In spring after the roads clear, the approach from the west is easier, but routefinding is difficult as there is no established mountaineering trail and no blazes or markings. For the best bet, go in late spring, and gather as much information about road, trail, and snow conditions as possible. Be prepared for routefinding with a map, a compass, an altimeter, and a GPS.

The Diamond Lake area can be the easiest or the most difficult trip you've ever done. If you attempt Mounts Bailey and Thielsen in poor weather, you may have difficult routefinding. But unlike other volcanoes in the Cascades, the approaches for these Diamond Lake twin bergs are not too long, and the camping options are protected with thick trees. In the spring, after snow has melted from the approach trails, climbing to these peaks, all under 10,000 feet, can be relatively straightforward. Winter can get busy here with snowmobiles; late spring offers the most peaceful days with good weather.

There is another option on Mount Bailey. It is the only Oregon area that has a backcountry snowcat operation not linked to a developed ski resort. If you are a novice, Mount Bailey Snowcats has experienced guides to help you explore the wild southern Oregon snow. They can also give you info on the local conditions.

Mount Thielsen, marked by a rocky summit pinnacle, is rugged terrain and less traveled. It was first climbed by USGS survey ensign E. E. Hayden in 1883. Frequent lightning storms and the prominent summit pinnacle have given it the moniker, "Lightning Rod of the Cascades."

Besides the snowcats, there is a wealth of cross-country and snowmobile terrain here—and a lot of anglers on the lake in the spring and summer. So the place is busy. If you are making a multiday trip in the spring or summer, you have your choice of many campsites along the lake, but they may be closed due to snow, depending on the time of year. If you are an angler, bring your rod to cast a line after your tour. Diamond Lake Resort offers lodging for those driving from afar looking for a cushy trip.

WILLAMETTE PASS TO DIAMOND LAKE MAPS

- USFS Willamette National Forest
- USFS Umpqua National Forest
- Pacific Northwest Recreation Series Willamette Cascades
- USFS Rogue–Umpqua Divide, Boulder Creek, and Mount Thielsen Wildernesses
- Imus Geo-Graphics Diamond Peak Wilderness
- Imus Geo-Graphics Willamette Pass Ski Trails

PRIMARY INFORMATION CENTERS/RANGER DISTRICTS

- Umpqua National Forest Headquarters, Roseburg: (541) 672-6601, www.fs.fed.us/r6/umpqua
- Willamette National Forest Headquarters, Eugene: (541) 465-6521, www.fs.fed.us/r6/willamette
- Middle Fork (Willamette) Ranger District: (541) 782-2283
- Diamond Lake (Umpqua) Ranger District: (541) 498-2531

AVALANCHE/WEATHER/ROAD CONDITIONS

- Northwest Weather and Avalanche Center: (503) 808-2400, www.nwac.us.
- Oregon DOT Trip Check: (800) 977-6368, www.tripcheck.com

PERMITS

- Wilderness permits are required for Diamond Peak and Mount Thielsen wildernesses. Free, self-issued permits are available at the trailheads.
- A Sno-Park Pass is required for these routes between November 1 and April 30.
- A Northwest Forest Pass is required for these routes during the rest of the year.

WINTER RESORTS AND PATROLS

- Willamette Pass Resort: (541) 345-7669, www.willamettepass.com
- Diamond Lake Resort: (800) 733-7593, www.diamondlake.net
- Willamette Backcountry Ski Patrol: www.wbsp.org

GUIDES

- Mount Bailey Snowcats: (800) 733-7593, www.catskimtbailey.com

OVERNIGHT SHELTERS

- Maiden Peak Shelter, Maiden Peak, Willamette National Forest, Middle Fork Ranger District: (541) 782-2283, www.fs.fed.us/r6/willamette
- Hemlock Butte Shelter, Mount Bailey, Umpqua National Forest, Diamond Lake Ranger District: (541) 498-2531, www.fs.fed.us/r6/upmqua

Opposite: Choosing a line carefully on Diamond Peak's west shoulder

60 West Peak and Peak 2

Start Point : Willamette Pass Sno-Park, 5128 feet
High Point : Peak 2 summit, 6693 feet
Trail Distance : 2 miles
Trail Time : 2 hours
Skill Level : Beginner
Best Season : Winter
Map : USGS Willamette Pass

Willamette Pass is a short junket for Eugene and Corvallis locals. The small Willamette Pass Ski Resort lies on a couple of peaks just off the road. Because the area is closed Monday through Wednesday, those with weekdays off can make ample turns in the permit area. In addition, West Peak makes an excellent destination out of bounds.

GETTING THERE. From Eugene, drive southeast on OR-58 (Willamette Highway) 70 miles to Willamette Pass. Park at Willamette Pass Sno-Park, right at the ski resort on the left side of the road.

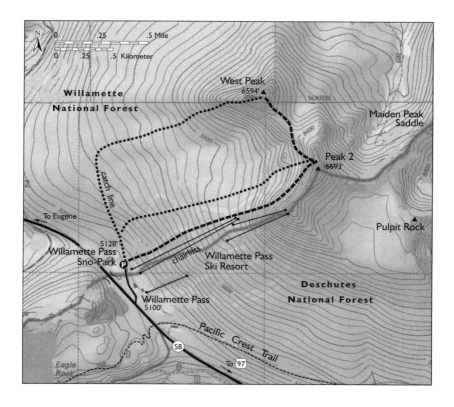

THE ROUTE. If the Willamette Pass Ski Resort is closed, ski up the resort runs. Peak 2 is a short distance from the top of the chairlifts' top terminus, up a ski trail. The top of the back-side chairlift is at the apex of Peak 2. To get to West Peak, skin to the northwest across the saddle between the two peaks, then directly through the wooded slopes up to the summit.

Descend the glades on the south or west flanks of the twin peaks. There is a cross-country ski trail, a catch line, you can take to skin back to the car.

Shoring up bootstraps to prevent blisters

61 Maiden Peak

Start Point	Willamette Pass Sno-Park, 5128 feet
High Point	Maiden Peak summit, 7818 feet
Trail Distance	14 miles
Trail Time	10 hours
Skill Level	Advanced
Best Season	Winter
Maps	USGS Willamette Pass, Odell Lake, The Twins

Maiden Peak isn't a technical climb, but it's a long ski, so it makes a good overnight, especially if you can book the shelter. Much of the route is in the woods along cross-country trails. If you can reserve the Maiden Peak Shelter, you can make a few laps up Maiden Peak if the snow is good. The Pacific Crest Trail around the Rosary Lakes is an alternate, but longer approach.

GETTING THERE. From Eugene, drive southeast on OR-58 (Willamette Highway) 70 miles to Willamette Pass. For either route, park at Willamette Pass Sno-Park, right at the ski resort on the left side of the road.

THE ROUTE. Ski up Willamette Pass Ski Resort (Route 60) to Peak 2. The downhill on the back side of the saddle drops you into the north side of the Rosary Lakes.

Alternatively, you can take the longer route around the east side of Willamette Pass Ski Resort along the Pacific Crest Trail, which leads you east and then north along the three Rosary Lakes. Find the Pacific Crest Trail by walking to the east end

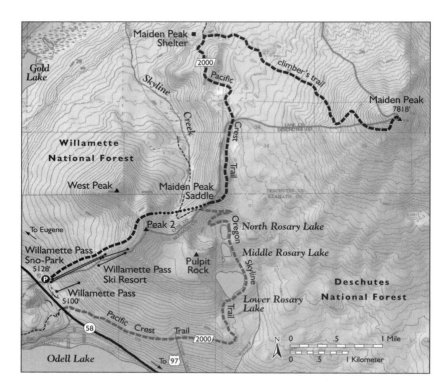

of the parking area, near the junction of OR-58 and the Willamette Pass Sno-Park access road.

From North Rosary Lake, skin 2 miles north on the Pacific Crest Trail to the Maiden Peak Shelter. If you are staying the night, set up camp. From the shelter, head east up the Maiden Peak Trail through the woods, following the primitive climber's trail. It takes you up the northwest flank of Maiden Peak.

With no trail in the thick trees, routefinding skills are essential on Diamond Peak.

Once on the summit, the descent follows the climber's trail back down to the shelter. Then, you have the trek back out the trail and over Peak 2.

62 Diamond Peak, West Shoulder

Start Point : Corrigan Lake trailhead, 5000 feet
High Point : Diamond Peak summit, 8744 feet
Trail Distance : 6 miles
Trail Time : 6 hours
Skill Level : Advanced
Best Season : Spring
Map : USGS Diamond Peak

Diamond Peak is a fabulous Oregon ski mountaineering objective because the turns can be spectacular, the views stunning, and the crowds nonexistent. It is so remote, the ski lines are uncrowded and clean in this spectacularly beautiful area of the state. Because the mountain biking is so great in this region, you might be able to combine a ski tour and a mountain bike ride.

The west approach for Diamond Peak is fairly difficult because the trail is primitive and the wilderness remote. If you time it right so that the road is open to the trailhead but there is still snow on the flanks of the mountain, the peak can be bagged and skied

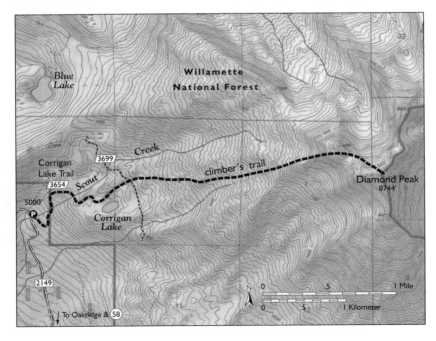

in one day. As always, plan for an unexpected night out if the weather turns poor and the route is obscured. Call the ranger district first to make sure the road is open.

GETTING THERE. From Eugene, drive southeast on OR-58 (Willamette Highway) 40 miles to Oakridge. From Oakridge, take Forest Road 21 south along Hills Creek Reservoir; the road turns east. After 30 miles, turn left on Forest Road 2149 and drive another 5 miles to the Corrigan Lake trailhead.

THE ROUTE. Hike east on the Corrigan Lake Trail 3654. In a mile it intersects Trail 3699. Continue past Trail 3699 where the Corrigan Lake Trail becomes a primitive climber's trail or nonexistent. Follow the main ridge northeast. You will be between the two branches of the Scout Creek headwaters. Hike through the woods, then at timberline climb Diamond Peak's west shoulder. There is a small lower summit and saddle at 8306 feet that makes a lower destination if snow or weather conditions higher up are not good. Otherwise, continue up the west side to the summit.

From the top of Diamond Peak you will see a huge, spectacular variety of lines you can drop in. But, as with any Cascade volcano, be careful you don't drop in a bowl and get too far away from the trailhead. If you ski off the steeper north side, for example, with every few hundred feet of descent you will be exponentially farther from the trailhead. The best option is to ski the west shoulder back to the Corrigan Lake Trail.

63　Mount Bailey, Southeast Ridge

Start Point : Mount Bailey trailhead, 5300 feet
High Point : Mount Bailey summit, 8363 feet
Trail Distance : 12 miles
Trail Time : 6 hours
Skill Level : Advanced
Best Season : Spring
Maps : USGS Diamond Lake, Pumice Desert West

Mount Bailey offers many turns, especially if you go with the snowcat operation. If you plan a winter trip, you will have an approach on the snow-covered forest roads. The best option for hiking is in late spring or early summer, when you can drive to the trailhead and the snowcat operation is closed for winter. There will still be plenty of snow up high, and you can do the route in a day.

GETTING THERE. From Roseburg, drive east on OR-138 (North Umpqua Highway) 80 miles to Diamond Lake. From the south end of the lake, head west on OR-230 a few hundred feet to Forest Road 6592. Turn right on FR 6592, heading north toward the South Shore camping area a quarter mile. Then turn left and head west on Forest Road 4795 for 2 miles. Finally, turn left and head south on Forest Road

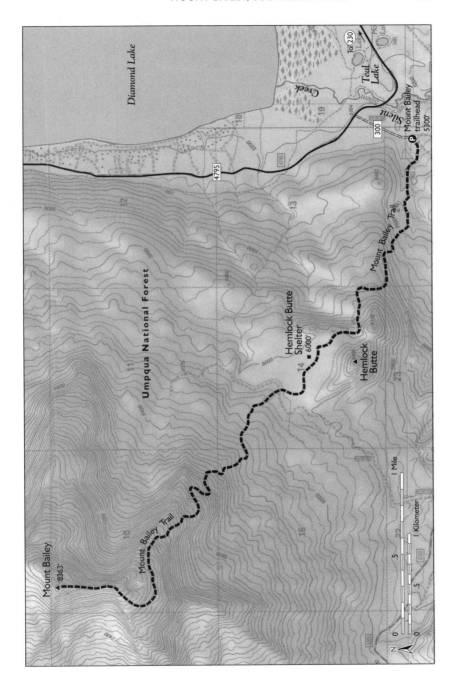

Good spot for lunch or a night out: Hemlock Butte Shelter (Jennifer Donnelly)

300 a few hundred feet to the Mount Bailey trailhead. At any point after OR-230, you could get stymied by snow on the road, and have a longer approach.

THE ROUTE. Head northwest through the woods on the Mount Bailey Trail. The trail meanders through the woods and is marked for cross-country skiers. In a broad meadow, you'll find the Hemlock Butte Shelter at 6000 feet.

The summit trail continues through the woods, then climbs the steep southeast ridge up above timberline. Watch for snowcat skiers and the snowcat guide operation, especially if they are doing avalanche control.

Descend the south bowl and southeast ridge.

64 Mount Bailey, Avalanche Bowl

Start Point	Mount Bailey trailhead, 5300 feet
High Point	Mount Bailey summit, 8363 feet
Trail Distance	12 miles
Trail Time	6 hours
Skill Level	Advanced
Best Season	Spring
Maps	USGS Diamond Lake, Pumice Desert West

Mount Bailey offers many routes, but Avalanche Bowl is one of the best. In winter, be wary of, yes, avalanches, and check in with Mount Bailey Snow Cats to find out about conditions and whether they are doing control work. Otherwise, make sure weather and snowpack are stable before dropping in the bowl. If in doubt, ski down Mount Bailey's southeast ridge (Route 63).

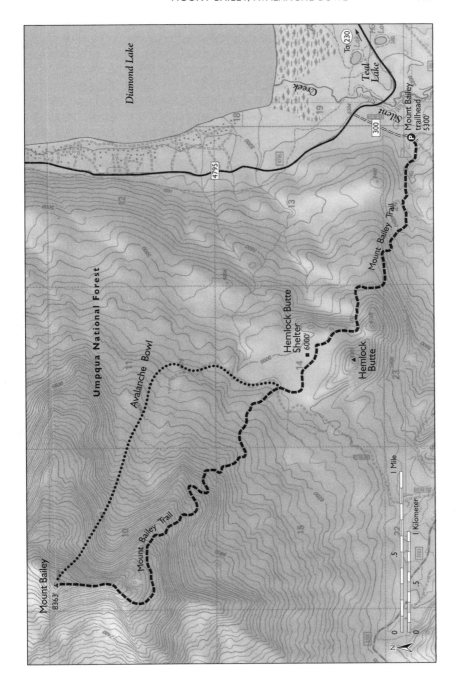

Mount Bailey from Diamond Lake shoreline camp, with Avalanche Bowl at left

GETTING THERE. From Roseburg, drive east on OR-138 (North Umpqua Highway) 80 miles to Diamond Lake. From the south end of the lake, head west on OR-230 a few hundred feet to Forest Road 6592. Turn right on FR 6592, heading north toward the South Shore camping area a quarter mile. Then turn left and head west on Forest Road 4795 for 2 miles. Finally, turn left and head south on Forest Road 300 a few hundred feet to the Mount Bailey trailhead. At any point after OR-230, you could get stopped by snow on the road, and have a longer approach.

THE ROUTE. Head northwest through the woods on the Mount Bailey Trail. The trail meanders through the woods and is marked for cross-country skiers. In a broad meadow, you'll find the Hemlock Butte Shelter at 6000 feet. The summit trail continues through the woods and up the southeast ridge above timberline.

If conditions are safe, descend Avalanche Bowl, the large east-facing cirque. You'll need to traverse back to the trailhead through thick woods to get back to the Hemlock Butte Shelter at 6000 feet to follow the approach trail back to the trailhead. There's an old road that leads back, if you can find it under the snow. Take a GPS, maps, and a compass, as these woods are thick.

65   Mount Thielsen, Northwest Bowl

Start Point	Mount Thielsen Sno-Park, 5400 feet
High Point	Mount Thielsen Northwest Ridge, 8500 feet
Trail Distance	6 miles
Trail Time	4 hours
Skill Level	Advanced
Best Season	Spring
Maps	USGS Diamond Lake, Mount Thielsen

If you have time, consider adding Mount Thielsen to your Diamond Lake trip and ski it along with both Bailey Routes 63 and 64. The turns are not as steep as Bailey's, but the approach is fairly straightforward and you can add another peak to your list. You can't ride off the summit, a rocky pinnacle that requires fifth-class rock-climbing skill. But skin up to the northwest ridge, make a few laps in the northwest bowl, and cruise back to your car by lunch. It's not an epic descent, but it is a beautiful climb.

GETTING THERE. From Roseburg, head east on OR-138 (North Umpqua Highway) for 80 miles to Diamond Lake. About 3 miles beyond the Diamond Lake Resort, park at the Mount Thielsen Sno-Park on the left, at the southeast end of the lake.

THE ROUTE. Head east up Mount Thielsen Trail 1456, marked with blue diamond cross-country ski blazes. After a long mile, it connects with and turns left on the Spruce Ridge Trail. This gains a ridge and cruises up through the forest. In 2 more miles, the trail passes Pacific Crest Trail 2000. Once on the North Ridge, you can skin up to the base of the craggy summit pinnacle.

For rock climbers, you can take the west ridge climber's trail to the summit, but leave your skis and snowboard at the base, about 8000 feet.

For descent, the northwest bowl is an easy drop. The slopes between 7000 and 8000 feet are best for skiing.

After you've made a few laps in the northwest bowl, skin back up to the ridge. Or, with firm snow and enough speed, you may be able to traverse to skier's left and gain the ridge. Then, it's down through the woods to your car.

Watching the clouds carefully while ascending the "Lightning Rod of the Cascades" (Jennifer Donnelly)

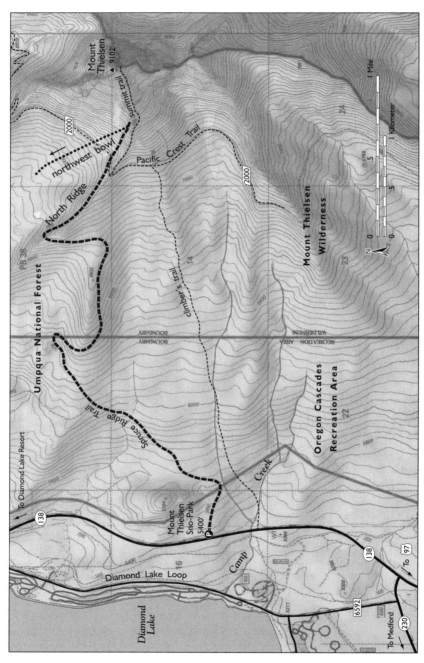

Opposite: Ski a circumnavigation of the deepest lake in the United States (Stefan Gumperlein)

CRATER LAKE
NATIONAL PARK

OREGON'S ONLY NATIONAL PARK, Crater Lake is a spectacularly scenic, historic, and geologic ski destination perched at the north end of the bucolic rural Klamath basin. The lake is a collapsed caldera of ancient Mount Mazama, unique because the crystalline water is surrounded by craggy shoreline peaks with no outlet stream. Only evaporation and seepage keep the water level constant. The 6-mile-wide lake is the deepest lake in the United States at 1932 feet. The water level is 500 feet below the rim, with very few trails down to the water's edge. In any case, it's unlawful to ski from the rim to the water; this is closed for safety and environmental preservation.

But no worries. Although the rim road is busy with cross-country skiers, the crags and their steep slopes that surround give plenty of options for short but sweet runs with loads of snow but nary another skier. Still an undiscovered spot for backcountry skiers, the snow piles up all winter and remains into early summer. Come spring, when the rim road is plowed and the cross-country options are minimal, backcountry skiers who are willing to climb can still find plenty of winter tour options and many patches of snow for 500–800-foot spring descents.

In winter, the south entrance road is plowed to park headquarters and up the hill to Rim Village on the south end of the lake. The north entrance road is not plowed, so you'll need a snowmobile or a bucketful of time for a long approach on skins.

In the spring, after the rim road is fully plowed around the lake, there's usually a long window for skiing the crags before the snow melts off the peaks. Sometimes, the rim road is plowed partway, to Kerr Notch on the south side.

The routes begin at park headquarters or farther up Rim Drive at Crater Lake Lodge at Rim Village. Poke your head into the historic lodge, akin to Mount Hood's Timberline Lodge with a beautiful panorama of the lake.

CRATER LAKE MAPS
- USNPS Crater Lake
- USFS Umpqua National Forest
- Oregon Recreation Upper Klamath Basin

PRIMARY INFORMATION CENTERS/RANGER DISTRICTS
- Crater Lake National Park: (541) 594-3000, www.nps.gov/crla
- Umpqua National Forest Headquarters: (541) 672-6601, www.fs.fed.us/r6/umpqua

AVALANCHE/WEATHER/ROAD CONDITIONS
- Northwest Weather and Avalanche Center: (503) 808-2400, www.nwac.us
- Oregon DOT Trip Check: (800) 977-6368, www.tripcheck.com

PERMITS
- A national park entrance fee is required at the north and south entrances.
- A backcountry overnight permit, which you can acquire at park headquarters, is required for multiday trips.

SPECIAL NOTE
Call in advance to find out if the rim road is open for quicker access to some routes.

The easy way home—hiking Rim Drive back from Mount Scott (Stefan Gumperlein)

66 Crater Lake Circumnavigation

Start Point	Rim Village, 7100 feet
High Point	Cloud Cap Overlook, 7960 feet
Trail Distance	33 miles
Trail Time	2 days
Skill Level	Advanced
Best Season	Winter
Maps	USGS Crater Lake East, Crater Lake West

Skiing the unplowed rim road midwinter around the lake is a classic cross-country adventure—one of the premier long routes in the entire West. It's a spectacularly scenic route marked by jagged peaks, rolling hills, and expansive views of the lake. The route is well marked since you follow the rim road. Be advised, you will find snowmobiles using the road as well. It's not actually much of a downhill, but for backcountry skiers looking for a classic tour, this is it. Consider light Nordic or scaled skinless telemark skis for maximum glide on the flats and the rolly-polly terrain.

The record for the route set in 1967 is 8 hours by John Day and Bill Pruitt and members of Italy's ski team. If you want to take on a burly multiday trip, combine the rim road loop with the three routes listed below (Routes 67, 68, and 69). But you may need a long weekend, or even four days.

GETTING THERE. From Medford, follow OR-62 (Crater Lake Highway) northeast, then east 72 miles to the south entrance of the park at Annie Spring.

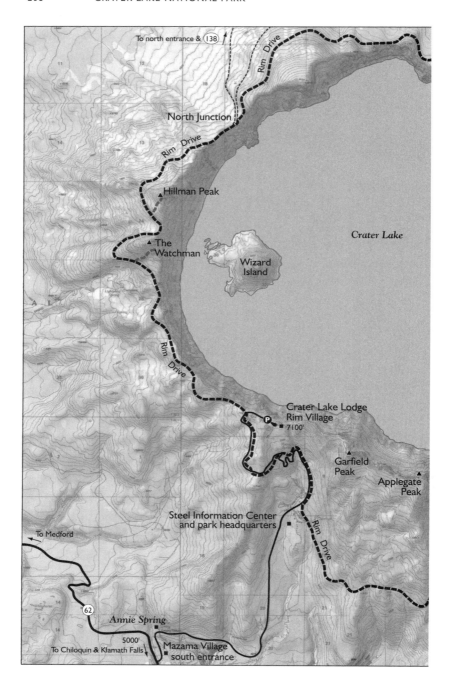

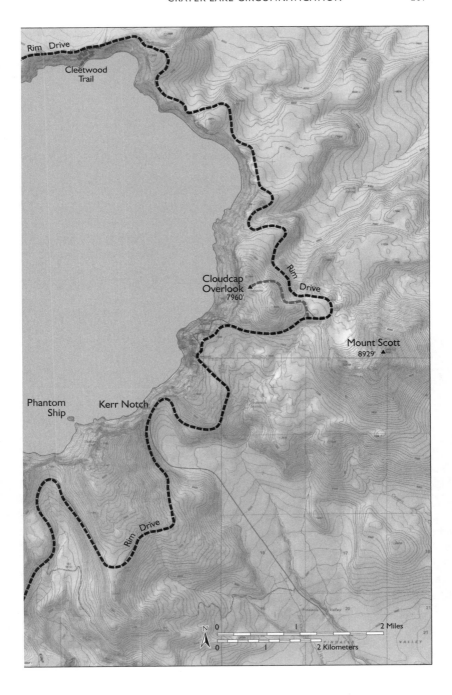

Once through the main entrance, stop at the Steel Information Center and park headquarters for last-minute info or an overnight permit. In another mile, up a few steep switchbacks, park at Crater Lake Lodge and the Rim Village Visitor Center, at the end of the plowed road.

THE ROUTE. Start at Crater Lake Lodge and follow the rim road (Rim Drive), which is mostly in sight of the lake, except on the east and southeast sides. Clockwise seems to be the most common direction, but with more elevation gain and loss on the south and east sides, skiing counterclockwise makes the last few miles easier.

You'll find plenty of ascents and descents, with upwards of 4000 feet elevation gain and loss. If you take multiple days, there are many opportunities for side trips with spectacular views, such as Cloud Cap Overlook, 7960 feet. If you go clockwise, here are the key points. Although not a detailed description, this gives circumnavigators a general idea of the route points and the bailouts.

From Crater Lake Lodge, ski west and north along Rim Drive to The Watchman and Hillman peaks (see Route 68). Here you'll have views of Wizard Island, the cinder cone in the lake.

Continue north and pass North Junction, and the road to the north entrance to the park, which is closed in winter.

Follow Rim Drive along the north side of the lake where a spur road, the Cleetwood Trail, leads down to the water to a summer tour-boat landing.

Ski south along the east side. About midway Rim Drive leaves the lake and passes Mount Scott, the highest point in the park (see Route 67) and a worthy side trip.

If you have time, take the short detour to Cloudcap Overlook at 7960 feet. Rim Drive then loops back to the lake, passing Kerr Notch and the Phantom Ship Overlook, two viewpoints along Rim Drive with spectacular scenery.

From Kerr Notch the southeast section of Rim Drive meanders through the woods, near and away from the lake, to finish the loop under the south flanks of Applegate and Garfield peaks, two other short ski tours described below in Route 69.

Descending a classic Oregon basalt lava flow

67 Mount Scott

Start Point : Mount Scott trailhead, 7695 feet
High Point : Mount Scott summit, 8929 feet
Trail Distance : 3 miles
Trail Time : 1 hour
Skill Level : Advanced
Best Season : Spring
Maps : Crater Lake East, Crater Lake West

Mount Scott offers some respectable turns, considering it's only a thousand feet of vertical. It's a short climb and ski, but for those on the circumnavigation, this makes a primo side junket to the highest point in Oregon's only national park.

If you are heading out just to ski Mount Scott, you can wait until the road is open to either Kerr Notch or better yet, all the way to the trailhead for the shortest approach.

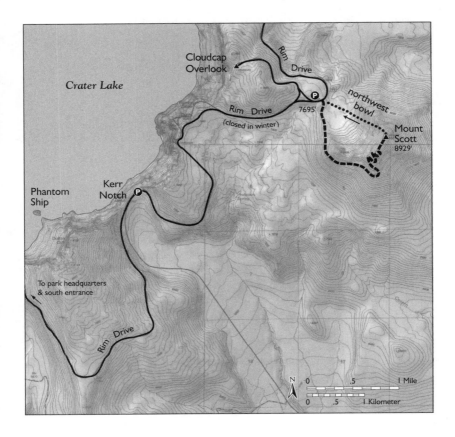

The Watchman standing guard over Wizard Island in Crater Lake (Dudley Chelton)

GETTING THERE. From Medford, follow OR-62 (Crater Lake Highway) northeast, then east 72 miles to the south entrance of the park at Annie Spring. Once through the main entrance, you can stop at the Steel Information Center and park headquarters for last-minute info or an overnight permit.

To get to the trailhead in early spring, you may be able to drive 8 miles to Kerr Notch, if the road is plowed that far. In midspring and summer, you should be able to drive to the Mount Scott trailhead.

THE ROUTE. Whether you park at park headquarters or Kerr Notch, ski up Rim Drive to the Mount Scott trailhead, just at the intersection to the spur road to Cloud Cap Overlook. Ascend the summer climber's trail, which leads you up the west side 1.5 miles to Mount Scott's summit.

For descent, the north- and northwest-facing cirques offer the best turns. When you hit the trees, skin west back to the road.

68 Hillman Peak and The Watchman

Start Point : Rim Drive, 7100 feet
High Point : Hillman Peak, 8151 feet; The Watchman, 8013 feet
Trail Distance : 8 miles
Trail Time : 4 hours
Skill Level : Intermediate
Best Season : Winter
Maps : Crater Lake East, Crater Lake West

Easy access and beautiful views make up for the short runs on this pair of peaks on the west side of the lake. Short but steep, both can be bagged in an easy half day from Rim Village, unless you stop for lunch at The Watchman Overlook to ogle the spectacular view. Yo-yo a few laps, or combine these peaks with a circumnavigation weekend (see Route 66).

GETTING THERE. From Medford, follow OR-62 (Crater Lake Highway) northeast, then east 72 miles to the south entrance of the park at Annie Spring. Once through the main entrance, you can stop at the Steel Information Center and park headquarters for last-minute info or an overnight permit. In another mile, up a few steep switchbacks, park at Crater Lake Lodge and the Rim Village Visitor Center, the end of the plowed road.

Carving Crater Lake powder (Won Kim)

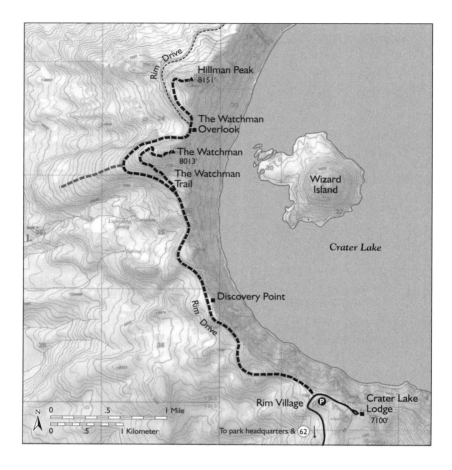

THE ROUTE. From Rim Village, ski west and north 2 miles along Rim Drive to The Watchman Trail. The trailhead is marked by a small picnic area with views of Wizard Island, the cinder cone in the lake. Follow the trail along The Watchman's west side; an unmarked summer climbing trail leads up the west flank to an old lookout on the summit. Ski down to Rim Drive.

After bagging The Watchman, continue another mile up Rim Drive to Hillman Peak. The trail to this second crag starts at The Watchman Overlook, a wayside with an in-your-face view of the lake. The peak has a shorter trail, 0.5 mile to the summit. From here, ski back down to Rim Drive.

Once back on Rim Drive, on the west side of the road west of The Watchman, there's an open meadow that makes for some low-angle turns. Drop down for 50 or 100 turns, then skin back up to Rim Drive and skin back to Rim Village.

Dropping in with a drop knee turn, below Rim Drive (Won Kim)

69 Garfield and Applegate Peaks

Start Point	Park Headquarters, 6400 feet
High Point	Garfield and Applegate aprons, 8000 feet
Trail Distance	5 miles
Trail Time	3 hours
Skill Level	Intermediate
Best Season	Winter
Maps	USGS Crater Lake East, Crater Lake West

The closest route to park headquarters, this is another short jaunt that provides two excellent runs at the base of two peaks. The route crosses open terrain, without established trails. The snow melts quickly on these south-facing slopes.

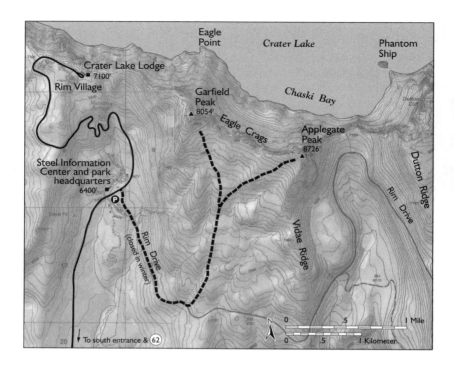

GETTING THERE. From Medford, follow OR-62 (Crater Lake Highway) north-east, then east 72 miles to the south entrance of the park at Annie Spring. Once through the main entrance, park at Steel Information Center and park headquarters. Stop in for last-minute info or an overnight permit.

THE ROUTE. From park headquarters, ski east along Rim Drive, which is not plowed in this direction in winter. In a mile, leave the road and head north through the woods and meadows toward the lower saddle between Garfield and Applegate peaks; the saddle is at 7750 feet. Before you reach the saddle, ski to the base of either peak. You can ski the south-facing apron and upper chutes of both peaks, although not likely from the summits, due to lack of snow and craggy boulders.

Don't attempt to descend the north side of these peaks toward the lake; there are cliffs here, Eagle Crags. And it is illegal to ski down to the lake.

Opposite: Powder hound sporting a powder grin (Pete Keane)

SOUTHERN OREGON

THE SOUTHERN OREGON CASCADES are a mixed lot. There's one big peak, Mount McLoughlin, and a handful of burly cinder cones worth climbing and descending. The main ski mountaineering objective is Mount McLoughlin, a large stratovolcano within the Sky Lakes Wilderness, part of the Fremont–Winema National Forest, the backyard for Klamath Falls, Ashland, Roseburg, and Medford residents. Several other buttes and cinder cones are worth tracking up too, especially in winter, like Brown Mountain and Pelican Butte. These peaks offer riders and skiers uncrowded lines and quality snow. Many times, there's no reason to go north or south in midwinter.

Over in the Siskiyou Mountains, Mount Ashland provides additional terrain, especially for those just starting out. Nary two dozen miles from Ashland and only a bit farther from Medford, Mount Ashland is nestled in the wildly scenic and sparsely populated Rogue River–Siskiyou National Forest.

If you make the trip down from the upper Willamette Valley, pay attention to conditions. You don't want to make the long drive for lousy snow. Mount Ashland's backcountry is a superb spot for winter yo-yos on the back side of the mountain. In spring, good corn and nice weather can make the turns worth the drive for the other peaks. Many a ski mountaineer has been known to combine one of these tours with a Mount Shasta ski (Routes 94 and 95).

If you are looking to blend culture with outdoors, plan a night in Ashland to see a play at the legendary Oregon Shakespeare Festival, which runs February through October.

SOUTHERN OREGON MAPS

- USFS Winema National Forest
- USFS Rogue–Siskiyou National Forest
- USFS Sky Lakes Wilderness

PRIMARY INFORMATION CENTERS/RANGER DISTRICTS

- Fremont–Winema National Forest Headquarters: (541) 947-2151, www.fs.fed.us/r6/frewin/
- Rogue River–Siskiyou National Forest: (541) 618-2000, www.fs.fed.us/r6/rogue-siskiyou
- Klamath Ranger District: (541) 883-6714
- Ashland Ranger District: (541) 552-2900

AVALANCHE/WEATHER/ROAD CONDITIONS

- Northwest Weather and Avalanche Center: (503) 808-2400, www.nwac.us
- Oregon DOT Trip Check: (800) 977-6368, www.tripcheck.com

WINTER RESORT AND SNOW REPORTS

- Mount Ashland Ski Area: (541) 482-2754, www.mtashland.com
- Warner Canyon: (541) 947-4892, www.lakecountychamber.org/skihill.html

PERMITS

- A wilderness permit is required for the Sky Lakes Wilderness Area. Free, self-issued permits are available at the trailhead.
- A Sno-Park Pass is required for these routes between November 1 and April 30.
- A Northwest Forest Pass is required for Mount McLoughlin.

Opposite: Sliding through southern Oregon snow (Pete Keane)

Big wind up high on the final pitch up the Southeast Ridge, Mount McLoughlin (Dave Waag)

70 Mount McLoughlin, Southeast Ridge

Start Point	Mount McLoughlin trailhead, 5600 feet
High Point	Mount McLoughlin summit, 9495 feet
Trail Distance	12 miles
Trail Time	6 hours
Skill Level	Advanced
Best Season	Spring
Map	USGS Mount McLoughlin

Located in the Sky Lakes Wilderness, part of the Fremont–Winema National Forest, this is a great trip for southern Oregon–based riders and skiers, especially those looking for a big-mountain climb and descent. This route can be combined with an extended trip to the Diamond Lake, Crater Lake, or Mount Shasta routes (Routes 63–65, 66–69, and 94–95). The challenging but nontechnical climb is marked by numerous lakes, rocky ground, and thick trees. Nontechnical doesn't mean low-angle. There's some steep skiing on this big mountain. Good weather makes this a great trip; poor weather and snow make the drive difficult, so plan carefully.

GETTING THERE. From Medford, head north on OR-62 (Crater Lake Highway) for 6 miles. Turn right and head east on OR-140 (Lake of the Woods Highway). In

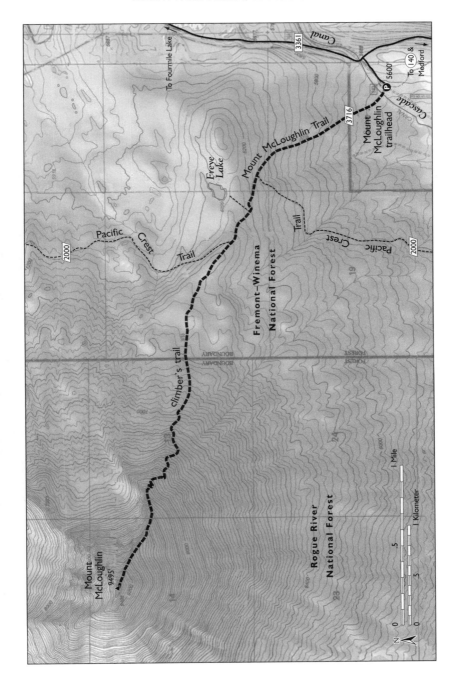

32 miles turn left and head north on Fourmile Lake Road (Forest Road 3650). After 2 miles, turn left on Forest Road 3361. Look for the Mount McLoughlin trailhead in a quarter mile and park there.

THE ROUTE. Take Mount McLoughlin Trail 3716, heading northwest. The trail winds through woods and among large rocks, and crosses the Cascade Canal. After a mile from the parking lot it joins the Pacific Crest Trail for a quarter mile. The climber's trail branches off the PCT and continues up steeper slopes. At timberline, it reaches the southeast ridge and follows the ridge to the summit.

On descent, ski down the southeast ridge. If you ride the bowls to the east or south, watch the ridgeline for descent. Don't get skewed from one side or the other, or you'll need to hike back at timberline to the trail.

71 Pelican Butte

Start Point : Cold Springs trailhead, 3800 feet
High Point : Pelican Butte, 8036 feet
Trail distance : 6 miles
Trail Time : 4 hours
Skill Level : Advanced
Best Season : Winter
Maps : USGS Pelican Butte, Crystal Spring

Pelican Butte is a local hot spot for Klamath Falls skiers. Just north of the Klamath Lake, its low elevation suffers from marginal snow but offers easy access. For north

The long bootpack to the top

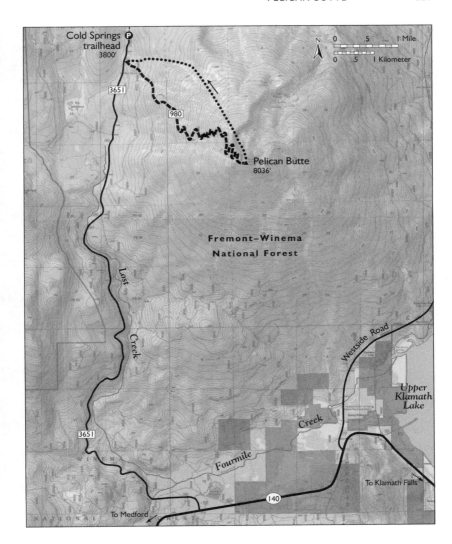

or central Oregon residents, combine this with a McLoughlin trip (Route 70) if the snow is good. In spring, timing is everything: You want the snow melted enough so you can drive to Cold Springs Campground, but enough on the upper slopes to ride. Be advised, there are snowmobiles on this route.

Keep in mind, this is a 4000-foot climb. It's a big butte and a long climb for a burly workout.

GETTING THERE. From Medford, head north on OR-62 (Crater Lake Highway) for 6 miles, then east on OR-140 (Lake of the Woods Highway). In 45 miles, turn

High above the clouds in southern Oregon

left and head north on Forest Road 3651 where it branches from OR-140. Follow this road about 8 miles north toward Cold Springs Campground. The summit road, Forest Road 980, is a quarter mile south of the Cold Springs trailhead on the right. The road is closed in winter.

THE ROUTE. From FR 3651, follow FR 980 up the west flank of Pelican Butte to the summit. Initially, the road is low-angle through forest. Then it climbs 2000 feet on a series of switchbacks. The summit is an old lookout site.

Descend along the road or use the summit as a base to ride Pelican Butte's northwest or southwest bowls.

72 Brown Mountain

Start Point : Brown Mountain trailhead, 4800 feet
High Point : Brown Mountain summit, 7311 feet
Trail Distance : 6 miles
Trail Time : 5 hours
Skill Level : Intermediate
Best Season : Winter
Maps : USGS Mount McLoughlin, Brown Mountain

Brown Mountain is more accessible and a shorter drive than some of the other southern Oregon peaks. An easier climb than Mount McLoughlin (Route 70), Brown Mountain can be combined with its neighboring peak for a double-summit weekend. Nestled in the Winema Wilderness, Brown Mountain lies in both the Fremont–Winema and Rogue River–Siskiyou national forests. The mountain, surrounded by lava fields, is a slag heap of a cinder cone like Black Butte in central Oregon (Route 40). In winter, there can be plenty of snow, but later in the spring, bring rock

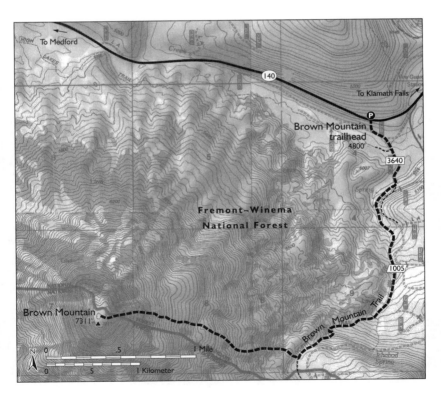

skis—there's a load of talus and scree. Watch for snowmobilers, and be ready for a long trek in on the road.

GETTING THERE. From Medford, drive north on OR-62 (Crater Lake Highway) 8 miles, then drive east on OR-140 (Lake of the Woods Highway) 30 miles. Two miles past Summit Sno-Park, park at the large turnoff on the left (north) side of the road or at the Brown Mountain trailhead across the road. The trail heads up the east side of the mountain.

THE ROUTE. From the Brown Mountain trailhead, ski up Forest Road 3640, which is closed in winter. Head south and catch the Brown Mountain Trail 1005 after about a half mile. When you reach the open lava fields, follow the wide-open slopes of Brown Mountain's east flank to the summit.

There are a lot of spots to descend back down the east side you climbed up. Just make sure you catch the trail home.

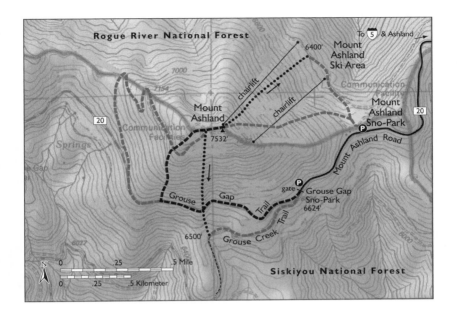

73 Mount Ashland

Start Point : Grouse Gap Sno-Park, 6624 feet
High Point : Mount Ashland summit, 7532 feet
Trail Distance : 2 miles
Trail Time : 2 hours
Skill Level : Intermediate
Best Season : Winter
Map : USGS Mount Ashland

Nestled in the rugged, remote, and beautiful Siskiyou Mountains, Mount Ashland is the southernmost ski resort in Oregon, just outside of the quaint town of Ashland, known for its Shakespeare plays. The ski area lies on the north-facing slope of the mountain, which is good for some early-season in-bounds hiking or the occasional uphill traffic tour. But, there are also plenty of lines on the south-facing backcountry of Mount Ashland, easily accessed by the Grouse Gap Nordic Ski trail system. For side- and backcountry skiing, this is an easy drive for Medford and Ashland locals, about as close as you can get.

Opposite: Mount Ashland rain and fog
sometimes stifle an early season tour

GETTING THERE. From Ashland, drive south 8 miles on I-5. Take Exit 6, follow the exit road for a mile, then turn right and head west on Mount Ashland Road (Forest Road 20). Drive 8 more miles up the winding, cliff-side mountain road to Mount Ashland Ski Area. Pass the Mount Ashland Sno-Park, and drive to the back of the lot, a few hundred feet past the ski resort, to the Grouse Gap Sno-Park where the road is blocked by a gate.

THE ROUTE. For in-bounds touring, you can skin up the ski resort right from the parking lot. The runs drop below the parking lot, so you'll have to skin back out.

To access the south-side backcountry, skin up the Grouse Gap Trail for a mile. The trail zigzags up the southwest side of Mount Ashland to the summit.

For descent, you will find some south-facing steep shots, treed old-growth glades, and meadows. Stop your descent at the Grouse Gap Trail, so you can make the flat skin to get back to the car. Or, if you drop lower, catch the lower Grouse Creek Trail back to the car.

Opposite: Finding dry powder in the "Alps"
of Oregon (Mark Flaming)

WALLOWA MOUNTAINS

THE EAGLE CAP WILDERNESS and the Wallowa Mountains are remote, uncrowded, and beautiful. This area is frequented by northeast Oregon locals. But the backcountry skiing and snowboarding have been discovered: more and more snow gliders from the west side of the state and beyond are venturing here. It is a backcountry destination worthy of a long weekend, or a whole week if you have the time to explore. The mountainscape is marked by high alpine lakes, rugged peaks, and large basins. The peaks are so picturesque and unlike the stratovolcanoes, cinder cones, and rolling hills of the Cascades, that the Wallowa Mountains have been dubbed "Oregon's Alps." Because of the drier climate, the snow conditions can be excellent—as in, deep, dry, light powder.

The hub of the Wallowa backcountry scene is the small town of Joseph and neighboring Enterprise. In these twin rural farming towns, you will find lodging and restaurants. But don't be overwhelmed by the high-end luxury. You'll find inexpensive motels, quaint bed-and-breakfasts, and brew pubs.

Day trips can be made from several sno-parks just south of Joseph, in particular Salt Creek Summit, McCully Basin, and South Wallowa Lake. For the most part these are winter and early spring routes, as the snow melts much faster here than on the glaciated peaks of the Cascades.

For those traveling from afar, guided trips are an excellent option. Two guide services offer overnight hut trips, and one offers multiday avalanche seminars. If you are a beginner or an intermediate, consider the multiday hut avalanche seminar. Not only will you get a multitude of turns in this area, but you will also drive away much more knowledgeable about avalanche safety. Another option is to rent out a hut or cabin without a professional guide. The do-it-yourself hut trips are an excellent option for advanced and expert backcountry skiers and snowboarders with skills in overnight trips. They require some planning and logistics, but that is often part of the fun of long-weekend backcountry adventures.

WALLOWA MOUNTAINS MAPS

- Geo-Graphics Wallowa Mountains Eagle Cap Wilderness
- USFS Wallowa–Whitman National Forest

PRIMARY INFORMATION CENTERS/RANGER DISTRICTS

- Wallowa–Whitman National Forest Headquarters: (541) 523-6391, www.fs.fed.us/r6/w-w
- Wallowa Mountains Visitor Center, Enterprise: (541) 426-4978
- Eagle Cap Ranger District: (541) 426-4978
- Whitman Ranger District: (541) 523-4476
- Pine Ranger Station: (541) 742-7511

AVALANCHE/WEATHER/ROAD CONDITIONS

- Wallowa Avalanche Center: www.wallowaavalanchecenter.org
- Northwest Weather and Avalanche Center: (503) 808-2400, www.nwac.us
- Oregon DOT Trip Check: (800) 977-6368, www.tripcheck.com

SKI AREAS

- Ferguson Ridge Ski Area: (541) 398-1167, www.skifergi.com
- Wallowa Lake Tramway: (541) 432-5331, www.wallowalaketramway.com. (Currently, the tram is only open May to September, but in past years it operated in winter.)

PERMITS

- A wilderness permit is required for the Eagle Cap Wilderness Area. Free, self-issued permits are available at the trailheads.
- A Sno-Park Pass is required for these routes between November 1 and April 30.
- A Northwest Forest Pass is required for these routes in spring.

OVERNIGHT SHELTERS

- Wing Ridge and Big Sheep Huts, Wing Ridge Ski Tours: (800) 646-9050, www.wingski.com
- McCully Basin and Norway Basin Huts, Wallowa Alpine Huts: (541) 398-1989, www.wallowahuts.com

GUIDES AND COURSES

- Wallowa Alpine Huts: (541) 398-1989, www.wallowahuts.com
- Wing Ridge Ski Tours: (800) 646-9050, www.wingski.com

Opposite: Finding fresh tracks in the fog (Pete Keane)

74 Wing Ridge

Start Point : Salt Creek Summit Sno-Park, 6120 feet
High Point : Wing Ridge, 8800 feet
Trail Distance : 4 miles
Trail Time : 4 hours
Skill Level : Intermediate
Best Season : Winter
Maps : USGS Aneroid Mountain, Lick Creek

Wing Ridge is one of the most accessible routes in this region. This is a short, popular route that can be crowded on weekends but offers the closest, and some of the best, turns near your car. From Salt Creek Summit Sno-Park, you can access the varied slopes of Wing Ridge fairly quickly. You'll find plenty of steep shots off the ridge, but in the northeast-facing basin, low-angle and gladed slopes provide plenty of turns if avalanche danger is high or if your skills aren't up for couloirs. If you don't make any of the other Wallowa routes in this book, you can easily fill a weekend doing laps here.

GETTING THERE. From Joseph, drive southeast on OR-350 (Imnaha Road) for 8 miles. Turn right on County Road 4602 and head south; it becomes Forest Road 39 (also called Wallowa Mountain Loop Road and Hells Canyon Scenic Byway). In 10 miles you reach Salt Creek Summit Sno-Park at the end of the plowed road

Low angle fresh tracks: skiing safely on Wing Ridge

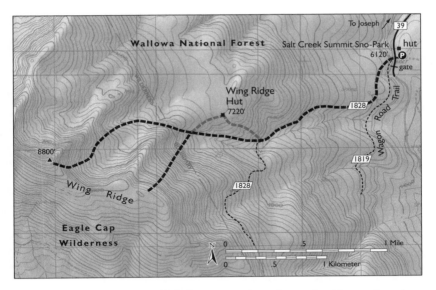

(see Route 75 map). Here you'll find a warming hut, plenty of parking, and maybe a couple of locals who can give you info on the conditions.

THE ROUTE. The route follows Wagon Road Trail 1819 south for a few hundred feet, then branches west (right) up the short, steep pitch through thick but short trees to a large gully. The Wing Ridge Hut is to climber's right, but the ski route to Wing Ridge continues southwest toward the ridge. When you break out of the trees, you see the large northeast-facing basin below the ridge.

You can continue to the summit of Wing Ridge and ski the steeper lines in the trees, or make laps lower down in the basin, which has safer, lower-angle slopes. If you ski or snowboard the northeast-facing chutes of Wing Ridge, pay close attention to avalanche danger. Descend through the trees back to the car the way you came up.

75   Big Sheep Basin

Start Point	Salt Creek Summit Sno-Park, 6120 feet
High Point	Wing Ridge, 8800 feet
Trail Distance	10 miles
Trail Time	10 hours
Skill Level	Advanced
Best Season	Winter
Maps	USGS Aneroid Mountain, Lick Creek

Skiing Big Sheep Basin, the south side of Wing Ridge, has a much longer approach than the Wing Ridge route above (Route 74). If you are renting out the Big Sheep

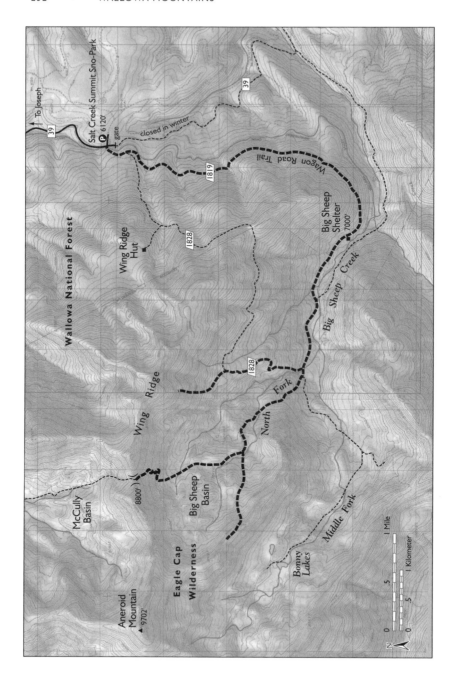

Shelter or taking a guided trip, this provides plenty of turns. Otherwise, it's a long approach, probably too much for a day tour, considering the option of the Wing Ridge route above.

GETTING THERE. From Joseph, drive southeast on OR-350 (Imnaha Road) for 8 miles. Turn right on County Road 4602 and head south; it becomes Forest Road 39 (also called Wallowa Mountain Loop Road and Hells Canyon Scenic Byway). In 10 miles you reach Salt Creek Summit Sno-Park at the end of the plowed road. Here you'll find a warming hut, plenty of parking, and maybe a couple of locals who can give you info on the conditions.

THE ROUTE. The route follows Wagon Road Trail 1819 south about 3 miles to the Big Sheep Shelter. It's relatively flat, so a large pack or sled is

Backcountry in style at the Wing Ridge Hut (Mark Flaming)

needed to schlog in overnight gear if you are hunkering in for three or four days of ski touring. This is not a great day trip because of this long, flat ski, but many cross-country skiers use this flat track.

Once you unload at the shelter, ski another few miles up the road that wraps around to the west through the trees. When you break out into Big Sheep Basin, you'll see the south side of Wing Ridge. From here you can ski multiple slopes in the basin, climbing one or more of the south-facing gullies and couloirs of Wing Ridge.

76 McCully Basin

Start Point	McCully Basin Sno-Park, 5520 feet
High Point	Wing Ridge, 8700 feet
Trail Distance	14 miles
Trail Time	10 hours
Skill Level	Advanced
Best Season	Winter
Maps	USGS Joseph, Kinny Lake, Aneroid Mountain

McCully Basin is another long approach to Big Sheep Basin. Like the Big Sheep Basin tour (Route 75), this is best saved for a multiday trip with the guide service

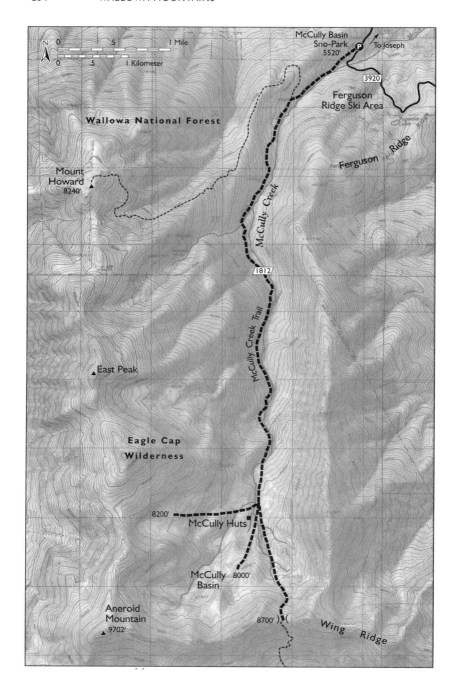

McCully Basin
Sno-Park
5520'

To Joseph

3920

Ferguson
Ridge Ski Area

Wallowa National Forest

Ferguson Ridge

Mount Howard
8240'

McCully Creek

1812

McCully Creek Trail

East Peak

Eagle Cap
Wilderness

8200'

McCully Huts

McCully 8000'
Basin

Aneroid
Mountain
9702'

8700'

Wing Ridge

0   .5   1 Mile

0   .5   1 Kilometer

Touring magnificent McCully Basin with Wallowa Alpine Huts guides
(Jennifer Donnelly)

and hut rental for a couple of nights. The upper basin has many steep shots: a long weekend's worth, if you have the time. The lower trail is used by cross-country skiers.

GETTING THERE. From Joseph, drive southeast on OR-350 (Imnaha Road) for 5 miles. Turn right on County Road 633 (Tucker Downs Road), which continues south for 3 miles and becomes Forest Road 3920. About a mile past Ferguson Ridge Ski Area, the road ends at McCully Basin Sno-Park.

THE ROUTE. From the sno-park, follow McCully Creek up Trail 1812 south into McCully Canyon. The trail follows an old road through the woods, then along McCully Creek for 5 miles to McCully Basin. At timberline around 7600 feet, the basin opens up. The McCully Huts, run by Wallowa Alpine Huts, are 5 miles in. From here, one can continue southeast up to the saddle on Wing Ridge. Other options include skiing and riding the west basin flanks. There are numerous routes up to around 8000 feet on the north slopes of the basin, which is the north-facing aspect of Wing Ridge. If you haven't been up the canyon before, hire a guide to give you the tour of this complex and scenic basin.

77 Mount Howard

Start Point : McCully Basin Sno-Park, 5520 feet
High Point : Mount Howard, 8240 feet
Trail Distance : 5 miles
Trail Time : 3 hours
Skill Level : Intermediate
Best Season : Winter
Maps : USGS Joseph, Kinny Lake, Aneroid Mountain

For a shorter trip than the ski up to McCully Basin (Route 76), you can climb the back side of Mount Howard. It's another popular cross-country route, but you can find some steeper turns in a small bowl off the top of Mount Howard worthy of a couple of 500-foot laps. The approach is a workout and an easy glide down.

GETTING THERE. From Joseph, drive southeast on OR-350 (Imnaha Road) for 5 miles. Turn right on County Road 633 (Tucker Downs Road), which continues south for 3 miles and becomes Forest Road 3920. About a mile past Ferguson Ridge Ski Area, the road ends at McCully Basin Sno-Park.

THE ROUTE. From the sno-park, follow McCully Creek up Trail 1812. The trail follows an old road through the woods, then branches in a mile. Take the right fork,

Heading deep into Oregon's Alps (Jennifer Donnelly)

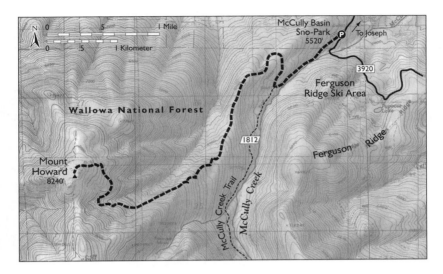

another logging road, which turns north for a half mile, then doubles back and heads south. The road meanders through the forest, zigzagging in and out of clearcuts and viewpoints, up a ridge.

After 2 miles, you reach the base of a steep, open slope, the back side of Mount Howard. Ascend to the top. You can yo-yo the slope a few times, and then ski back out the cross-country trail.

78 Aneroid Lake Basin

Start Point : Wallowa Lake Sno-Park, 4670 feet
High Point : Tenderfoot Pass, 8500 feet
Trail Distance : 16 miles
Trail Time : 8 hours
Best Season : Winter
Skill Level : Advanced
Maps : USGS Joseph, Aneroid Mountain

Aneroid Lake is the third of the long approaches, the grand tours of the Wallowa Mountains. Like Big Sheep and McCully basins, this is either a multiday snow-camping trip or a long day, with more of a workout skinning in than in making multiple laps of epic descents.

In years past, private cabins (Aneroid Lake Cabins) were rented by one of the guide services, but currently there are no guided trips here. There are also some private cabins on the lake 4.4 miles up the trail at 7500 feet.

Taking a midday break, Wallowa Mountains (Jennifer Donnelly)

After your tour, you can stop by the Wallowa Lake Inn for hot chocolate and lunch.

GETTING THERE. From Joseph, head south on OR-82 for 5 miles to Wallowa Lake. The road ends at the Wallowa Lake Sno-Park and the Trail 1804 trailhead at the south end of the lake.

THE ROUTE. From Wallowa Lake, the route follows Trail 1804 up the East Fork Wallowa River. It follows switchbacks through the forest, past a dam, and into Eagle Cap Wilderness. The trail continues through meadows and up to Aneroid Lake Cabins, about 7 miles from the trailhead.

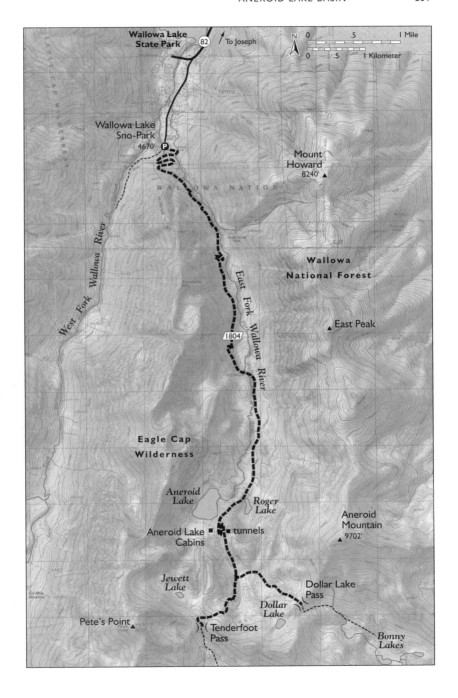

Wallowa Lake
State Park

82 / To Joseph

N 0   .5   1 Mile

0   .5   1 Kilometer

Wallowa Lake
Sno-Park
4670'

P

Mount
Howard
8240'

WALLOWA NATION

West Fork Wallowa River

East Fork Wallowa River

Wallowa
National Forest

East Peak

1804

Eagle Cap
Wilderness

Aneroid
Lake

Roger
Lake

Aneroid
Mountain
9702'

Aneroid Lake
Cabins

tunnels

Jewett
Lake

Dollar Lake
Pass

Dollar
Lake

Pete's Point

82

Tenderfoot
Pass

Bonny
Lakes

You can hike and ski the large Aneroid Basin or the flanks of Aneroid Mountain. Be cautious of avalanche danger here. For more options, skin south to Tenderfoot Pass or southeast to Dollar Lake Pass.

79 Norway Basin

Start Point : Clear Creek Sno-Park, 3200 feet
High Point : Red Mountain, 9555 feet
Trail Distance : 20 miles
Trail Time : 2 days
Skill Level : Expert
Best Season : Winter
Maps : USGS Krag Peak, Cornucopia

The south side of the Wallowa Mountains doesn't get as much activity as the north, but this is a newer destination for Wallowa Alpine Huts. It is a long trek in, so if you don't book the yurt, it is way too much for a day jaunt. You'll find this expansive, majestic basin less crowded, but then, nothing is really crowded in these more remote peaks. Book a yurt trip and head into this basin to explore a multitude of pristine slopes and peaks. You can do a full guided, catered trip or a self-guided, self-catered trip if you have skills and snowmobiles for the sled in. It's best to hire a guide and rent out the yurt because the area is so vast.

Midseason powder turns (Pete Keane)

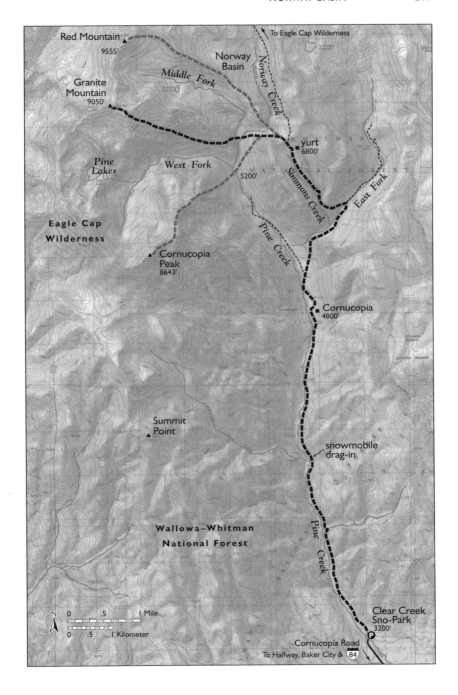

GETTING THERE. From I-84 at Baker City, take exit 304 and drive east on OR-86 for 50 miles to Halfway. From Halfway, drive 7 miles north on Cornucopia Road. The plowed section of the road ends at Clear Creek Sno-Park.

THE ROUTE. It's a 6-mile-long skin up a road before you climb to the basin, so this is typically a route for snowmobiles. Wallowa Alpine Huts pulls you in behind snowmobiles to the summer cabin community of Cornucopia. From Cornucopia, you skin 2.5 miles up a 2000-foot climb to the yurt at the head of Norway Basin. The yurt is near the confluence of Norway Creek and Middle Fork Pine Creek at 7400 feet.

The basin is huge. The guides have numerous objectives, from low-angle treed slopes to high alpine peaks. Check out Red Mountain, Cornucopia Peak, and Granite Mountain.

Opposite: The last signs of winter above Hoffer Lakes

BLUE MOUNTAINS, ELKHORN
AND STRAWBERRY RANGES

THE BLUE MOUNTAINS, including the small but spectacular Elkhorn Range, are some of the least skied, but have some of the best snow in Oregon. A smaller area than the Wallowa Mountains and much less visited, these peaks are just starting to be discovered by Beaver State ski and snowboard mountaineers.

The Elkhorn Range is slightly closer than the Wallowas to the urban centers of Portland and the Willamette Valley, and access is easy. And the snow can be ideal: drier and longer lasting than the famed Cascade Cement. The range is only 18 miles long but has plenty of skiable lines. Glacier-free, large basins are marked by huge boulders exposed by erosion. High alpine lakes, thin lodgepole pine forests, expansive meadows, and polished granite make for stunning scenery.

History abounds in these valleys, too. In spring you'll find remnants of gold mines, including old mine shacks, large dredges, tailings, and walls built by Chinese laborers. The towns of Baker City and La Grande are quaint and historic. The Baker Valley has spectacularly large farms of cattle and bucolic, serene fields with antique barns.

BLUE MOUNTAINS, ELKHORN AND STRAWBERRY RANGES MAPS
- USFS Wallowa–Whitman National Forest
- USFS Malheur National Forest
- USFS Umatilla National Forest
- USFS Strawberry Mountain Wilderness

PRIMARY INFORMATION CENTERS/RANGER DISTRICTS
- Wallowa–Whitman National Forest Headquarters: (541) 523-6391, www.fs.fed.us/r6/w-w
- Malheur National Forest: (541) 575-3000, www.fs.fed.us/r6/malheur
- La Grande Ranger District: (541) 963-7186
- Blue Mountain Ranger District: (541) 575-3000

AVALANCHE/WEATHER/ROAD CONDITIONS
- Wallowa Avalanche Center: www.wallowaavalanchecenter.org
- Northwest Weather and Avalanche Center: (503) 808-2400, www.nwac.us
- Oregon DOT Trip Check: (800) 977-6368, www.tripcheck.com

WINTER RESORTS
- Anthony Lakes Mountain Resort: (541) 856-3277, www.anthonylakes.com
- Spout Springs Ski Area: (541) 566-0327, www.spoutsprings.com

PERMITS
- A Sno-Park Pass is required for these routes between November 1 and April 30.
- For the Strawberry Mountain Wilderness, a self-issue wilderness permit is available at trailheads.

The spectacular view of bucolic Anthony Lake alone is worth the trip.

80 Anthony Lake Basin

Start Point	Anthony Lakes Sno-Park, 7160 feet
High Point	Anthony Lake Basin, 8000 feet
Trail Distance	2 miles
Trail Time	2 hours
Skill Level	Intermediate
Best Season	Winter
Map	USGS Anthony Lakes

To explore this spectacular snow and terrain, start simple. The easiest place to begin tracking up this area is at Anthony Lakes Mountain Resort and the cross-country trails around Anthony Lake. This is a spectacular alpine trip: accessible, steep, and scenic. The runs are short, and the ski resort makes the trip easier by allowing skiers one ride up to gain the first ridge, at least at the time of writing. It's now under new ownership, so check with ski patrol first. Steep chutes require caution with respect to avalanches, and the deep basins have deep lakes that may be snow covered but have thin ice. You'll find plenty of powder midwinter and it likely won't be tracked up, given the dearth of backcountry skiers and riders here.

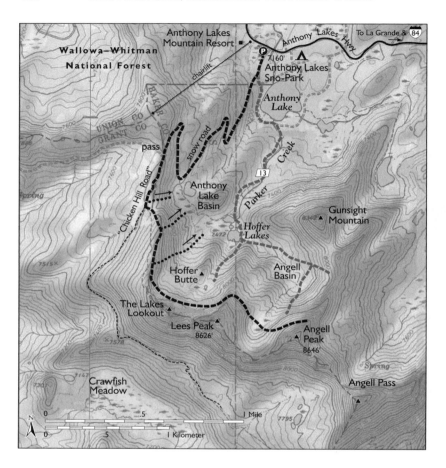

GETTING THERE. From I-84 at North Powder, 25 miles south of La Grande, take Exit 285. Head southwest on North Powder River Lane, which becomes OR-73 (Anthony Lakes Highway). After several miles of meandering through the Baker Valley farmlands, you will reach the foothills of the climb into the Elkhorns. Ascend the twisty mountain road 3000 feet over 10 miles to Anthony Lakes Mountain Resort. Turn left and park at the Anthony Lakes Sno-Park at the ski resort.

THE ROUTE. To access the basin above Anthony Lake and the Hoffer Lakes, you have three options. One is to climb the ski resort's snowcat service road to gain a pass at 7800 feet. Another is to buy a one-ride ticket and catch the lift. Either way, from the small pass at 7800 feet, ski up "Chicken Hill Road" out of bounds to the south. The first peak you'll see looming to the south is The Lakes Lookout, as the road ascends the ridge at the edge of Anthony Lake Basin. In less than a half mile, you'll see the crags above the Hoffer Lakes: from west to northeast, they are Hoffer Butte,

The Lakes Lookout, Lees Peak, Angell Peak, and Gunsight Mountain.

From the ridge at 8000 feet, you can drop northeast into the basin for the first of many 500-foot laps. You don't need to ski to the summit of these crags, but stay on the lower aprons.

At the bottom of the basin where the trees become thick, skin back up to the ridge and take the next line. You can ski the north-facing slopes and couloirs of all three peaks, including several steep couloirs that make fabulous, but advanced descents. Be careful of avalanches, and, if in doubt, stick to the lower aprons.

A third option is to ski up cross-country ski trail 13, the backcountry access trail. The trail skirts Anthony Lake, follows the Hoffer Lakes Trail through thick lodgepole pine forest, and then continues up to the saddle between Lees and Angell peaks. This accesses the same aprons below the peaks as the first two options. If you choose, you can skin to the next basin to the east, Angell Basin, for more turns.

Descend the climbing route. When exiting, be careful you go around, not over, the Hoffer Lakes—or take the ski resort runs back.

81 Angell Peak, Northeast Basin

Start Point : Anthony Lakes Sno-Park, 7160 feet
High Point : Angell Pass, 8200 feet
Trail Distance : 5 miles; circumnavigation 12 miles
Trail Time : 5 hours
Skill level : Advanced
Best Season : Winter
Map : USGS Anthony Lakes

A more advanced, longer tour, the Angell Peak, Northeast Basin is a wide-open, scenic bowl with big views and bigger runs. It's a much longer tour around the back side of Gunsight Peak and Angell Peak, compared to the easy access of Angell Basin above Hoffer Lakes (Route 80). For a burly overland cross-country trip, you can circumnavigate the collection of peaks and meet up with the Crawfish Basin Trail via Dutch Flat Saddle, a popular cross-country tour.

GETTING THERE. From I-84 at North Powder, 25 miles south of La Grande, take Exit 285. Head southwest on North Powder River Lane, which becomes OR-73 (Anthony Lakes Highway). After several miles of meandering through the Baker Valley farmlands, you will reach the foothills of the climb into the Elkhorns. Ascend the twisty mountain road 3000 feet over 10 miles to Anthony Lakes Mountain Resort. Turn left and park at the Anthony Lakes Sno-Park at the ski resort.

THE ROUTE. Leaving the sno-park, head east through the campground or walk down the road. Catch the Elkhorn Crest Trail at Anthony Lakes Highway; the

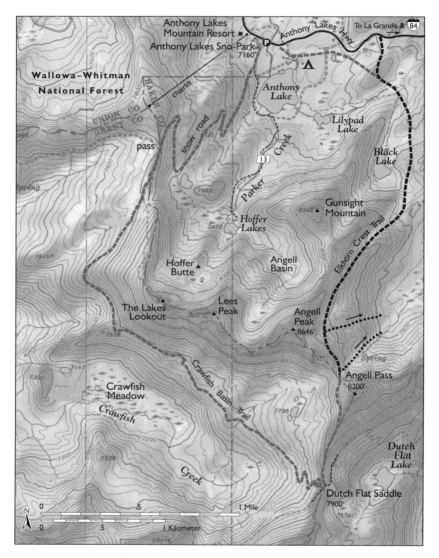

trailhead is about a half mile south of the ski area sno-park. Follow the Elkhorn Crest Trail south as it heads past Black Lake, up a ridge, and underneath the east-facing cliff of Gunsight Mountain. Follow the traverse under Angell Peak to Angell Pass.

You can ski all the way to Angell Pass or drop in anywhere the snow looks good below Gunsight Mountain or Angell Peak. The glades here provide some safety when avalanche danger is significant.

For the full circumnavigation, continue past the narrow notch of Angell Pass along an old road cut sidehill into the forested slope; follow the 8500-foot contour to

Scouting for just a few more patches of snow, Angell Peak

Dutch Flat Saddle. From Dutch Flat Saddle, you can exit on the Crawfish Basin Trail as described in Route 82. The Crawfish Basin Trail leads you under the cliffs of Angell and Lees peaks back to the ski area.

82 Crawfish Basin

Start Point	Anthony Lakes Sno-Park, 7160 feet
High Point	Dutch Flat Saddle, 7900 feet
Trail Distance	5 miles
Trail Time	4 hours
Skill Level	Intermediate
Best Season	Winter
Maps	USGS Anthony Lakes, Crawfish Basin

Crawfish Meadow is less steep than the other two routes in the Elkhorns, but still has many avalanche areas. The gladed runs may be safer and sunnier, as the route is on the west and southwest-facing slopes of Lees Peak. It is a fun intermediate tour, and you may be able to catch a paid snowcat tour of the area with Anthony Lakes Mountain Resort.

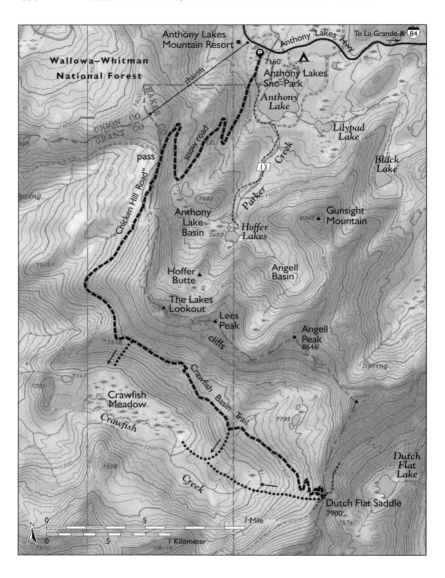

GETTING THERE. From I-84 at North Powder, 25 miles south of La Grande, take Exit 285. Head southwest on North Powder River Lane, which becomes OR-73 (Anthony Lakes Highway). After several miles of meandering through the Baker Valley farmlands, you will reach the foothills of the climb into the Elkhorns. Ascend the twisty mountain road 3000 feet over 10 miles to Anthony Lakes Mountain Resort. Turn left and park at the Anthony Lakes Sno-Park at the ski resort.

High alpine vista

THE ROUTE. To access Crawfish Meadow, you have two options. One is to climb the ski resort's snowcat service road to gain a pass at 7800 feet. Another is to buy a one-ride ticket and catch the lift. Either way, from the small pass at 7800 feet, ski up "Chicken Hill Road" out of bounds to the south. This trail becomes the Crawfish Basin Trail.

The trail heads south under the cliffs of the peak called "The Lakes Lookout," Lees Peak, and then Angell Peak, all on skier's left. The trail follows the 7600-foot contour for 2 miles. The last section is a moderate slope, and the trail zigzags up to Dutch Flat Saddle. You may not find trail markers, so make sure your routefinding skills are honed. At the saddle, you'll find a sign and a vista overlooking another basin and Dutch Flat Lake.

For descent, you can drop down through any of the glades before the saddle, under the Lees Peak and Angell Peak cliffs. On this upper traverse, you can ski the bowls below the trail into the Crawfish Meadow basin. Yo-yo a few times in the glades. The open, flat meadow is at 7120 feet.

Once finished, ski back out the Crawfish Basin Trail to the ski resort.

83 Spout Springs

Start Point	Spout Springs Sno-Park, 5000 feet
High Point	Spout Springs, 5448 feet
Trail Distance	1 mile
Trail Time	1 hour
Skill Level	Beginner
Best Season	Winter
Map	USGS Tollgate

Bald Mountain and Spout Springs isn't necessarily a destination tour; you wouldn't want to drive here from Portland. But for locals in La Grande, Pendleton, or Walla Walla, Washington, this is a short drive to an accessible, simple, entry-level junket, a beginner route in a ski area on a small hill, right off the road in the north part of

Low-angle freshies (Pete Keane)

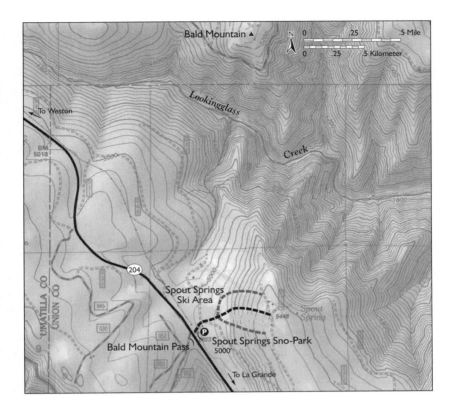

the Blue Mountains. It's not unlike Glade Trail (Route 2) on Mount Hood or Cinder Cone (Route 56) on Mount Bachelor. If you're heading to other northeast Oregon spots like the Elkhorn or Wallowa mountains, you may just stop here along the way. As with many eastern and southern Oregon passes, the slope is not hugely vertical and the snowpack may not be deep. But the sky is often clear and the snow is often drier. Because this is in Spout Springs Ski Area, check to see if the resort is operating and which runs are open for lift operations. This tour is pretty short, so plan on an hour or two, or yo-yo for several laps.

GETTING THERE. From Pendleton, head north on OR-11 for 25 miles. In the community of Weston, turn right (east) on OR-204. Follow this winding mountain road 20 miles to Bald Mountain Pass. Park at the sno-park at Spout Springs Ski Area.

THE ROUTE. The ski route ascends directly up one of the cleared slopes of Spout Springs Ski Area or the cross-country slope that gets you to the top of the mountain, a mere 400 feet. Steer clear of resort operations if open. If not, pick the path of least resistance. Take any one of the runs back, and burn another lap.

High-speed midsummer trench digging among the lava fields

(84) Strawberry Mountain

Start Point : Onion Creek trailhead, 5200 feet
High Point : Strawberry Mountain summit, 9038 feet
Trail Distance : 10 miles
Trail Time : 6 hours
Skill Level : Advanced
Best Season : Winter
Map : USGS Strawberry Mountain

Whereas Spout Springs (Route 83) is an entry-level short tour on the north end of the Blue Mountains, Strawberry Mountain is a peak in the southern end of the Blues. It lies in the Strawberry Range and wilderness areas of the same name, just outside of the town of John Day. This area is as remote as Steens Mountain (Routes 85 and 86). It's a long way for one summit, so consider combining this route with another adventure: either a tour in the Elkhorn Range to the north, or a spring junket to Steens Mountain. Like others in this book, this route is a cross-country trail turned backcountry tour by an ascent of the peak.

GETTING THERE. From John Day, drive east on US 26 (John Day Highway) 13 miles to Prairie City. Drive south on County Road 60 (Strawberry Road), along

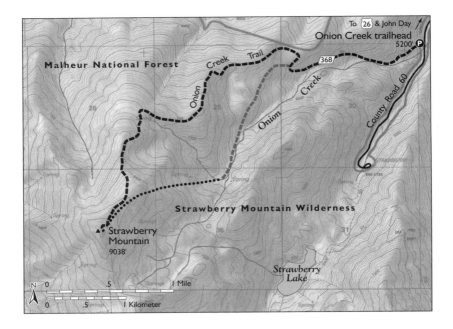

Strawberry Creek, about 10 miles to the end of the plowed road and park there, or drive a few miles farther to the Onion Creek trailhead if the road is clear.

THE ROUTE. From the Onion Creek trailhead, skin up the Strawberry Creek valley, on Onion Creek Trail 368, a low-angle ascent, 5 miles to summit. There are some cliffs to avoid northeast of the summit. Otherwise, make turns wherever you can find good snow, down the Onion Creek drainage back to the trail. Without well-practiced routefinding skills, you can get lost in these remote drainages. So if in doubt, retrace the Onion Creek Trail back to your car.

Opposite: Remote, rugged, wild: up the Pike Creek Trail, way out in the desert

STEENS MOUNTAIN

REMOTE, RUGGED, BEAUTIFUL, Steens Mountain is part of a desert and basin range, one of a hundred small ranges that stretch out in Oregon and Nevada between the Cascades and the Rocky Mountains. This is one of the most isolated corners of the state. The range here is much unlike the Cascades or northeast Oregon's Blue, Wallowa, and Elkhorn mountains. Natural hot springs appear in dry, barren lake beds of the Alvord Desert. Wild horses, pronghorn antelope, and bighorn sheep run wild in the basins and foothills. Rattlesnakes are a hazard on the approach trails. Sunrises are spectacularly unmarred by hills and peaks. Huge U-shaped canyons are filled with rushing waters. The lowlands are marked by sages and grasses, and a few quaking aspens stands. But the higher mountain is all rock.

It's dry here: cold nights but clear, hot, dry days of spring make for excellent conditions—if you time it right. Little snowfall in some years allows easy car/foot access but sometimes only a short weather window for making turns. A long drive for a few thousand feet of turns can be disheartening if the hot desert melts the snow too quickly. In winter the dry snow can be blissful, but the cold nights and lack of trees can make whiteouts dangerous and lightning a significant hazard if thunderstorms develop. The best window for snow conditions is to go early in the spring during good weather, after a big-snow winter.

STEENS MOUNTAIN MAPS
- BLM Burns District North Half Map
- BLM Burns District South Half Map
- Pacific Northwest Recreation Steens High Desert Country

PRIMARY INFORMATION CENTERS/RANGER DISTRICTS
- Burns District, Oregon Bureau of Land Management, Hines: (541) 573-4400, www.or.blm.gov/steens or www.blm.gov/burns

AVALANCHE/WEATHER/ROAD CONDITIONS
- Northwest Weather and Avalanche Center: (503) 808-2400, www.nwac.us
- Oregon DOT Trip Check: (800) 977-6368, www.tripcheck.com

PERMITS
Currently no permits are required to access Steens Mountain's east or west sides, unless you want to drive past the gate on the Steens Loop Road on the west side, for which you can get a permit from the Burns District of the BLM as listed below in Route 86.

85 Pike Creek

Start Point : Pike Creek Campground, 4200 feet
High Point : Steens Mountain ridge, 7000 feet
Trail Distance : 7 miles
Trail Time : 5 hours
Skill Level : Advanced
Best Season : Spring
Maps : USGS Wildhorse Lake, Fish Lake

The beauty of Pike Creek, and the east side of Steens Mountain escarpment, is that this is one of the most remote corners of Oregon. If you ski this route, you'll be one of probably a few dozen who have skied or snowboarded here. Of the 70-mile-long escarpment, there are many canyons on the east side that are skiable. Most are expansive, rugged, and without approach trails. One of the few with a trail is Pike Creek, an accessible drainage just south of the true summit of Steens Mountain. Pike Creek has an easy place to park right off the road, a relatively short hike to the snow, an excellent camping spot in a basin, and a multitude of slopes for yo-yoing.

The trail is another story: it's rugged and primitive, and the slopes are upward of 40 degrees; some parts may be snow covered and others rough talus.

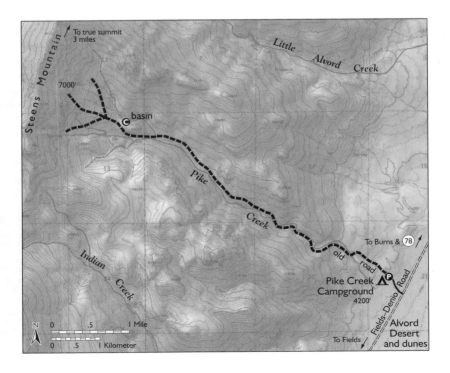

In spring a two-day trip gives you time to drive, hike up to the snow-filled basins, and ski. Generally your best skiing will be in the morning, so you'll want to get up the canyon the night before. In the afternoon, the hot desert sun can cook the snow into slush. Afternoon wet slides are likely on this east- and southeast-facing slope.

GETTING THERE. From Burns, drive east on OR-78 (Steens Highway) about 60 miles. You will see the large north end of the Steens Mountain escarpment to your right. Turn right on Folly Farm Road, also called Fields–Denio Road. This gravel road begins at the north end of the escarpment and parallels it on the east side. The trailhead for Pike Creek is 41 miles down this road. You will pass Alvord Ranch in about 35 miles; continue 6 miles farther to Pike Creek Campground, on the right side of the road. The trailhead is opposite the Alvord Desert and dunes. If you've made it to Alvord Lake, the large desert lake and hot springs, you've gone about 10 miles too far.

THE ROUTE. From the campground, follow a primitive mining double track up the drainage. Cross a few streams, traverse heavy-gauge talus, climb steep switchbacks. You'll pass an old mine shaft on the south wall of the canyon. After a few miles and hours, the stream bifurcates. Follow the left drainage to a large, flat step at 6000 feet. This flat spot provides a decent campsite and a panoramic view of multiple couloirs and small bowls. From this point, you can hike to the bottom of one of several couloirs, and continue to the top of the ridge.

Steens Mountain's true summit, with a radio facility, is 3 miles farther north along the ridge. Because it's a long slog, save the summit-bagging for the West Escarpment route (Route 86).

Yo-yo a few laps if you find good snow on the lower aprons. Take a dip in Alvord hot springs after the trip.

86 West Escarpment

Start Point : Page Springs, 4200 feet
High Point : Steens Mountain summit, 9733 feet
Trail Distance : 40 miles
Trail Time : 3 days
Skill Level : Advanced
Best Season : Winter
Maps : USGS Page Springs, Fish Lake, McCoy Ridge, Wildhorse Lake

Whereas the steep east side of Steens Mountain (see Route 85) has hundreds of potential routes for expert glissé alpinists, the west side of the 70-mile-long escarpment is a cross-country ski destination. Gentle slopes and a summit road make access straightforward and routes easy. This is the beautiful Malheur National Wildlife Refuge. It's worthy of a big backcountry trip, one or two days, to check out this side. But it's a long trek into skiable terrain.

GETTING THERE. From Burns, drive 60 miles south on OR-205 to the small town of Frenchglen, at the Malheur National Wildlife Refuge. Once through town, turn left and head east on Steens Mountain Road (North Loop Road). In 3 miles, stop at the gate at the end of the road at Page Springs, where there's a campground.

In some seasons and light snow years, you may be able to drive to the snow line, as far as Fish Lake Campground, shrinking the 40-mile three-day trip into a 20-mile one- or two-day tour. Skiers wanting to drive past the gate can submit a winter recreation application a week before the trip to the Burns District of the Bureau of Land Management. You can pick up the permit and key to the gate for no charge.

THE ROUTE. The ski route follows the unplowed road (continuation of Steens Mountain Road) through sagebrush, grasses, and desert shrubbery, which may be snow covered if early in the season. You'll pass Lily and Fish lakes. Fish Lake is a spot to camp if you are on a two-day trip.

From Fish Lake, continue to the summit via the road. You'll spy several huge canyons: Kiger Gorge to the left, and the Little Blitzen and Big Indian gorges to the right. To reach the summit, take the half-mile spur trail on your left. You'll know you are at the high point when you see the radio towers.

Descend the climbing route on the road. Don't plan on making too many turns; it is more of a cross-country tour than a descent.

Opposite: Ogling a very small slice of the 70-mile-long Steens Mountain escarpment, after fixing the flat tire

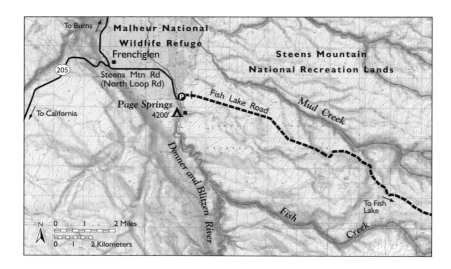

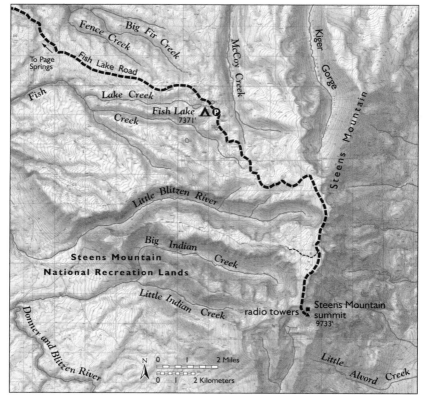

*Opposite: Reaching the top is only half the trip: descending
Mount Rainier after a successful summit*

SOUTHWEST WASHINGTON

THE TWIN GIANTS, Mount Adams and Mount St. Helens, in southwest Washington, combined with Mount Hood, are part of the standard trifecta of objectives for ski and snowboard mountaineers in Oregon. In fact, many Willamette Valley skiers and snowboarders make an annual jaunt to both Washington peaks. Mounts Adams and St. Helens are close to the Portland metro area and offer spectacular climbs and descents for intermediate to advanced ski and snowboard mountaineers. Fabulous fall lines, spectacular scenery, and burly ascents make both peaks worthy of many trips.

Mount Adams, at 12,276 feet, is the second largest peak in Washington. Much of it lies in the Mount Adams Wilderness, but the east flank is part of the Yakama Indian Reservation; the routes here lie in the wilderness lands. The Klickitat and Yakama tribes called this peak Pahto, son of the Great Spirit. It was given its current name by Thomas Farnham in 1843, named after President John Adams back when the Cascade Mountains were known as the President Range.

The first ascent was reported in 1854 by A. G. Aiken, Edward J. Allen, and Andrew Burge, and since then the south-side summit climb has seen a lot of activity. In the 1920s a lookout tower was stationed on the summit, and in the 1930s a sulfur mine operated out of a shack, remnants of which are still visible in late summer on a light-snow year. The first descent on skis was by a group led by University of California ski coach Walter Mosauer in 1932.

Mount St. Helens, at 8365 feet, is shorter and one of the most well-known Cascade volcanoes after the May 18, 1980, eruption that blew half the mountain away including the top 1321 feet. The natives called the mountain Loowit; the Klickitat tribes translated this to "fair maiden" and the Salish, "smoking one." On April 10, 1792, explorer Captain George Vancouver spied this peak from the Columbia River and named it after Britain's court ambassador to Madrid.

The first ascent of Mount St. Helens was by the *Oregonian* newspaper founder Thomas Dryer in 1853. The first ski descent was probably in 1961 by famed Pacific Northwest mountaineer and guidebook author Fred Beckey. The mountain was skied much from the north and south until the eruption in 1980 closed access for years. Since it reopened in 1987, climbing routes have been exclusively from the south. The crater and the entire blown-out north side are closed to climbing and skiing.

The third big Washington objective for Oregonians is the famed Mount Rainier. At 14,411 feet, Rainier is the tallest peak in the Pacific Northwest and epicenter of Pacific Northwest mountaineering. It was called Tahoma (or one of several variations) by the Native Americans. British Captain George Vancouver spied the mountain in 1792 and named it for British Naval Officer Rear Admiral Peter Rainier. In 1899 it became the United States' fifth national park. The first ascent was in 1870 by local mountaineers Hazard Stevens and Philemon Van Trump. The first ski ascent was in 1939 by Sigurd Hall. Now, nearly 10,000 people attempt to climb to the summit yearly; about half make it. Mount Rainier is worth including in an Oregon guidebook because it is both a common objective and a spectacular ski.

Combine these three volcanoes with a winter route on Silver Star, and you have an entire mountaineering season's worth of turns.

SOUTHWEST WASHINGTON MAPS

- USFS Gifford Pinchot National Forest
- USFS Mount Adams Wilderness
- USFS Wind River Ranger District (for Silver Star)
- USFS Mount Adams Ranger District
- USFS Mount St. Helens National Volcanic Monument
- NPS Mount Rainier National Park
- Geo-Graphics Mount St. Helens National Volcanic Monument
- Green Trails Mount St. Helens No. 364, Mount St. Helens NW No. 364S, Mount Adams East, Mount Adams West, Mount Rainier East No. 270, Mount Rainier West No. 269 and Paradise No. 270S

PRIMARY INFORMATION CENTERS/RANGER DISTRICTS

- Gifford Pinchot National Forest Headquarters: (360) 891-5000; Climber's Recording (360) 891-5015; www.fs.fed.us/gpnf
- Mount St. Helens National Volcanic Monument: (360) 449-7800; Climber's Recording (360) 247-3961; www.fs.fed.us/gpnf/mshnvm
- Mount Rainier National Park Headquarters: Information (360) 569-2211; Climber's Recording (360) 569-2211; www.nps.gov/mora
- Mount Adams Ranger District: (509) 395-3400 (for Mount Adams)
- Paradise Ranger District: (360) 569-2211 (for Mount Rainier)

AVALANCHE/WEATHER/ROAD CONDITIONS

- Northwest Weather and Avalanche Center: (503) 808-2400 or (206) 526-6677, www.nwac.us
- Washington DOT: (800) 695-7623; wsdot.wa.gov/traffic

PERMITS

For Mount Adams, a Cascade Volcano Pass is required from June 1 through September 30. The cost is $15 for a weekend, $10 for weekday pass, and $30 for an annual pass for multiple trips. The pass and climber's registration can be obtained at the Mount Adams Ranger Station. No pass is required for climbing below 7000 feet or from October 1 to May 31.

For Mount St. Helens, a climbing permit is required year-round for making tracks above 4800 feet. From November 1 to March 31, permits are free and are obtained at Lone Fir Resort in Cougar, Washington, www.lonefirresort.com or (360) 238-5210. From April 1 to October 31, the permits cost $22 a day and are available at www.mshinsitute.org. There is no limit from April 1 to May 15. From May 15 through October 31, the permits are limited to one hundred a day.

For Mount Rainier National Park, you need to pay the entrance fee. You will only need a climbing permit above 10,000 feet, which doesn't include the Muir Snowfield route described herein.

A Sno-Park Pass is required from November 1 to April 30 for designated lots. Washington will honor a valid Oregon permit on an Oregon-licensed vehicle.

The Mount St. Helens routes require a Northwest Forest Pass when the sno-park season is over. For Mount Adams, a parking pass is included in the Cascade Volcano Pass.

GUIDES

* Mount St. Helens Institute: www.mshinstitute.org
* Rainier Mountaineering: www.rmiguides.org

SPECIAL NOTES

For Mount Adams, call ahead to check if the road from Morrison Creek to Cold Springs is open. Usually this is after Memorial Day. For Mount St. Helens Monitor Ridge, call ahead to see if the road is open to Climber's Bivouac.

87 Silver Star

Start Point : Grouse Creek Vista, 2400 feet
High Point : Pyramid Rock, 3200 feet
Trail Distance : 2 miles
Trail Time : 3 hours
Skill Level : Beginner
Best Season : Winter
Maps : USGS Larch Mountain, Bobs Mountain

Silver Star Mountain, 4390 feet, is located in the far southwest corner of Gifford Pinchot National Forest and on land managed by the Washington Department of Natural Resources. Just above the cities of Vancouver and Camas, the snowcap can

The closest tracks to PDX: a hidden stash of midwinter pow on Silver Star

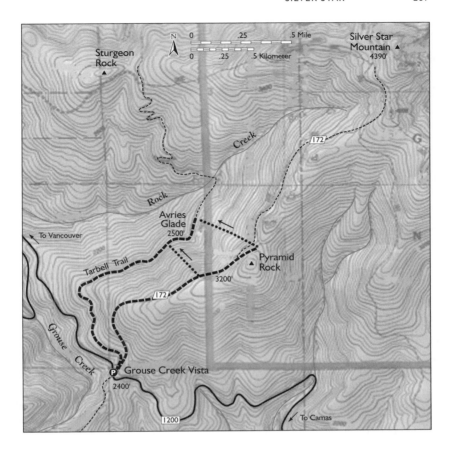

be seen from Portland and Interstate 84 when driving up the Columbia River Gorge. Although this is a popular summer hike, it is a rarely visited winter backcountry destination.

Silver Star is at risk of getting little snow some years. But in big snow years in midwinter, it offers a wilderness experience close to home, sans developed ski resorts or the long drive.

The roads are not plowed to the trailhead in the winter. In some years you may have a good month to ride Silver Star and a mile hike on slush to the trailhead. In light winters, the days may be few that snow persists on the slopes.

GETTING THERE. From Washougal, Washington (east of Vancouver), head east on WA-14, and turn left at 140th/15th Street, marked by a Washougal River Recreation Area sign. Follow Washougal River Road north and east for 7 miles. Turn left on Hughes Road, which becomes Miller Road. After 2 miles on Miller Road, the road forks. Take Department of Natural Resources Road 1200 about 10 miles to Grouse

Creek Vista, a wide spot in the road with room for parking at the saddle. Hopefully, you can drive all the way to Grouse Creek Vista, but you may get stymied a mile or so before the trailhead by snow.

THE ROUTE. The Tarbell Trail and Trail 172 jointly leave the road and head north. After a few hundred yards, the trail forks and is marked by a sign. Head right on Trail 172 up a steep drainage toward Silver Star peak. After a few miles winding up the wooded drainage, it opens up to the ridge with Pyramid Rock in view and Silver Star Mountain beyond. Climb the knoll just to the south of Pyramid Rock for the best and closest line of descent.

The descent drops around 1000 feet until the trees and brush get too thick to ride through. At this point, you can skin or snowshoe back up for multiple runs. On your last run down, continue through the trees to the Tarbell Trail below the slope for the hike back to Grouse Creek Vista.

88 Mount Adams, Suksdorf Ridge

Start Point	Cold Springs, 5600 feet
High Point	Mount Adams summit, 12,276 feet
Trail Distance	10 miles
Trail Time	8 hours
Skill Level	Advanced
Best Season	Summer
Map	USGS Mount Adams East

Suksdorf Ridge, more commonly known as "South Climb," is the most popular glissé and climbing route on Mount Adams, and one of the most popular mountaineering routes in the Pacific Northwest. A classic, the climb is a great place to get big-mountain experience if you have only a weekend to spare. On nice summer weekends it can get overcrowded. This is considered a nontechnical summit climb, but snow-riders should still have mountaineering experience to make the ascent. On hard snow, crampons and an ice ax may be necessary. Self-arrest grip poles are handy, too.

Many climb and glide Mount Adams in two days, camping on midmountain. However, it can be climbed and skied easily in a day round trip from Cold Springs with a predawn start; that will almost surely necessitate car camping at the trailhead or getting a super-early start for the two-hour drive to the trailhead from Portland. A few climb it in winter or spring before the road is clear. The section between Morrison Creek and Cold Springs will not be passable until late May or June, so call ahead or be prepared for a long hike up the road, or a bramble-filled drainage, to timberline.

For snowriders lacking time, skill, or experience for the summit climb, the Crescent Glacier is a fun route in the late spring or summer. If the snow is good, you can hike up and make several runs on the glacier bowl.

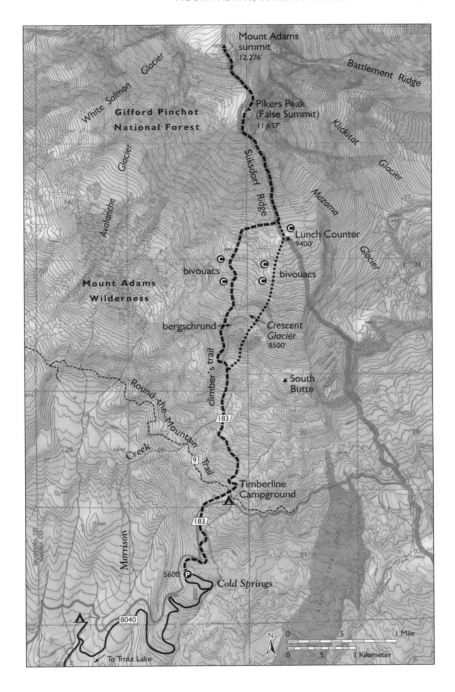

*Big mountain experience:
mid-August ascent of Crescent
Glacier, Mount Adams*

GETTING THERE. From Hood River, cross the Hood River toll bridge to White Salmon, Washington; turn left on WA-14, and drive 2 miles. Turn right and drive north on WA-141 for 25 miles to Trout Lake. At Trout Lake, the road forks. Take the left fork to the ranger station, a mile north of town on the left, to obtain a climbing permit. After obtaining a permit, drive back to Trout Lake and follow the right fork north. In a few miles, turn left on Forest Road 80, marked by a South Climb sign. After a few miles, continue straight on Forest Road 8040. Pass Wicky Creek Shelter, and drive another 6 miles to the trailhead. The final section of road from Morrison Creek Horse Camp to Cold Springs is rough and unimproved. You should have a sturdy vehicle with high clearance, although some passenger cars can travel the road in good conditions. The road may be open Memorial Day, but usually not until June.

THE ROUTE. A trail register and gate mark an old road, Trail 183, that leads north to Timberline Campground, 0.5 mile from the trailhead. (If you plan to camp, consider setting up camp here or at the trailhead.) Follow Trail 183 north, then take the climber's trail to the bottom of the Crescent Glacier. From here, gain the top of the glacier by climbing directly up the face to the north or northeast. Poles may be in place to mark this route. If you are only out for a few turns on the Crescent Glacier, you can make as many laps as you have time for between 7000 and 8000 feet.

At the top of the Crescent Glacier, about 8500 feet, you should reach the first of many rock shelter bivouacs on either side of the snowfield. These are scattered in the lava up to a wide, flat spot at 9400 feet called Lunch Counter. If you are camping midmountain, find a bivouac and set up camp.

From Lunch Counter the route is straight up Suksdorf Ridge to Pikers Peak, also called the False Summit. From the False Summit, the true summit is visible on a clear day across the saddle and to the northwest. The last pitch leading to the summit is steep. On light-snow years in midsummer, you'll see the remnants of the summit mine shack.

89 Mount Adams, Southwest Chute

Start Point : Cold Springs, 5600 feet
High Point : False Summit, 11,657 feet
Trail Distance : 9 miles
Trail Time : 8 hours
Skill Level : Advanced
Best Season : Summer
Map : USGS Mount Adams East

The Southwest Chute is one of the finest descents in this book. This narrow gully has been dubbed Chute 333: 30 feet wide, 30-degree slope, 3000-foot descent. It is a clean fall line and a spectacular ski or snowboard descent. Because of its steepness, timing is important. This should be ridden in early summer, early in the day. With fresh snow or slush late in the day, avalanche danger is significant. With hardpack ice, risk of a fall can send you to the bottom into rocks.

Many people ride this in one day with an early start from Cold Springs. For an overnight, consider camping at Timberline Campground, 0.5 mile from the trailhead. If you camp at Lunch Counter, you will need to carry your overnight gear with you on the descent or hike back up and retrieve it after you ride the chute. The best option: round trip in one day from your car at Cold Springs.

GETTING THERE. From Hood River, cross the Hood River toll bridge to White Salmon, Washington; turn left on WA-14, and drive 2 miles. Turn right and drive

Midsummer cloud cap on Mount Adams, viewed from the porch after another good climb

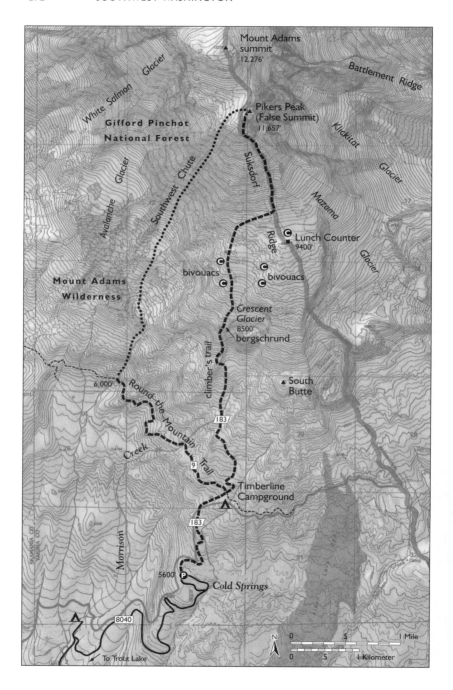

north on WA-141 for 25 miles to Trout Lake. At Trout Lake, the road forks. Take the left fork to the ranger station, a mile north of town on the left, to obtain a climbing permit. After obtaining a permit, drive back to Trout Lake and follow the right fork north. In a few miles, turn left on Forest Road 80, marked by a South Climb sign. After a few miles continue straight on Forest Road 8040. Pass Wicky Creek Shelter, and drive another 6 miles to the trailhead. The final section of road from Morrison Creek Horse Camp to Cold Springs is rough and unimproved. You should have a sturdy vehicle with high clearance, although some passenger cars can travel the road in good conditions. The road may be open Memorial Day, but usually not until June.

THE ROUTE. A trail register and gate mark an old road, Trail 183, that leads north to Timberline Campground. Follow Trail 183 north, then take the climber's trail to the bottom of the Crescent Glacier. From here, gain the top of the glacier by climbing directly up the face to the north or northeast. Poles may be in place to mark this route. At the top of the Crescent Glacier, about 8500 feet, you should reach the first of many rock shelter bivouacs on either side of the snowfield. These are scattered in the lava up to Lunch Counter, a wide, flat camping spot at 9400 feet. From here, continue climbing straight up Suksdorf Ridge to Pikers Peak, also called the False Summit, at 11,657 feet.

The chute drops right off the False Summit, an hourglass-shaped snowfield, 3000 feet to the south. Once the main snowfield peters out, you may be able to continue down the gully on snow all the way to timberline, around 6000 feet. Once down to timberline, hike back to Cold Springs on the Round-the-Mountain Trail, which follows the 6000-foot contour. Trees and snow cover at timberline may make the trail back to Cold Springs (Trail 183) difficult to find: it won't be marked with blazes, and it's not a well-traveled trail, especially in early summer. Be prepared to hike overland using a map and compass.

90   Mount St. Helens, Monitor Ridge

Start Point : Climber's Bivouac, 3800 feet
High Point : Mount St. Helens summit; 8365 feet
Trail Distance : 8 miles
Trail Time : 6 hours
Skill Level : Advanced
Best Season : Summer
Map : USGS Mount St. Helens

The Monitor Ridge route is the main summer ski on Mount St. Helens whereas Swift Creek (Route 91) is primarily a spring jaunt. Monitor Ridge is one of the most popular ski mountaineering routes in this guide. And it is a sweet glide. Like the

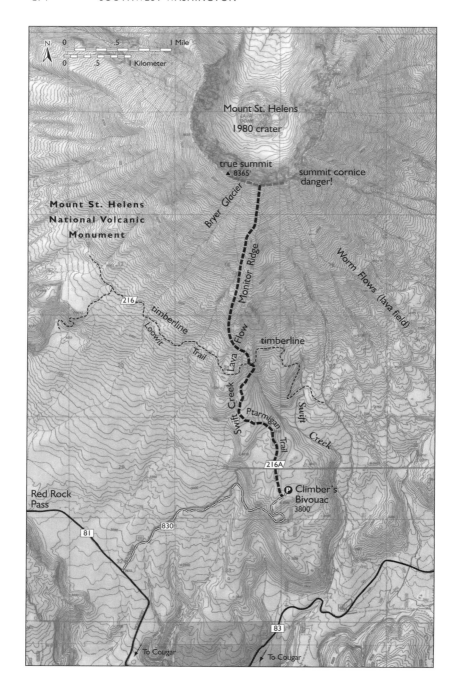

Bootpacking up the sleeping, steaming Mount St. Helens

Suksdorf Ridge/South Climb on Mount Adams, this glissé descent is a great place to get mountaineering experience without gnarly crevasses or super-steep chutes and cliffs. This tour is a short, beautiful hike through the woods, a steady climb to summit, and a fascinating look into the hissing, steaming crater. It is a Northwest classic.

One caution, though: the cornice is perched on the cliff of the crater. It's a 2000-foot fall. People have died here by getting too close to the edge; the cornice breaks off, and they tumble into the crater. Use caution at the rim.

GETTING THERE. From Portland, follow I-5 north into Washington for 21 miles to Woodland and take Exit 21. From Woodland drive east on WA-503 (Lewis River Road) 30 miles to Cougar. Continue right (east) at Cougar as WA-503 becomes Forest Road 90, just before the dam that holds Swift Creek Reservoir. Turn left on Forest Road 83 and follow it east for 3 miles, then turn left on Forest Road 81 and follow it for a mile. Turn right onto gravel Forest Road 830 to Climber's Bivouac. Call first to make sure the road is clear all the way to Climber's Bivouac.

THE ROUTE. From Climber's Bivouac, follow the Ptarmigan Trail 216A about 2 miles to timberline, where you pass the Loowit Trail 216. Continue north on 216A and when you break out of the trees, hike up a short slope to Monitor Ridge; the trail may be marked by wood poles. The trail follows the ridge north directly to the summit rim, alternating on snow and lava rock ridges.

The descent follows one of the main snowfields along Monitor Ridge. Descend the west side of the Monitor Ridge, following one of several snowfields but staying close to the ascent route. Don't drop into the east side of the ridge or the cornice, the east-facing rim of Monitor Ridge, or you will have to skin back out of the basin. Use caution here on the west side, too: if you carve turns too far down one of the west-side drainages, it will take you far west of the Ptarmigan Trail, and you'll have to hike back over lava to the trail. If in doubt, just follow your climbing route.

91 Mount St. Helens, Swift Creek

Start Point : Marble Mount Sno-Park, 2640 feet
High Point : Mount St. Helens summit, 8365 feet
Trail Distance : 9 miles
Trail Time : 7 hours
Skill Level : Advanced
Best Season : Spring
Map : USGS Mount St. Helens

Swift Creek is the second of the two main routes on Mount St. Helens. Whereas Monitor Ridge (Route 90) is a primary summer route, Swift Creek is best in spring. It is also known as Worm Flows, although Worm Flows lava field is east of, and separate from, the route. Although not as popular as the summer route, there will still be a lot of people here, especially in May, when the snow is good. Most people get up early and ski this in one day. A few will camp just above timberline near the flats at the Swift Creek headwaters. You'll probably hear the roar of snowmobiles in the surrounding areas.

The road is plowed all the way to the sno-park, so if you time it right, you should be able to skin up the trail right from the car. Which means, on descent, you can ski all the way back to your car.

One caution: the cornice is perched on the cliff of the crater. It's a 2000-foot fall. People have died here by getting too close to the edge; the cornice breaks off, and they tumble into the crater. Use caution at the rim.

GETTING THERE. From Portland, follow I-5 north into Washington for 21 miles to Woodland and take Exit 21. From Woodland drive east on WA-503 (Lewis River Road) 30 miles to Cougar. Continue right (east) at Cougar as WA-503 becomes Forest Road 90, just before the dam that holds Swift Creek Reservoir. Turn left on Forest

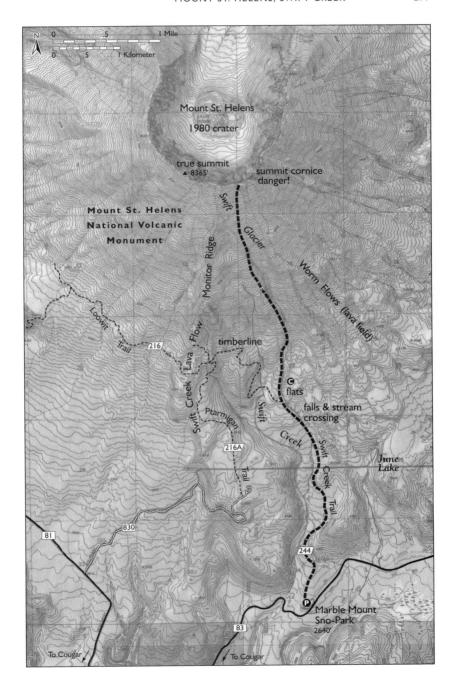

N

0   .5   1 Mile

0   .5   1 Kilometer

Mount St. Helens
1980 crater

true summit
▲ 8365'

summit cornice
danger!

Mount St. Helens
National Volcanic
Monument

Swift

Glacier

Monitor Ridge

Worm Flows (lava field)

Loowit

Trail

216

Lava Flow

timberline

Swift Creek

Ptarmigan

flats

Swift

falls & stream
crossing

216A

Creek

Trail

Swift Creek Trail

June
Lake

81

830

244

83

P Marble Mount
Sno-Park
2640'

To Cougar

To Cougar

Racing the corn window, clambering up Loowit's Swift Creek

Road 83 and follow it east for 5 miles to Marble Mount Sno-Park. The route is popular and should be marked by signs.

THE ROUTE. Head north on the Swift Creek Trail 244 as it winds through the woods just to the east of Swift Creek. After 2 miles, the trail reaches timberline and crosses the Loowit Trail 216. Continue north and cross over the Swift Creek headwaters just above a small waterfall. From the flats, skin or snowshoe up the obvious main ridge toward the summit; it may be marked by poles.

Once on the crater rim, the true summit is a few hundred feet west, so you may choose to traverse if you really need to bag the actual peak.

The descent follows the main snowfield on the west or east of the climbing route. Steer clear of Monitor Ridge to the west, as frequent avalanches occur here and slide close to the Swift Creek route. Drop down to the flats and catch the Swift Creek Trail back to your car. If you've timed your ski before early in the spring, you should be able to ski all the way to your car. Snowboarders will want poles while cruising down the trail.

92 Mount St. Helens, Butte Dome

Start Point : Red Rock Pass, 3116 feet
High Point : Mount St. Helens summit, 8365 feet
Trail Distance : 10 miles
Trail Time : 8 hours
Skill Level : Advanced
Best Season : Spring
Map : USGS Mount St. Helens

This is a less popular route for skiing and snowboarding, mostly because the approach is significantly longer than the other routes. However, if you've done Mount St. Helens by Monitor Ridge (Route 90) and Swift Creek (Route 91) and are looking for another challenge, this ascent will round out the south-side trio. In spring, you may have to park at Cougar Sno-Park and skin up the road for 2 miles if the snow level is low. Even if you can park at Red Rock Pass, this route is still longer than the other two.

One caution: the cornice is perched on the cliff of the crater. It's a 2000-foot fall. People have died here by getting too close to the edge; the cornice breaks off, and they tumble into the crater. Use caution at the rim.

Evening cirrus rolling in over Mount St. Helens

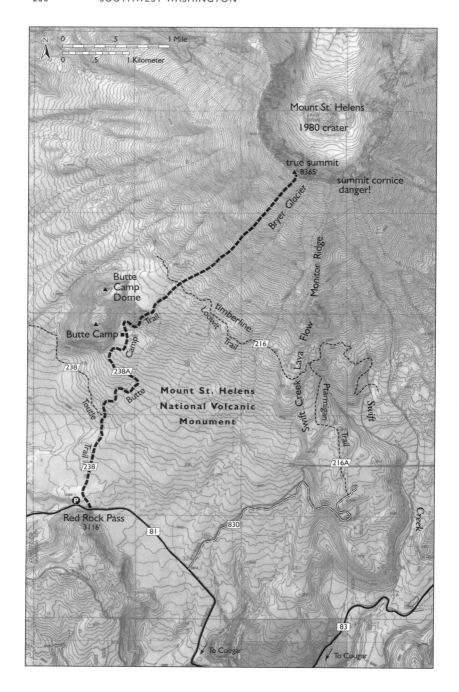

GETTING THERE. From Portland, follow I-5 north into Washington for 21 miles to Woodland and take Exit 21. From Woodland drive east on WA-503 (Lewis River Road) 30 miles to Cougar. Continue right (east) at Cougar as WA-503 becomes Forest Road 90, just before the dam that holds Swift Creek Reservoir. Turn left on Forest Road 83 and follow it east for 3 miles. Then turn left on Forest Road 81 and follow it for a mile. If there is snow on the road, park at Cougar Sno-Park at the junction of FR 83 and 81; FR 81 will be gated. In spring and summer, follow FR 81 for 2 miles to Red Rock Pass.

THE ROUTE. Head north on the Toutle Trail 238 for a mile, then continue on the Butte Camp Trail 238A for 2 miles to Butte Camp, at 4000 feet, under Butte Camp Dome, a small cinder cone just west of the trail. In another mile, the trail passes the Loowit Trail 216 at timberline.

From timberline, follow the ridge to the summit. Because this route is unmarked, use caution in poor weather. Consider marking your trail with wands, and identify landmarks at timberline so you can find the trail home when you descend. The route puts you on the crater rim at the true summit of Mount St. Helens.

The descent follows the ascent route closely. Watch for landmarks to get back to the Butte Camp Trail. Veer too far in either direction, and you may miss the trail home. There are numerous gullies and drainages here that eventually take you down to the Loowit Trail.

93 Mount Rainier, Muir Snowfield

Start Point : Paradise, 5400 feet
High Point : Camp Muir, 10,100 feet
Trail Distance : 9 miles
Trail Time : 6 hours
Skill Level : Intermediate
Best season : Summer
Maps : USGS Mount Rainier East, Mount Rainier West

Although it is a long drive, this mountain is a Pacific Northwest classic and a trip all Oregon ski and snowboard mountaineers should make at one time or another. Detailed descriptions of the myriad climbs and descents are found in other guidebooks, but one is worth mentioning here: the Muir Snowfield. It is not just a must for all Pacific Northwest glissé alpinists, but a favorite route in the summer for intermediate to advanced skiers and snowboarders. It is also the approach to Disappointment Cleaver, the main climbing route, named after the gully higher on the mountain. This is one of the easiest routes to the summit, so it can be crowded with mountaineers ascending the big peak.

Mount Rainier—a Pacific Northwest classic

The snowfield was named after naturalist and mountaineer John Muir, after he climbed to this camp in 1883. If you catch this in late spring or early summer, shoot for a few days of clear weather and high pressure. If there is any chance of foul weather rolling in from the Pacific, make alternate plans. It is a long drive just for rain.

There are some glide cracks, but no crevasses, and the route is straightforward. But in bad weather this is a big burly mountain, so be careful.

GETTING THERE. Head north on I-5 from Portland for about 70 miles to Exit 68. Head east on WA-12 for 32 miles to Morton. At Morton, turn north on WA-7 and drive 17 miles to Elbe. At Elbe, turn east on WA-706 and drive 20 miles to the Nisqually entrance to Mount Rainier National Park at Longmire. After you pay to enter, continue about 10 miles to Paradise. At Paradise, park in the overnight parking area. Sign in at the ranger station, obtain a climber's permit only if you are venturing above 10,000 feet, and check conditions.

THE ROUTE. From the Paradise parking lot, head north up the Skyline Trail to Alta Vista and Glacier Vista, at 6300 feet. In winter, this trail is well traveled; in summer, it is paved. Continue on to Panorama Point, at 6400 feet, by following either the low-angle south-facing slope or the switchbacks on the west-facing slope. Both will be well marked and well traveled.

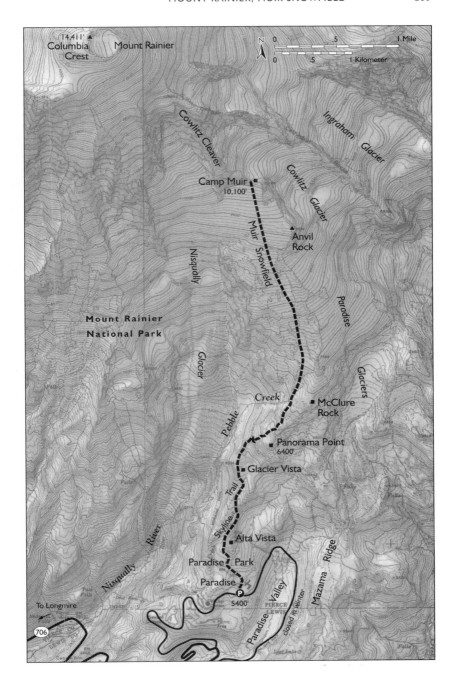

Continue north above Panorama Point to Pebble Creek where you reach the terminus of the Muir Snowfield; McClure Rock will be to the east. From here it is a long trudge up the low-angle pitch to Camp Muir, at 10,100 feet, resting in a little notch below Disappointment Cleaver and the Nisqually Glacier. About halfway up you will see Anvil Rock off to the right. You might cross a few glide cracks, usually marked with wands by the rangers.

At Camp Muir, check out the overnight shelter for a future trip. There's also a ranger hut here.

The descent is a beautiful ride 4000 feet down the Muir Snowfield, then down the steep sections below Panorama Point. It pretty much follows the route up. Depending on the snow coverage, you may have to hike out the last few miles.

Opposite: Step into the wild and scenic
Mount Shasta–Trinity Alps Wilderness

NORTHERN CALIFORNIA

THE PEAKS IN NORTHERN CALIFORNIA are beautiful, large, and plentiful. For Oregonians, Shasta is, like the Muir Snowfield on Mount Rainier, a must-do out-of-state junket. The bold fall lines are thrilling, the snow good through midsummer, and the views stunning. Other routes on Etna Summit and Lassen are easy to reach for southern Oregon riders and skiers. The Trinity Alps provide scores of routes and thousand of turns.

The second highest peak in the Cascade Range, Mount Shasta is slightly shorter than Mount Rainier by a few hundred feet. It's known for glaciers that are not quite as steep or crevassed as those of its northern cousins, Jefferson and Hood. It's a huge mountain by volume, and provides excellent and numerous route options for all levels of ski and snowboard mountaineers.

The "gentle giant" was held in awe by the Modoc, Wintum, and Shas-ti'ca tribes. They called the mountain "Great White" or "Great Purity." It was first spied by Fray Narcisco Duran, a Spanish explorer, in 1817. The first ascent was in 1854 by E. D. Pierce and a group of eight climbers. The first ski descent was by Fletcher Hoyt and climbing partners in 1947.

NORTHERN CALIFORNIA MAPS
- USFS Shasta Trinity National Forest
- USFS Mount Shasta Wilderness
- Wilderness Press Mount Shasta
- Wilderness Press Lassen Volcano National Park
- Lassen Peak National Volcanic Monument

PRIMARY INFORMATION CENTERS/RANGER DISTRICTS
- Shasta Trinity National Forest: (530) 226-2500, www.fs.usda.gov/stnf
- Lassen Volcano National Park: (530) 595-4480, www.nps.gov/lavo
- Mount Shasta Ranger District: (530) 926-4511

AVALANCHE/WEATHER/ROAD CONDITIONS
- Mount Shasta Avalanche Center: (530) 926-9613, www.shastaavalanche.org
- Oregon DOT: (800) 977-6368, www.tripcheck.com
- California DOT: www.dot.ca.gov/hq/roadinfo

WINTER RESORTS
- Mount Shasta Ski Park: (530) 926-8686, www.skipark.com

PERMITS
- For Mount Shasta, a wilderness permit and a $20 summit pass are required, obtained at a self-service station at the trailheads.
- For Lassen, there is a national park entrance fee.

GUIDES AND COURSES
- Shasta Mountain Guides: (530) 926-3117, www.shastaguides.com
- SWS Mountain Guides: (888) 797-6867, www.swsmtns.com

Mount Shasta and Shastina on a crystalline summer morning, en route to a ski mountaineering ascent

94   Mount Shasta, Avalanche Gulch

Start Point : Bunny Flat trailhead, 6900 feet
High Point : Mount Shasta summit, 14,162 feet
Trail Distance : 11 miles
Trail Time : 8 hours
Skill Level : Expert
Best Season : Summer
Maps : USGS Mount Shasta, McCloud, Hotlum

Avalanche Gulch is the easiest and most popular route up Mount Shasta—technically easy, but that's as far as mountaineering goes. For backcountry skiers attempting a big mountain, you should be an expert. It's marked by rock- and icefall, as well as avalanches, hence the moniker Avalanche Gulch. And, a large number of people of varying

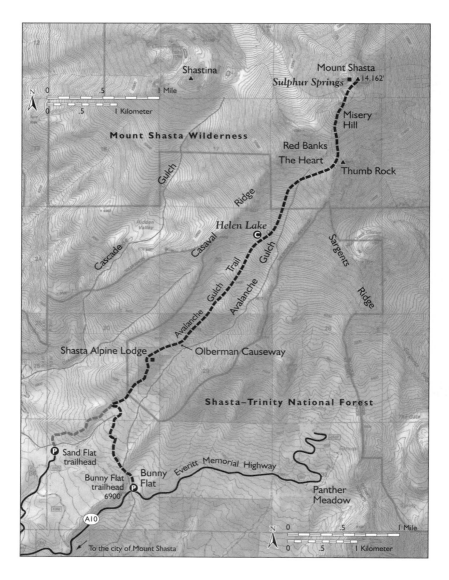

levels of experience on this route can make it dangerous. In the spring, it is a fabulous ski, often with good weather and great snow all the way to the base of the mountain.

GETTING THERE. Drive south on I-5, the long haul to the California state line, and continue 60 miles to the city of Mount Shasta. From there, take the Everitt Memorial Highway (CA-A10) to the Bunny Flat trailhead. Alternatively, you can start from the Sand Flat trailhead, a few miles' drive west of Bunny Flat.

THE ROUTE. From either trailhead, hike about a mile to the Sierra Club Shasta Alpine Lodge. From the lodge, follow the Olberman Causeway, built to access the hut up the mountain. It turns into the Avalanche Gulch Trail, then heads up the mountain. After a few miles, reach the bench with Helen Lake at 10,400 feet, a good spot to break and camp.

From Helen Lake, climb the 2000-foot snowfield and gain the ridge. This veers to climber's right of Avalanche Gulch and passes below and to the right of the famous rock formations called The Heart and Red Banks. Once atop Red Banks, follow the ridge up Misery Hill to the summit.

The descent follows the route down. Be watchful of rockfall late in the day.

95 Mount Shasta, Hotlum–Bolum Ridge

Start Point	North Gate trailhead, 6990 feet
High Point	Hotlum Glacier, 13,000 feet
Trail Distance	12 miles
Trail Time	10 hours
Skill Level	Expert
Best Season	Summer
Maps	USGS Mount Shasta, McCloud, Hotlum

The Hotlum–Bolum ridge is reported to be one of the safer routes on the north side of Shasta. It's more remote and less crowded than Avalanche Gulch (Route 94). And it's a better ski, with good fall lines, wide-open snowfields, and spectacular scenery. Both the Hotlum and Bolum glaciers don't have nearly the number or size of crevasses and seracs as other Cascade volcanoes. The lower slopes should have plenty of snow in spring and into early summer. The upper glaciers and snowfield, known as "the ramp," are steep and snow-filled until late in the season. The best skiing is between 9000 and 13,000 feet. Although there are many reports of skiers descending from the summit, that final 1000 feet is exposed and for experienced mountaineers.

GETTING THERE. From Portland, drive south on I-5, the long haul to the California state line, and continue 50 miles to the town of Weed. Exit and turn north on US 97. Drive 10 miles to Military Pass Road, which will be on your right. Follow this road a mile, passing under a railroad bridge, then turn right on Forest Road 42N16. This is a rough, rocky dirt road; it will be slow going. Luckily, the 8-mile road to the North Gate trailhead is well marked with signs.

THE ROUTE. Start at the North Gate Trail and in a mile, and at the first gully, head up the drainage. This is to the southeast of North Gate hill, a good reference point you'll need for descent. The route meanders another 2 miles up a gully sandwiched between a rocky lava flow to the east and two rocky cones to the west. Be

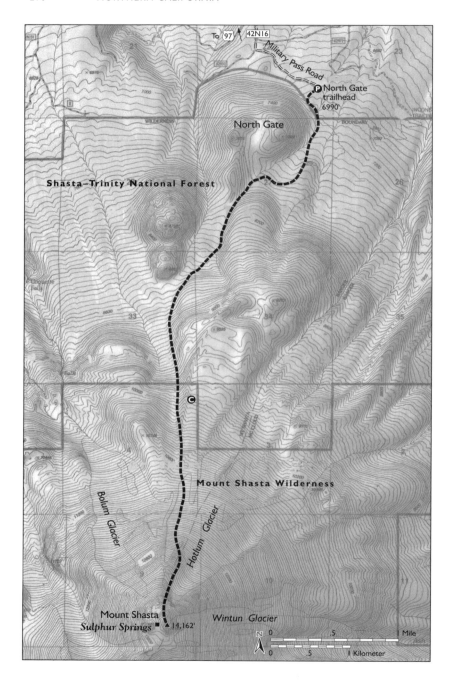

Early morning summer ascent of the Hotlum–Bolum Ridge

advised, routefinding can be difficult on the way down, so mind your landmarks. Once up to 10,000 feet, 4 miles from the trailhead, there are areas to camp in the snow or in rock bivy sites.

Continue up the ridge to 11,000 feet where you traverse southeast across the top of the Hotlum Glacier. There are two prominent snowfields or ramps. The first is less steep, the second is much closer to the seracs of the Hotlum Glacier. At the top of the ramps you will find a large, flat shelf to have lunch, just below the Hotlum headwall.

The best skiing is from the top of either ramp down the ridge. If you continue to the summit, you may be able to ski off the top or hike back down with your skis to 11,000 feet. Descend the climbing route, pack up your camp, and head down to North Gate, using caution so you don't go astray in the numerous gullies and drainages.

96 Lassen Peak, Southeast Face

Start Point Lassen Peak trailhead, 8500 feet; Lassen Chalet, 5700 feet
High Point Lassen Peak summit, 10,457 feet
Trail Distance 2 miles from Lassen Peak trailhead;
10 miles from Lassen Chalet
Trail Time 2 hours from Lassen Peak trailhead,
8 hours from Lassen Chalet
Skill Level Intermediate
Best Season Spring
Maps USGS Lassen Peak, Reading Peak, West Prospect Peak,
Manzanita Lake

Lassen Peak is the southernmost peak in the Cascade Range and, after Mount St. Helens, the last one to erupt. It is a target for Oregon ski mountaineers usually when combined with Mount Shasta (Routes 94 and 95). But it can be a

Prepping for the climb—blister prevention

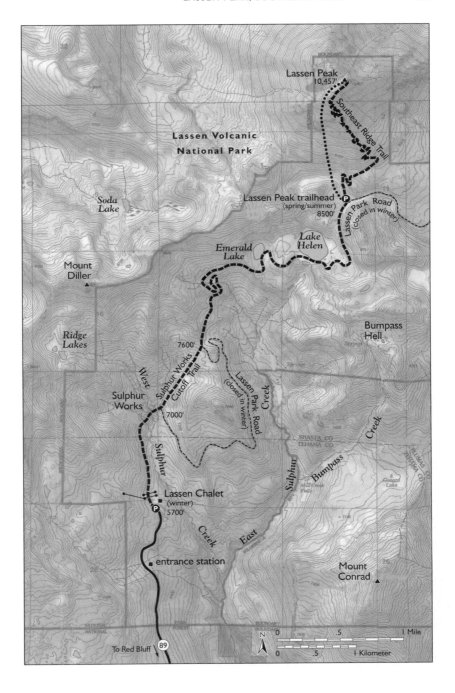

destination in itself. It's a plug dome, the largest in the world, and has a few permanent snowfields.

It's not as big or tall as Mount Shasta. And, access is much easier because in the spring you can drive to 8500 feet, one of the highest trailheads in this book.

GETTING THERE. From Portland, drive the long haul south on I-5 to the California state line, and continue 150 miles to Red Bluff. From Red Bluff, follow CA-36 for 55 miles to Mineral, then 2 more miles to CA-89. Follow CA-89 for 4 miles north to the southeast entrance to Lassen Volcanic National Park. Pay the entrance fee and follow CA-89 (Lassen Peak Highway) into the park. In winter and spring, you may have to stop at the Lassen Chalet trailhead at 5700 feet, almost a mile from the entrance station. In late spring or early summer, you can drive 4 miles farther to the Lassen Peak trailhead at 8500 feet.

THE ROUTE. In winter, if the road is snow-covered, start from the Lassen Chalet, a now defunct ski area. This adds 4 miles one-way to the route and 3000 feet of elevation gain, but it's an easy ski up the road, and you can bypass 1 mile by taking the Sulphur Works Cuttoff Trail to get to the Lassen Peak trailhead.

Follow the Lassen Peak Southeast Ridge Trail as it zigzags up the summit for a mile. Descend the south or southeast face with an alternative lap down the north face.

California high country

97 Etna Summit

Start Point : Etna Summit, 5956 feet
High Point : Etna Summit, 5956 feet
Trail Distance : 2 miles
Trail Time : 2 hours
Skill Level : Beginner
Best Season : Winter
Map : Etna Summit

Etna Summit is within striking distance of southern Oregon, for Medford, Ashland, and Klamath Falls locals. For a big road trip from the Willamette Valley, combine this hill with a trip south to Lassen Peak (Route 96) and Mount Shasta (Routes 94 and 95). This short slope on the Sawyers Bar Road (not Etna Mountain, the peak a few miles to the east) offers short runs easily accessed by car. It's the only route you can drive to the top and ski down. This allows you to use a car shuttle if you are resistant to earning your turns by hiking. More importantly, it offers a great place to begin backcountry skiing with the security of a road and vehicle close by. Try it if you are in the neighborhood.

Big snow year in California's Shasta–Trinity Alps Wilderness

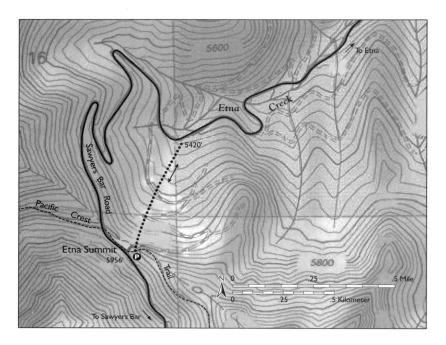

GETTING THERE. From Medford, drive south on I-5 into California 20 miles. Exit at Yreka, and take US 3 south 26 miles to the town of Etna. At Etna, drive west on Sawyers Bar Road 11 miles to the summit at 5956 feet.

THE ROUTE. The best skiing is on Etna's north-facing slopes, on the east side of the road. Ski off the summit into the Etna Creek drainage, which you drove up along. You'll be paralleling the road. After you pass three switchbacks, catch the road. Some skiers car shuttle for quicker laps; purists skin back up.

Opposite: Fueling up at Mount Rainier's Camp Schurman

APPENDICES

RESOURCES

BELOW IS A GENERAL LIST OF RESOURCES where you can get more information on backcountry skiing in Oregon.

GENERAL WEBSITES
Cascade Climbers, www.cascadeclimbers.com
Cascade Volcano Observatory, www.vulcan.wr.usgs.gov
National Forest Region Six, www.fs.fed.us/r6
Northwest Mountaineering Journal, www.mountaineers.org/nwmj
Ski Mountaineer, www.skimountaineer.com
Skiing the Backcountry, www.skiingthebackcountry.com
Traditional Mountaineering, www.traditionalmountaineering.com
Turns All Year, www.turnsallyear.com

ROAD CONDITIONS
California Department of Transportation, www.dot.ca.gov/hq/roadinfo
Oregon Department of Transportation, (800) 977-6368,
    www.tripcheck.com
Washington Department of Transportation, www.wsdot.wa.gov/traffic

AVALANCHE AND WEATHER CONDITIONS
Central Oregon Avalanche Association, www.coavalanche.org
Mount Shasta Avalanche Center, (530) 926-9613, www.shastaavalanche.org
Northwest Avalanche Center, (503) 808-2400, www.nwac.us
Wallowa Avalanche Center, www.wallowaavalanchecenter.org

WINTER RESORTS
Anthony Lakes Mountain Resort, (541) 856-3277, www.anthonylakes.com
Cooper Spur Mountain Resort, (503) 230-2084, www.cooperspur.com
Ferguson Ridge Ski Area, (541) 398-1167, www.skifergi.com
Hoodoo Ski Area, (541) 822-3337, www.hoodoo.com
Mount Ashland Ski Area, (541) 482-2754, www.mtashland.com
Mount Bachelor Ski Resort, (541) 382-7888, www.mtbachelor.com
Mount Hood Meadows Ski Resort, (503) 227-7669, www.skihood.com
Mount Hood Ski Bowl, (503) 222-2695, www.skibowl.com
Mount Shasta Ski Park, (530) 926-8686, www.skipark.com
Ski Bluewood, (509) 382-4725, www.bluewood.com
Spout Springs Ski Resort, (541) 566-0327, www.spoutsprings.com

Summit Ski Area, (503) 272-0256, www.summitskiarea.com
Timberline Lodge, (503) 222-2211, www.timberlinelodge.com
Warner Canyon, (541) 947-4892, www.lakecountychamber.org/skihill.html
Willamette Pass Resort, (541) 345-7669, www.willamettepass.com

SELECTED BOOKS
Route Information

Barnett, Steve. *The Best Ski Touring in America*. San Francisco: Sierra Club, 1988.

Beckey, Fred. *Cascade Alpine Guide: Climbing and High Routes, Volume 1: Columbia River to Stevens Pass*, 3rd ed. Seattle: The Mountaineers Books, 2000.

Bergdorfer, Rainier. *100 Classic Backcountry Ski and Snowboard Routes in Washington*. Seattle: The Mountaineers Books, 1999.

Blair, Seabury Jr. *Backcountry Ski Washington: The Best Trails and Descents for Free-Heelers and Snowboarders*. Seattle: Sasquatch Books, 1998.

Bogar, Mike. *Best Groomed Cross-Country Ski Trails in Oregon*. Seattle: The Mountaineers Books, 2002.

Burns, Cameron, and Stephen Porcella. *Climbing California's Fourteeners*. Revised. Seattle: The Mountaineers Books, 2008.

Dawson, Louis W. *Wild Snow: A Historical Guide to North American Ski Mountaineering*. Golden, CO: American Alpine Club, 1998.

Dodge, Nicholas A. *A Climber's Guide to Oregon*. Portland, OR: Mazamas, 1968.

Hall, Don. *On Top of Oregon*. Corvallis, OR: Western Guide, 1975.

Humes, Jim, and Sean Wagstaff. *Boarderlands: The Snowboarder's Guide to the West Coast*. San Francisco: HarperCollinsWest, 1995.

Kirkendall, Tom, and Vicky Spring. *Cross-country Ski Tours: Washington's South Cascades and Olympics*, 2nd ed. Seattle: The Mountaineers Books, 1995.

Mueller, Ted. *Northwest Ski Trails*. Seattle: The Mountaineers Books, 1968.

Mueller, Ted, and Marge Mueller. *Exploring Washington's Wild Areas: A Guide for Hikers, Backpackers, Climbers, Cross-country Skiers, and Paddlers*. Seattle: The Mountaineers Books, 1994.

Smoot, Jeff. *Climbing the Cascade Volcanoes*, 2nd ed. Helena, MT: Falcon, 1999.

Sullivan, William. *Exploring Oregon's Wild Areas: A Guide for Hikers, Backpackers, Cross-Country Skiers and Paddlers*, 2nd ed. Seattle: Mountaineers Books, 2002.

Thomas, Jeff. *Oregon High: A Climbing Guide to Nine Cascade Volcanoes*. Portland, OR: Keep Climbing Press, 1991.

Vielbig, Klindt. *Cross-Country Ski Routes Oregon*, 2nd ed. Seattle: The Mountaineers Books, 1994.

Waag, David. *Oregon Descents: A Backcountry Ski Guide to the Southern Cascades*. Portland, OR: Free Heel Press, 1997.

Avalanche Safety

Ferguson, Sue, and Edward LaChapelle. *The ABCs of Avalanche Safety*, 2nd ed. Seattle: The Mountaineers Books, 2003.

Fredston, Jill, and Doug Fesler. *Snow Sense: A Guide to Evaluating Snow Avalanche Hazard*, 5th ed. Anchorage: Alaska Mountain Safety, 1999.

Moynier, John. *Avalanche Aware: The Essential Guide to Avalanche Safety*, 2nd ed. Helena, MT: Falcon, 2007.

Tremper, Bruce. *Staying Alive in Avalanche Terrain*, 2nd ed. Seattle: The Mountaineers Books, 2008.

Weather

Renner, Jeff. *Mountain Weather: Backcountry Forecasting and Weather Safety for Hikers, Campers, Climbers, Skiers and Snowboarders*. Seattle: The Mountaineers Books, 2005.

Ski, Snowboard, and General Mountaineering

Bien, Vic. *Mountain Skiing*. Seattle: The Mountaineers Books, 1982.

Eng, Ron. *Mountaineering: The Freedom of the Hills*, 8th ed. Seattle: The Mountaineers Books, 2010.

Van Tilburg, Christopher. *Backcountry Snowboarding*. Seattle: The Mountaineers Books, 1998.

Volken, Martin, Scott Schell, and Margaret Wheeler. *Backcountry Skiing: Skills for Ski Touring and Ski Mountaineering*. Seattle: The Mountaineers Books, 2007.

First Aid and Survival

Carline, Jan, Martha Lentz, and Steven MacDonald. *Mountaineering First Aid: A Guide to Accident Response and First-Aid Care*, 5th ed. Seattle: The Mountaineers Books, 2004.

Forgey, William. *Wilderness Medicine: Beyond First Aid*, 5th ed. Helena, MT: Falcon, 1999.

Van Tilburg, Christopher. *Emergency Survival: A Pocket Guide*. Seattle: The Mountaineers Books, 2001.

Van Tilburg, Christopher. *First Aid: A Pocket Guide*. Seattle: The Mountaineers Books, 2001.

Wilkerson, James, Ernest Moore, and Ken Zafren. *Medicine for Mountaineering and Other Wilderness Activities*, 6th ed. Seattle: The Mountaineers Books, 2010.

MOUNTAINEERING CLUBS

American Alpine Club, Golden, Colorado, www.americanalpineclub.org

Cascade Mountaineers, Bend, Oregon, www.cascademountaineers.org

Chemeketans, Salem, Oregon, www.chemeketans.org

Mazamas, Portland, Oregon, www.mazamas.org

Mountaineers, Seattle, Washington, www.mountaineers.org

Obsidians, Eugene, Oregon, www.obsidians.org

Oregon Mountaineering Association, www.i-world.net/oma

Oregon Nordic Club, www.onc.org (multiple chapters across state)
Ptarmigans, Vancouver, Washington, www.ptarmigans.org
Santiam Alpine Club, Salem, Oregon, www.santiamalpineclub.org

MOUNTAIN RESCUE UNITS

Corvallis Mountain Rescue, www.corvallismountainrescue.org
Deschutes County Search and Rescue, www.dcsarinc.org
Eugene Mountain Rescue, www.eugenemountainrescue.org
Hood River Crag Rats, www.cragrats.org
Portland Mountain Rescue, www.pmru.org

BACKCOUNTRY AND FRONTCOUNTRY SKI PATROLS

Crater Lake Nordic Patrol, www.craterlakeskipatrol.org
Mount Bachelor Ski Patrol, www.mtbachelornsp.org
Mount Hood Ski Patrol, www.mthoodskipatrol.org
National Ski Patrol Oregon Region, www.nsp-orre.org (with links to all Oregon
    patrols)
Santiam Pass Ski Patrol, www.santiampassskipatrol.org
Willamette Backcountry Ski Patrol, www.wbsp.org

GUIDES

Mount Bailey Snow Cats, (800) 733-7593, www.catskimountbailey.com
Tam MacArthur Rim, (541) 549-8101, www.threesistersbackcountry.com
Timberline Mountain Guides, (541) 312-9242, www.timberlinemtguides.com
Shasta Mountain Guides, (530) 926-3117, www.shastaguides.com
Silcox Hut, Timberline Lodge, (503) 272-3311, www.timberlinelodge.com
SWS Mountain Guides, (888) 797-6867, www.swsmtns.com
Wallowa Alpine Huts, (541) 398-1980, www.wallowahuts.com
Wing Ridge Ski Tours, (800) 646-9050, www.wingski.com

OVERNIGHT SHELTERS

Helmock Butte Shelter, Mount Bailey, Umpqua National Forest and Edelweiss Ski
    Club, Diamond Lake Ranger District, (541) 498-2531
Jeff View Shelter, Tam McArthur Rim, Deschutes National Forest, Bend–Fort Rock
    Ranger District, (541) 383-4000, www.fs.fed.us/r6/deschutes
Kwohl Butte Shelter, Kwohl Butte, Deschutes National Forest, Bend–Fort Rock
    Ranger District, (541) 383-4000, www.fs.fed.us/r6/deschutes
Maiden Peak Shelter, Maiden Peak, Willamette National Forest and Eugene Nordic
    Club, (541) 782-2283, www.fs.fed.us/r6/willamette/recreation/tripplanning
    -winter/shelters/index.html#maidenpeak or Middle Fork Ranger District
McCully Basin, Wallowa Mountains, Wallowa Alpine Huts, Joseph, Oregon,
    www.wallowahuts.com

Tilly Jane A-frame and Guard Station, Mount Hood, Mount Hood National Forest and Oregon Nordic Club, Portland, Oregon, www.onc.org or Hood River Ranger District, (541) 352-6002

Wing Ridge and Big Sheep Shelters, Wallowa Mountains, Wing Ridge Ski Tours, Joseph, Oregon, (800) 646-9050, www.wingski.com

SKI AND SNOWBOARD MOUNTAINEERING COURSES

The Mazamas, (503) 227-2345, www.mazamas.org

Mount St. Helens Institute, (360) 449-7883, www.mshinstitute.org

Rainier Mountaineering, (888) 892-5462, www.rmiguides.com

Shasta Mountain Guides, (530) 926-3117, www.shastaguides.com

SWS Mountain Guides, (888) 797-6867, www.swsmtns.com

Timberline Mountain Guides, (541) 312-9242, www.timberlinemtguides.com

AVALANCHE COURSES

Mountain Savvy, (503) 780-9300, mountainsavvy.com

Portland Mountain Rescue, www.pmru.org

Shasta Mountain Guides, (530) 926-3117, www.shastaguides.com

SWS Mountain Guides, (888) 797-6867, www.swsmtns.com

Three Sisters Backcountry, www.threesistersbackcountry.com

Timberline Mountain Guides, (541) 312-9242, www.timberlinemtguides.com

Wallowa Alpine Huts, (541) 398-1980, www.wallowahuts.com

AVALANCHE BEACON PARKS

Mount Bachelor Ski Resort, www.mtbachelor.com, hosted by Backcountry Access (www.backcountryaccess.com)

EQUIPMENT LIST FOR A DAY TOUR

HERE IS A GENERAL LIST of equipment needed for a typical day tour. You may not take all of these items on every tour, but for the most part, you should be prepared with most of the items on this list. Importantly, you must know how to use them.

PACK

Backpack: Avalung, airbag, or standard toploading pack (approximately 2000 cubic inches)

CLOTHING

Hat
Helmet
Neck gaiter
Goggles and sunglasses
Gauntlet gloves and lightweight gloves
Zip undershirt
Insulating vest or sweater
(lightweight fleece or synthetic fill)
Insulating sweater
(bulky, fleece, or synthetic fill)
Soft-shell jacket
Hard-shell jacket, waterproof and windproof
Long underwear
Mountaineering pants, lightweight
Hard-shell pants, waterproof and windproof
Ski or snowboard socks

SKIS/SNOWBOARD

Alpine touring, telemark, or light Nordic skis, or split snowboard
Boots with compatible bindings
(there are many versions of ski, telemark, and snowboard boot/binding systems)
Poles, adjustable
Climbing skins
Skin wax
Ski/snowboard crampons
If hiking with a solid snowboard or alpine skis (the kind used in a ski resort), you'll need a mode of ascent, usually snowshoes

AVALANCHE

Avalung or airbag backpack
Beacon
Probe, 2–3 meters
(do not substitute probe ski poles)
Shovel, metal (not plastic)

FIRST-AID, SURVIVAL, REPAIR KIT (MINIMUM)

First aid

Tape, Johnson & Johnson waterproof

Compression wrap, Coban

Benzalkonium chloride or alcohol gel/
    wipes

Clot bandage

Sunscreen and lip balm

Water purification tablets

Dressings, nonstick, and/or adhesive-
    strip bandages

Survival

Matches, lighter, or flint with firestarter

Bivy sack

Compass, GPS, map(s)

Extra batteries

Chemical heat packs

Perlon cord

Whistle

Headlight

Cell phone

Personal locator beacon or Mountain
    Locator Unit (unique to Mount
    Hood)

Repair

Multitool

Duct or hockey tape

Steel wool/thread

Extra binding screw

Wire, safety pins

Plastic cable ties

Polyurethane straps

BASIC MOUNTAINEERING GEAR

Full-frame crampons

Instep crampons

Ice ax

Rope

Harness

Prusik cords and/or ascenders

Pully

Three locking carabiners

Descender

Pickets

OTHER ESSENTIALS

Food

Water

OVERNIGHT GEAR (NOT A DETAILED LIST)

Large pack

Extra food and water

Extra socks, gloves, hat

Stove and fuel

Tent

Sleeping bag

Sleeping pad

Tarp

Warm down parka

Down booties

Personal toiletries

OREGON LAWS PERTAINING TO SKIING AND SNOWBOARDING

BELOW ARE THE TWO MOST IMPORTANT LAWS that pertain to backcountry skiing and snowboarding in Oregon. The first is the Skier Responsibility law and the second is the law that allows county sheriffs to bill a person for search-and-rescue.

SKI AND SNOWBOARD RESPONSIBILITY

30.970 Definitions for ORS 30.970 to 30.990. As used in ORS 30.970 to 30.990:

(1) "Inherent risks of skiing" includes, but is not limited to, those dangers or conditions which are an integral part of the sport, such as changing weather conditions, variations or steepness in terrain, snow or ice conditions, surface or subsurface conditions, bare spots, creeks and gullies, forest growth, rocks, stumps, lift towers and other structures and their components, collisions with other skiers, and a skier's failure to ski within the skier's own ability.

(2) "Injury" means any personal injury or property damage or loss.

(3) "Skier" means any person who is in a ski area for the purpose of engaging in the sport of skiing or who rides as a passenger on any chairlift device.

(4) "Ski area" means any area designated and maintained by a ski area operator for skiing.

(5) "Ski area operator" means those persons, and their agents, officers, employees, or representatives, who operate a ski area. [1979 c.665 §1]

30.975 Skiers assume certain risks. In accordance with ORS 31.600 and notwithstanding ORS 31.620 (2), an individual who engages in the sport of skiing, alpine or Nordic, accepts and assumes the inherent risks of skiing insofar as they are reasonably obvious, expected or necessary. [1979 c.665 §2]

30.980 Notice to ski area operator of injury to skier; injuries resulting in death; statute of limitations; informing skiers of notice requirements.

(1) A ski area operator shall be notified of any injury to a skier by registered or certified mail within 180 days after the injury or within 180 days after the skier discovers, or reasonably should have discovered, such injury.

(2) When an injury results in a skier's death, the required notice of the injury may be presented to the ski area operator by or on behalf of the personal representative of the deceased, or any person who may, under ORS 30.020, maintain an action for the wrongful death of the skier, within 180 days after the date of the death which resulted from the injury. However, if the skier whose injury resulted in death presented a notice to the ski area operator that would have been sufficient under this section had the skier lived, notice of the death to the ski area operator is not necessary.

(3) An action against a ski area operator to recover damages for injuries to a skier shall be commenced within two years of the date of the injuries. However, ORS 12.160 and 12.190 apply to such actions.

(4) Failure to give notice as required by this section bars a claim for injuries or wrongful death unless:

(a) The ski area operator had knowledge of the injury or death within the 180-day period after its occurrence;

(b) The skier or skier's beneficiaries had good cause for failure to give notice as required by this section; or

(c) The ski area operator failed to comply with subsection (5) of this section.

(5) Ski area operators shall give to skiers, in a manner reasonably calculated to inform, notice of the requirements for notifying a ski area operator of injury and the effect of a failure to provide such notice under this section. [1979 c.665 §3]

30.985 Duties of skiers; effect of failure to comply.

(1) Skiers shall have duties which include but are not limited to the following:

(a) Skiers who ski in any area not designated for skiing within the permit area assume the inherent risks thereof.

(b) Skiers shall be the sole judges of the limits of their skills and their ability to meet and overcome the inherent risks of skiing and shall maintain reasonable control of speed and course.

(c) Skiers shall abide by the directions and instructions of the ski area operator.

(d) Skiers shall familiarize themselves with posted information on location and degree of difficulty of trails and slopes to the extent reasonably possible before skiing on any slope or trail.

(e) Skiers shall not cross the uphill track of any surface lift except at points clearly designated by the ski area operator.

(f) Skiers shall not overtake any other skier except in such a manner as to avoid contact and shall grant the right of way to the overtaken skier.

(g) Skiers shall yield to other skiers when entering a trail or starting downhill.

(h) Skiers must wear retention straps or other devices to prevent runaway skis.

(i) Skiers shall not board rope tows, wire rope tows, j-bars, t-bars, ski lifts or other similar devices unless they have sufficient ability to use the devices, and skiers shall follow any written or verbal instructions that are given regarding the devices.

(j) Skiers, when involved in a skiing accident, shall not depart from the ski area without leaving their names and addresses if reasonably possible.

(k) A skier who is injured should, if reasonably possible, give notice of the injury to the ski area operator before leaving the ski area.

(l) Skiers shall not embark or disembark from a ski lift except at designated areas or by the authority of the ski area operator.

(2) Violation of any of the duties of skiers set forth in subsection (1) of this section entitles the ski area operator to withdraw the violator's privilege of skiing. [1979 c.665 §4]

30.990 Operators required to give skiers notice of duties. Ski area operators shall give notice to skiers of their duties under ORS 30.985 in a manner reasonably calculated to inform skiers of those duties. [1979 c.665 §5]

SEARCH-AND-RESCUE COSTS

401.590 Reimbursement of public body for search-and-rescue by benefited persons; amount; exceptions.

(1) A public body may collect an amount specified in this section as reimbursement for the cost of search-and-rescue activities when the public body conducts search and rescue activities for the benefit of hikers, climbers, hunters and other users of wilderness areas or unpopulated forested or mountainous recreational areas in this state.

(2) The public body may collect moneys as authorized by this section from each person for whose benefit search-and-rescue activities are conducted. The public body may not collect more than $500 from an individual under this section and may not collect more than the actual cost of the search-and-rescue activities from all of the individuals for whose benefit the activities are conducted.

(3) A public body may obtain reimbursement under this section only when: (a) Reasonable care was not exercised by the individuals for whose benefit the search-and-rescue activities are conducted; or (b) Applicable laws were violated by such individuals.

(4) Any individual who is charged a fee for reimbursement under this section may appeal the charge or the amount of the fee to the public body that charged the fee.

(5) For the purposes of subsection (3) of this section, evidence of reasonable care includes:

(a) The individuals possessed experience and used equipment that was appropriate for the known conditions of weather and terrain.

(b) The individuals used or attempted to use locating devices or cellular telephones when appropriate.

(c) The individuals notified responsible persons or organizations of the expected time of departure and the expected time of return and the planned location or route of activity.

(d) The individuals had maps and orienteering equipment and used trails or other routes that were appropriate for the conditions.

(6) As used in this section, "public body" means any unit of state or local government that conducts or has authority to conduct search-and-rescue activities. [1995 c.570 §1]

ROUTES BY BEST SEASON

Route	Winter	Spring	Summer
MOUNT HOOD SOUTH			
Tom, Dick, and Harry Mountain	•		
Glade Trail	•		
Alpine Trail	•		
Palmer Glacier and Triangle Moraine		•	
Illumination Saddle and Upper Zigzag Glacier		•	
South Climb, Hogsback Ridge		•	
South Climb, West Crater Rim		•	
Salmon River Canyon	•		
Barlow Butte	•		
Boy Scout Ridge	•		
White River Canyon	•		
Frog Lake Buttes	•		
Mount Hood Circumnavigation		•	
MOUNT HOOD EAST			
Bennett Pass	•		
Mount Hood Meadows Bowls	•		
Mitchell Creek Bowl and Iron Canyon	•		
Vista Ridge	•		
Lower Heather Canyon	•		
Upper Heather and Clark Canyons		•	
Newton Canyon	•		
Superbowl via Vista Ridge		•	
Superbowl via Heather Canyon		•	
Wy'east Face		•	
Gunsight Ridge	•		
MOUNT HOOD NORTH			
Tilly Jane Trail	•		
Pollalie Canyon	•		
Old Wagon Road and Ghost Ridge	•		
Cooper Spur and Upper Tilly Jane		•	
Snowdome			•
Langille Bowls			•
Barrett Spur		•	

Route	Winter	Spring	Summer
SANTIAM PASS TO MCKENZIE PASS			
Mount Jefferson, Jefferson Park Glacier			•
Mount Jefferson, Russell Glacier			•
Mount Jefferson, Park Butte			•
Potato Hill	•		
Hoodoo Butte and Hayrick Butte	•		
Mount Washington, Northwest Bowl		•	
Cache Mountain	•		
Three Fingered Jack		•	
Black Butte	•		
Black Crater	•		
Belknap Crater	•		
THREE SISTERS WILDERNESS AND BEND			
North Sister, Southeast Ridge			•
Middle Sister, Southeast Ridge			•
Middle Sister, Hayden Glacier			•
Middle Sister, Collier Glacier			•
South Sister, Green Lakes			•
South Sister, Moraine Lake			•
Broken Top, Crater Bowl		•	
Broken Top, Southwest Ridge		•	
Ball Butte	•		
Moon Mountain	•		
Todd Lake Rim	•		
Tam McArthur Rim	•		
Tumalo Mountain	•		
Cinder Cone	•		
Mount Bachelor		•	
Kwohl Butte	•		
Paulina Peak	•		
WILLAMETTE PASS TO DIAMOND LAKE			
West Peak and Peak 2	•		
Maiden Peak	•		
Diamond Peak, West Shoulder		•	
Mount Bailey, Southeast Ridge		•	
Mount Bailey, Avalanche Bowl		•	
Mount Thielsen, Northwest Bowl		•	

Route	Winter	Spring	Summer
CRATER LAKE NATIONAL PARK			
Crater Lake Circumnavigation	•		
Mount Scott		•	
Hillman Peak and The Watchman	•		
Garfield and Applegate Peaks	•		
SOUTHERN OREGON			
Mount McLoughlin, Southeast Ridge		•	
Pelican Butte	•		
Brown Mountain	•		
Mount Ashland	•		
WALLOWA MOUNTAINS			
Wing Ridge	•		
Big Sheep Basin	•		
McCully Basin	•		
Mount Howard	•		
Aneroid Lake Basin	•		
Norway Basin	•		
BLUE MOUNTAINS, ELKHORN AND STRAWBERRY RANGES			
Anthony Lake Basin	•		
Angell Peak, Northeast Basin	•		
Crawfish Basin	•		
Spout Springs	•		
Strawberry Mountain	•		
STEENS MOUNTAIN			
Pike Creek		•	
West Escarpment	•		
SOUTHWEST WASHINGTON			
Silver Star	•		
Mount Adams, Suksdorf Ridge			•
Mount Adams, Southwest Chute			•
Mount St. Helens, Monitor Ridge			•
Mount St. Helens, Swift Creek		•	
Mount St. Helens, Butte Dome		•	
Mount Rainier, Muir Snowfield			•
NORTHERN CALIFORNIA			
Mount Shasta, Avalanche Gulch			•
Mount Shasta, Hotlum–Bolum Ridge			•
Lassen Peak, Southeast Face		•	
Etna Summit	•		

ROUTES BY SKILL LEVEL

Route	beg	inter	adv	expert	guided
MOUNT HOOD SOUTH					
Tom, Dick, and Harry Mountain		•			
Glade Trail	•				
Alpine Trail	•				
Palmer Glacier and Triangle Moraine		•			
Illumination Saddle and Upper Zigzag Glacier			•		
South Climb, Hogsback Ridge				•	•
South Climb, West Crater Rim				•	•
Salmon River Canyon		•			
Barlow Butte		•			
Boy Scout Ridge		•			
White River Canyon		•			
Frog Lake Buttes		•			
Mount Hood Circumnavigation				•	•
MOUNT HOOD EAST					
Bennett Pass		•			
Mount Hood Meadows Bowls		•			
Mitchell Creek Bowl and Iron Canyon		•			
Vista Ridge		•			
Lower Heather Canyon		•			
Upper Heather and Clark Canyons			•		
Newton Canyon			•		
Superbowl via Vista Ridge			•		
Superbowl via Heather Canyon			•		
Wy'east Face				•	
Gunsight Ridge			•		
MOUNT HOOD NORTH					
Tilly Jane Trail	•				
Pollalie Canyon			•		
Old Wagon Road and Ghost Ridge		•			
Cooper Spur and Upper Tilly Jane			•		
Snowdome			•		
Langille Bowls			•		
Barrett Spur			•		

Route	beg	inter	adv	expert	guided
SANTIAM PASS TO MCKENZIE PASS					
Mount Jefferson, Jefferson Park Glacier			•		
Mount Jefferson, Russell Glacier			•		
Mount Jefferson, Park Butte			•		
Potato Hill	•				
Hoodoo Butte and Hayrick Butte		•			
Mount Washington, Northwest Bowl			•		
Cache Mountain		•			
Three Fingered Jack			•		
Black Butte		•			
Black Crater		•			
Belknap Crater		•			
THREE SISTERS WILDERNESS AND BEND					
North Sister, Southeast Ridge			•		
Middle Sister, Southeast Ridge		•			
Middle Sister, Hayden Glacier			•		
Middle Sister, Collier Glacier			•		
South Sister, Green Lakes		•			
South Sister, Moraine Lake		•			
Broken Top, Crater Bowl		•			
Broken Top, Southwest Ridge		•			
Ball Butte	•				
Moon Mountain	•				
Todd Lake Rim	•				
Tam McArthur Rim		•			•
Tumalo Mountain	•				
Cinder Cone	•				
Mount Bachelor	•				
Kwohl Butte	•				
Paulina Peak	•				
WILLAMETTE PASS TO DIAMOND LAKE					
West Peak and Peak 2	•				
Maiden Peak		•			
Diamond Peak, West Shoulder		•			
Mount Bailey, Southeast Ridge		•			•
Mount Bailey, Avalanche Bowl		•			•
Mount Thielsen, Northwest Bowl		•			
CRATER LAKE NATIONAL PARK					
Crater Lake Circumnavigation		•			
Mount Scott		•			
Hillman Peak and The Watchman	•				
Garfield and Applegate Peaks	•				

Route	beg	inter	adv	expert	guided
SOUTHERN OREGON					
Mount McLoughlin, Southeast Ridge			•		
Pelican Butte			•		
Brown Mountain		•			
Mount Ashland		•			
WALLOWA MOUNTAINS					
Wing Ridge		•			•
Big Sheep Basin			•		•
McCully Basin			•		•
Mount Howard		•			•
Aneroid Lake Basin			•		
Norway Basin				•	•
BLUE MOUNTAINS, ELKHORN AND STRAWBERRY RANGES					
Anthony Lake Basin		•			
Angell Peak, Northeast Basin			•		
Crawfish Basin		•			
Spout Springs	•				
Strawberry Mountain			•		
STEENS MOUNTAIN					
Pike Creek			•		
West Escarpment			•		
SOUTHWEST WASHINGTON					
Silver Star	•				
Mount Adams, Suksdorf Ridge			•		
Mount Adams, Southwest Chute			•		
Mount St. Helens, Monitor Ridge			•		•
Mount St. Helens, Swift Creek			•		•
Mount St. Helens, Butte Dome			•		
Mount Rainier, Muir Snowfield		•			•
NORTHERN CALIFORNIA					
Mount Shasta, Avalanche Gulch				•	•
Mount Shasta, Hotlum–Bolum Ridge				•	•
Lassen Peak, Southeast Face		•			
Etna Summit	•				

INDEX

ABOUT THE AUTHOR

CHRISTOPHER VAN TILBURG, MD, specializes in medical and safety aspects of outdoor recreation, adventure travel, and mountaineering. He is author of eight books including *Mountain Rescue Doctor: Wilderness Medicine in the Extremes of Nature*, which was a finalist for Oregon Book Awards and Banff Festival of Mountain Books.

Dr. Van Tilburg serves as editor in chief of *Wilderness Medicine*, contributing editor to *Backcountry*, member of Mountain Rescue Association Medical Committee, and member of Hood River Crag Rats Mountain Rescue team. He lives and works in Hood River, Oregon. Contact him through www.docwild.net.

(Jennifer Donnelly)

OTHER TITLES YOU MIGHT ENJOY FROM THE MOUNTAINEERS BOOKS

The Avalanche Handbook,
3rd Edition, *McClung & Schaerer*
The unrivaled resource used by the pros for avalanche information and snow conditions

Staying Alive in Avalanche Terrain,
2nd Edition, *Tremper*
"No one who plays in mountain snow should leave home without having studied this book."
— Rocky Mountain News

Hypothermia, Frostbite, and Other Cold Injuries, 2nd Edition,
Giesbrecht & Wilkerson
Standard reference for wilderness medical and rescue professionals

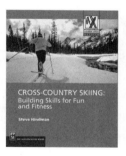

Cross-Country Skiing
Hindman
For the novice to intermediate cross-country skier: instruction by a member of the national Nordic Demonstration Team.

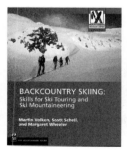

Backcountry Skiing,
Volken, Wheeler
The definitive manual of backcountry skiing

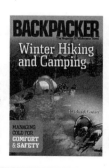

Winter Hiking and Camping: Managing Cold for Comfort and Safety, *Lanza*
Learn to camp in the cold rain and snow from the experts at *Backpacker* magazine

THE MOUNTAINEERS, founded in 1906, is a nonprofit outdoor activity and conservation club, whose mission is "to explore, study, preserve, and enjoy the natural beauty of the outdoors...." Based in Seattle, Washington, the club is now one of the largest such organizations in the United States, with seven branches throughout Washington State.

The Mountaineers sponsors both classes and year-round outdoor activities in the Pacific Northwest, which include hiking, mountain climbing, ski-touring, snowshoeing, bicycling, camping, canoeing and kayaking, nature study, sailing, and adventure travel. The club's conservation division supports environmental causes through educational activities, sponsoring legislation, and presenting informational programs.

All club activities are led by skilled, experienced volunteers, who are dedicated to promoting safe and responsible enjoyment and preservation of the outdoors.

If you would like to participate in these organized outdoor activities or the club's programs, consider a membership in The Mountaineers. For information and an application, write or call The Mountaineers, Club Headquarters, 7700 Sand Point Way NE, Seattle, WA 98115; (206) 521-6001. You can also visit the club's website at www.mountaineers.org or contact The Mountaineers via email at clubmail@mountaineers.org.

The Mountaineers Books, an active, nonprofit publishing program of the club, produces guidebooks, instructional texts, historical works, natural history guides, and works on environmental conservation. All books produced by The Mountaineers Books fulfill the club's mission. Visit www.mountaineersbooks.org to find details about all our titles and the latest author events, as well as videos, web clips, links, and more.

The Mountaineers Books
1001 SW Klickitat Way, Suite 201
Seattle, WA 98134
(800) 553-4453
mbooks@mountaineersbooks.org

The Mountaineers Books is proud to be a corporate sponsor of The Leave No Trace Center for Outdoor Ethics, whose mission is to promote and inspire responsible outdoor recreation through education, research, and partnerships. The Leave No Trace program is focused specifically on human-powered (nonmotorized) recreation.

Leave No Trace strives to educate visitors about the nature of their recreational impacts, as well as offer techniques to prevent and minimize such impacts. Leave No Trace is best understood as an educational and ethical program, not as a set of rules and regulations.

For more information, visit www.lnt.org, or call (800) 332-4100.